Dance Movement Therapy

This thoroughly updated edition of *Dance Movement Therapy* echoes the increased worldwide interest in dance movement therapy and makes a strong contribution to the emerging awareness of the nature of embodiment in psychotherapy. Recent research is incorporated, along with developments in theory and practice, to provide a comprehensive overview of this fast-growing field.

Helen Payne brings together contributions from experts in the field to offer the reader a valuable insight into the theory and practice of dance movement therapy. The contributions reflect the breadth of developing approaches, covering subjects including:

- Dance movement therapy with people with dementia
- Group work with people with enduring mental health difficulties
- Transcultural competence in dance movement therapy
- Freudian thought applied to authentic movement
- Embodiment in dance movement therapy training and practice
- Personal development through dance movement therapy

Dance Movement Therapy will be a valuable resource for anyone who wishes to learn more about the therapeutic use of creative movement and dance. It will be welcomed by students and practitioners in the arts therapies, psychotherapy, counselling and other health and social care professions.

Helen Payne is an accredited psychotherapist and senior registered dance movement therapist. She is Reader in Counselling and Therapeutic Studies at the University of Hertfordshire, facilitates authentic movement groups and runs a small private practice.

Contributors: Sara Bannerman-Haig, Sara Boas, Jill Bunce, Jill Hayes, Vicky Karkou, Ute Kowarzik, Jeannette MacDonald, Bonnie Meekums, Helen Payne, Kedzie Penfield, Rosa Shreeves, Allison Singer, Monika Steiner Celebi.

Dance Movement Therapy

Second edition

Theory, Research and Practice

Edited by Helen Payne

Routledge
Taylor & Francis Group

LONDON AND NEW YORK

First edition published 1992 by Routledge
11 New Fetter Lane, London, EC4P 4EE

Reprinted 1996, 1998, 1999, 2002, 2004

This edition published 2006 by Routledge
27 Church Road, Hove, East Sussex BN3 2FA

Simultaneously published in the USA and Canada
by Routledge
270 Madison Avenue, New York, NY 10016

Routledge is an imprint of the Taylor and Francis Group, an informa business
© 2006 selection and editorial matter, Helen Payne; individual
chapters, the contributors

Typeset in Times by RefineCatch Limited, Bungay, Suffolk
Printed and bound in Great Britain by
TJ International Ltd, Padstow, Cornwall
Paperback cover design by Lisa Dynan

This publication has been produced with paper manufactured to
strict environmental standards and with pulp derived from
sustainable forests.

British Library Cataloguing in Publication Data
A catalogue record for this book is available from the British Library

Library of Congress Cataloging in Publication Data
Dance movement therapy : theory and practice / edited by
Helen Payne.—2nd ed.
    p. cm.
  Includes bibliographical references and index.
  ISBN 1-58391-702-0 — ISBN 1-58931-703-9 (pbk.)
  1. Dance therapy.   I. Payne, Helen, 1951–

  RC489.D3D36 2006
  616.89'1655—dc22
                                            2005054295

ISBN13: 978-1-58391-702-2 hbk
ISBN13: 978-1-58391-703-9 pbk

ISBN10: 1-58391-702-0 hbk
ISBN10: 1-58391-703-9 pbk

This book is dedicated to my daughters, Sarah and Lucie

Contents

List of figures and tables   ix
List of contributors   x
Preface   xv
Acknowledgements   xvii
Postscript   xix

1   **Introduction: Embodiment in action**   1
    HELEN PAYNE

2   **Opening doors: Dance movement therapy with people
    with dementia**   17
    UTE KOWARZIK

3   **Dance movement therapy in the community: Group work
    with people with enduring mental health difficulties**   31
    VICKY KARKOU

4   **Dancing with demons: Dance movement therapy and
    complex post traumatic stress disorder**   49
    JEANETTE MACDONALD

5   **Dance movement therapy with patients with
    Parkinson's disease**   71
    JILL BUNCE

6   **Stretching, tensing and kicking: Aspects of infantile
    movement in dance movement therapy with children and
    adolescents in special education**   87
    SARA BANNERMAN-HAIG

7   Hidden treasures, hidden voices: An ethnographic study into the
    use of movement and creativity in psychosocial work with
    war-affected refugee children in Serbia   101
    ALLISON JANE SINGER

8   The body of culture: Transcultural competence in dance
    movement therapy   112
    SARA BOAS

9   Another royal road: Freudian thought applied to authentic
    movement   132
    KEDZIE PENFIELD

10 Birth moves: Dance movement therapy and holistic birth
    preparation   149
    MONIKA STEINER CELEBI

11 Embodiment in dance movement therapy training and practice   167
    BONNIE MEEKUMS

12 The lived experience of students in a dance movement
    therapy group: Loss, physical contact and the dance movement
    therapy approach   184
    HELEN PAYNE

13 Dance movement therapy with undergraduate dance students:
    'Special ingredients' in the development of playfulness,
    self-confidence and relationship   207
    JILL HAYES

14 Full circle: From choreography to dance movement therapy
    and back   232
    ROSA SHREEVES

Appendix   246
Author index   251
Subject index   257

Figures and tables

Figures

4.1	Alice's picture made at the start of DMT	66
4.2	Alice's picture made at the end of DMT	67
8.1	The Transcultural Competence model	116
9.1	Verbal to Movement Form continuum	135
10.1	Repertory grid interview	159
10.2	Cluster analysis of Jane's grid	160
11.1	The WISE/EMPoweR model of therapeutic change	172
11.2	The spiral process in psychological therapies	177

Tables

2.1	LMC assessment tool	20
3.1	List of theoretical principles	39
3.2	List of clinical principles	40
10.1	Evaluation of holistic birth preparation classes	156
10.2	Themes emerging from antenatal classes: those components which women valued	157
10.3	Themes emerging from antenatal classes: those components which concerned women	158

Contributors

Sara Bannerman-Haig MA, SRDMT has been working with children and adolescents in primary and special school settings for many years. A great deal of her experience has been in the area of learning disability. She has taught on two of the MA/postgraduate training courses in dance movement therapy. She served on the Council for ADMTUK between 1996 and 2001 and has previously published and presented.

Sara Boas, MA, RDMT works with creative dialogue and movement, to enable individual and collective transformation. She has pioneered holistic approaches to professional development and is the founding director and principal coach of **boas**, an international consultancy committed to transforming leadership in business, the public sector, research, NGOs and the arts. She coaches the senior leadership of international businesses and public sector bodies, practises as a dance movement therapist and provides training and supervision for professionals in clinical, managerial and advisory roles. In 2003 Sara established the Foundation for the Arts in Social Transformation (FAST), a global voluntary organisation which uses artistic processes to enable young people and members of vulnerable or marginalised groups to realise their creative potential and take a leading role in their own communities. For more information on her research and activities: www.boastl.com, www.fastchange.org and www.lifedance.info.

Jill Bunce, Cert. Ed., BA (Hons), PG Dip, MA, SRDMT, ITLMA, UKCP is a Senior Registered Dance Movement Therapist who has been in private practice since 1991 and is an Honorary member of the neurological department of a Midlands Hospital. She has worked in Staffordshire, Derbyshire and London and has travelled nationally and internationally, lecturing and providing workshops for medical professionals, including specialist nurses. She has also worked extensively in education with children with learning difficulties and autism. She is registered with the UKCP as an educational therapist and has made links in her work between early neurological development with attachment difficulties. She is at present a senior lecturer in dance movement therapy, is subject leader for dance and movement studies in the combined subject programme and is disability advisor for the School of Education and Health Science at the University of Derby. She has supported the development of dance movement therapy in Russia, Greece, Finland and Poland and at the University of Derby. She presented at the Conference for Neurological Illness in Spain in 2001 and is at the moment studying for her Doctor of Practice in Education at the University of Derby where she is researching curriculum design for dance education. The PD and MS societies and the University of Derby support her work as a practitioner in dance movement therapy.

Monika Steiner Celebi, MA, UKCP, SRDMT has many years experience of working in hospitals and psychiatric institutions in England and abroad. She has taught on the University of Hertfordshire postgraduate diploma in dance movement therapy. She is a qualified yoga teacher and undertook special training in yoga for pregnancy. She is a trained National Childbirth Trust antenatal teacher. In recent years she has led numerous classes for pregnant women, expecting couples and has taught antenatal educators. She has a private psychotherapy and movement therapy practice and teaches yoga. She has published articles and contributed to books.

Dr Jill Hayes, MA, PhD, SRDMT has worked in education using the arts with young people with cognitive and emotional learning difficulties in Germany, the USA and England for 15 years. For the past ten years she has been facilitating experiential learning in the arts therapies at undergraduate and postgraduate levels. Her doctoral thesis analysed dance students' perceptions of an experiential DMT group, with reference to choreography and performance. She is currently writing a book on embodiment in dance and therapy.

Dr Vicky Karkou, MSc, PhD, RDMT is a Lecturer at Queen Margaret University College, Edinburgh. She is also a Postdoctoral Research Fellow and Programme Leader in MA Advanced in Arts Therapies at the University of Hertfordshire, Hatfield. She is trained as a dance movement therapist, a teacher and a researcher and has worked in community settings and schools for several years. She has been involved in professional registration and training in the UK and abroad, and has published widely. Some of her recent publications include the book co-authored with Dr Patricia Sanderson: *Arts Therapies: A Research-Based Map of the Field*.

Ute Kowarzik, MA, SRDMT is a qualified dance movement therapist and researcher. Over the last eight years she has worked with different client groups including women who have experienced domestic violence, refugee women, and older people including people with dementia living in a residential care home. For many years she has conducted research studies on social and health issues, and more recently has been involved in studies investigating the effects of dance movement therapy. The foci of these studies were people with dementia living in a residential care home and chronic pain suffers being treated in a primary care setting. One of her interests is the development of research methods which are more sensitive to capturing clients' experience of the dance movement therapy process and to this end she has explored use of video recordings as a way of tracking this process and the effects on clients' non-verbal communication in a therapeutic setting.

Jeannette MacDonald, BA (Hons), ARAD, SPDMT trained at the Royal Ballet School, London and is a life member of The Royal Academy of Dance where she is a Tutor for Professional Studies. Jeannette danced professionally in Europe and the UK before pioneering dance movement therapy within the National Health Service (NHS). She is Senior Dance Movement Therapist for the Creative Therapy Service (NHS) in Exeter and is in private practice in Exeter and London. Director of Exeter Dance Centre from 1988 to 2001 and Chairperson of the Association for Dance Movement Therapy UK (ADMTUK) from 1998 to 2002, Jeannette is a member of the Executive Council and has represented the profession at the Health Professions Council (HPC) working towards State Registration for DMT. She was a member of the CNAA Validation panel for the first postgraduate DMT course in the UK. She is a member of the Accreditation Panel of the Council for Dance Education and Training (CDET). Jeannette is clinical supervisor to senior colleagues, students in training and other arts therapists. She teaches and lectures nationally and internationally.

Dr Bonnie Meekums, BSc (Hons), MPhil, PhD, UKCP, SRDMT has been developing her approach to DMT for around 30 years. She began her academic life as a physiologist/biochemist, then trained in dance and theatre at the ground-breaking Dartington College of Arts, where her teachers included Mary Fulkerson (release work) and Steve Paxton (contact improvisation). Of late, she has rediscovered an interest in neuroscience, through the recent developments linking attachment experiences and brain development. Her research career has similarly spanned a wide spectrum from experimental science to narrative research. She is perhaps best known for her books *Creative Group Therapy for Women Survivors of Child Sexual Abuse* and *Dance Movement Therapy*. She currently teaches both in Poland and at the University of Leeds (UK), and maintains a private practice. Above all, she treasures the meaningful relationships in her life that help her to keep on growing, learning and just plain being.

Dr Helen Payne, M Phil, PhD, UKCP, SRDMT and Fellow ADMT.UK was previously Head of Counselling and Psychotherapy at the University of Hertfordshire, England where she is now a Reader. She pioneered the development of DMT in the UK co-creating the professional association (ADMT.UK) for which she was Chair for five years, designing and leading the first nationally validated UK postgraduate training, writing and researching. Her books include *Creative Movement and Dance in Group-work, Dance Movement Therapy, Theory and Practice, A Handbook of Inquiry in the Arts Therapies* and *Ethical Practice and the Abuse of Power in Social Responsibility*. She trained in person-centred, psychodynamic and group analytic approaches, and studied authentic movement for many years with Janet Adler. She educates counsellors, supervises doctoral candidates, researches and teaches authentic movement and dance movement therapy worldwide, together with having a private practice in integrative movement psychotherapy. Recently she inspired the co-creation of the new international journal *Body, Movement and Dance in Psychotherapy* (h.l.payne@herts.ac.uk).

Kedzie Penfield, BA, CMA, MPA, SRDMT studied dance movement therapy with Liljan Espanak at Flower and Fifth Avenue Hospitals in NYC. After qualifying as a Laban movement analyst she apprenticed with Irmgard Bartenieff in New York City in the early 1970s, helping to establish the first CMA training programmes and codifying the Fundamentals material. She came to the UK in 1975 to work at Dingleton Hospital as its first dance movement therapist and has lived in Scotland ever since. She worked as a teacher at the Laban Centre in London and as a freelance therapist, trainer and supervisor for various health boards and organisations in the public and private sectors throughout the UK and Europe. In the 1990s she studied with Janet Adler and trained at the Scottish Institute of Human Relations as a psychoanalytic psychotherapist. At present she has a private practice in Edinburgh in supervision and in individual movement and psychoanalytical psychotherapy.

Rosa Shreeves SRDMT, UKCP is a dance artist and therapist, trained at Spectrum Centre for Humanistic and Integrative Psychotherapy. She has worked as a choreographer, performer, broadcaster and choreographic mentor. Her solo shows have toured widely. She is the author of *Children Dancing, Imaginary Dances*, co-author of *Moves*, some published poetry, and has had an exhibition of her photographs. Rosa has worked in both the public and private sector with a wide range of individuals and groups, particularly in outdoor locations with, for example, children, psychiatric patients, special needs, health professionals, therapists and dancers and with many mixed population groups in the UK and Spain. She is also qualified in massage. Her ongoing study of Mexican dance and culture enriches her work.

Allison Singer, BA(Hons), PGDip DMT, MA originally trained in theatre at Dartington College of Arts, majoring in dance and choreography, and vocal improvisation. Postgraduate studies include a Masters in Ethnomusicology; training as a drama and movement therapist with the Sesame Institute; training as a yoga teacher and receiving a fellowship to study at Kaivalyadham Yogic Hospital in India. Her professional work has always moved between community work, therapy work, performance and research with a strong interest in intercultural and interdisciplinary work. Her community and therapeutic work includes working with war-affected refugee children; adults with profound and complex learning difficulties; elderly adults and professionals. She has presented her research nationally and internationally, including at the United Nations in Geneva. Currently completing her PhD thesis in dance ethnography at De Montfort University, Leicester, she is Programme Leader for the PGDip Dramatherapy, University of Derby; and works as a drama and movement therapist in private practice.

Preface

Dance movement therapy: theory, research and practice

Dance movement therapy (DMT) can be defined as the psychotherapeutic use of movement and dance founded on the principle of motion and emotion being inextricably entwined. This relationship is the channel through which a person can embody a deeper connection with the self.

Since the first edited book to document UK practice entitled *Dance Movement Therapy; Theory and Practice*, published in 1992, DMT has grown into adolescence. A number of books have been written and, most recently, an international journal has been established combining DMT with body psychotherapy. There is now a European Association for Dance Movement Therapy and over 30 DMT training programmes have been developed around the world. In the UK, dance movement therapy will become a state registered profession alongside the other arts therapies of art, music and drama within the next two years.

As can be seen from the chapters in this new edited book, DMT in the UK has emerged from pioneering practice in health, education, community mental health and social settings to consolidate that practice in those settings and to develop newer uses with high functioning groups and individuals in the community. This second edition of *Dance Movement Therapy: Theory, Research and Practice* (with the added term 'Research' in the subtitle) gives the practitioner, the allied professional and the trainee, both in the UK and worldwide, an in-depth understanding of DMT as currently practised in the UK. This volume makes a strong contribution to the emerging awareness of the nature of embodiment in psychotherapy and counselling together with building on neuroscience developments.

The contributions represent the diversity of DMT models including descriptive accounts and those reflecting findings from some of the first systematic research studies. This book honours the versatility of DMT as it moulds itself to the various populations and settings exemplified. Each chapter has a similar framework in order to clearly articulate the client material within theory, research and practice. There are reflections which reveal the *way* in which DMT is delivered together with theoretical underpinnings for each particular approach.

The second edition of *Dance Movement Therapy: Theory, Research and Practice*, edited by the same senior practitioner, builds upon the first edition to confirm the authority of DMT in the world of psychological therapies. It will be essential reading to all students, trainers and practitioners of DMT, to clients, counsellors and psychotherapists, body psychotherapists, mental health professionals, special educators, dance/movement teachers and dance artists.

Helen Payne, PhD is an accredited psychotherapist; senior registered movement psychotherapist and Reader in counselling and psychotherapy.

Acknowledgements

Primarily I would like to thank all those contributors who have celebrated their practice by putting it down for others to read. It takes courage to put into words a non-verbal therapy. It is also problematic to communicate this particular approach and methodology. Despite this, the chapters splendidly bear witness to the various guises of dance movement therapy. It has been an honour to work with them; they have been patient with my editorial comments and trusting of my appraisal.

My appreciation goes to those who have helped me to clarify my work: my clients, research participants, students, teachers, supervisors, and others for their support: including Nick Turner, Julia Buckroyd, Jill Clover, Jeni Boyd, and colleagues in ADMTUK and the University of Hertfordshire.

My thanks also to my family for being so supportive to me throughout this enterprise.

Helen Payne
May 2005

Please note where cases presented are not fictional, authors have assured the editor that all material in this book has received informed consent from the relevant clients and research participants whose identifying features have been changed.

Postscript

There is an exciting new development happening in DMT which builds on all that has gone before. It appears to be concerned with the body becoming the soul incarnate, through the soul in action – transpersonal dance. The being human called by the sacred to our soul's journey is to do with what it is to be human, where the tension between spirit and matter are in the suffering, honing the soul during its journey. Movement, whether symbolic or pre-symbolic, is a way in to the soul's transformation. Souls are revealed and contact with the divine may be made through moving in community or alone. In this way spirit and matter are held at the same time, embracing whatever might be wanting to become. The body holds the opposites within the creative impulse which can lead to pyschospiritual transformation. DMT in emphasising the body and energy through movement and transformational dance is uniquely placed to work with the psychospiritual aspects of the human condition. Without this, it could be argued, any change may not be fully integrated whereby ego has to surrender to the life-force's movement within.

Helen Payne
June 2005

Chapter 1

Introduction

Embodiment in action

Helen Payne

Background

Welcome to the new edited dance movement therapy (DMT) compilation. This book is a reflection of UK theory, research and practice in DMT fulfilling two connected aims. First, it updates the previous edition entitled *Dance Movement Therapy: Theory and Practice*, first published in 1992, reprinted a number of times and in several languages. Second, it aims to echo the increased interest worldwide in DMT and its inquiry. It does this by documenting a flavour of UK DMT theory, research and practice. Following the first edition more books on DMT were published in the UK and elsewhere; however, there are still far too few. This edition goes some way to bridging the gap on this subject in the literature.

In the years since the first edition of this book, DMT in the UK has developed considerably. The professional association ADMTUK (see Appendix for details) now accredits senior and registered therapists and assumes responsibility for the safe and ethical practice of DMT. Licence to practise is restricted to accredited members who abide by a code of ethics and principles for practice. The profession is now unionised and has a career structure in the new 'Agenda for Change' in the NHS. ADMTUK has successfully applied for membership of the Health Professions Council (HPC), the regulatory body for the health professions such as occupational therapy, speech and language therapy and physiotherapy. Once this procedure is finalised (in two years), DMT will have the same relationship to HPC as the other three arts therapies professions (art, music and drama). This is an enormously important step in the professional development of DMT. The Nuffield Trust's conference in 1998 on 'The Arts in Medicine' led to debate on the role of the arts in health professionals' training and the care of patients, to which DMT contributed. However, since then it has also grown in stature and recognition on the international stage. There are many more university postgraduate training programmes, professional associations and employment opportunities globally. The newly launched *International Journal of Body, Movement and Dance in Psychotherapy* is testimony to the overall worldwide growth in this field. For example, new publications from as far afield as India (Kashyap 2005) are evident, as well as Goodill (2005) whose material is based on American practice.

DMT is now informed and supported by national and international research. Stemming from the increase in practitioners who have completed research in DMT, this second UK edited book provides a range and depth of theory, integrated into research and practice hereto unavailable. Consequently, in this new edition there is more focus on the application of research to theory and practice. It is hoped that this will stimulate a number of different practitioners from a range of professions, not solely DMT, in their thinking about inquiry, theoretical issues, application of interventions and research processes, and practice outcomes. PhD and postdoctoral research in dance and DMT is growing, and, as with other newly developing professions on this journey, there is a greater need for practice-based research literature.

Purchases of the previous book were from the UK and Europe, although Australasia and the USA were also well represented. Dance movement therapists were an obvious audience. However, others included health professionals, counsellors/psychotherapists, dancers and dance departments. It is anticipated this volume will attract readers from these same professions globally, as well as those from special education, occupational therapy, psychology, social work, learning disability, mental health, and somatic studies.

Since that first edition, interest is much more prevalent in the general population towards the application of dance/movement/body to personal development, healing and change. Publications in the UK following the 1992 edition demonstrate this attention: for example, through the metaphoric body (Bartel and Ne'eman 1993); movement and drama (Pearson 1996); movement and the voice (Newman 1998); embodied psychotherapy (Shaw 2003); DMT (Meekums 2000); arts therapies (Payne 1993a; Meekums 2003); arts therapies and health (Jones 2004); body psychotherapy (Stanton 2002; Totton 1999, 2003, 2005; Aposhyan 2004); and the expressive body in life, therapy and art (Halprin 2003). Perhaps dance as a shamanic practice such as Roth (1990), together with the growing attraction of alternative and complementary approaches to medicine, has added to this surge in attention.

What is dance movement therapy?

Dance movement therapy in the UK developed from a creative approach to dance (Laban 1978) with numerous groups in hospitals, education, health and social settings, to a form of psychotherapy (Meekums 2003). DMT supports people whereby spontaneous movement is seen as symbolic of unconscious processes. It increases self-awareness and self-esteem, providing for growth, change and healing within a therapeutic relationship. Dance, improvisation, empathic embodiment (Cooper 2001), change and the self are in constant interaction in much DMT practice. It is a craft: a hybrid comprised of the theory and practice of psychological therapy and dance. Various services offer DMT as practitioners become qualified and registered with the professional association, The Association for Dance Movement Therapy, United Kingdom (ADMTUK), as a private practitioner or as working in one of the above services.

Dance movement therapy is defined as: 'the psychotherapeutic use of movement and dance through which a person can engage creatively in a process to further their emotional, cognitive, physical and social integration' (ADMTUK 2002: 1). DMT, also termed movement psychotherapy or dance therapy (all terms are protected), is a form of psychotherapy in which the creative use of movement and dance play a fundamental role within the therapeutic alliance. It is practised with groups and individuals in education, health and social care settings as well as private practice. Dance as a healing art is ancient. In historical genres the expression of feelings and emotions is common. However, nowadays DMT is informed by contemporary psychological theory and research, psychotherapeutic theory and practice, multicultural trends in dance, spiritual developments and body psychotherapy. It is anticipated that the new neuropsychology research, where sensory perception is closely linked to affective and cognitive processes in a kind of kinaesthetic thinking, will also affect DMT theory, research and practice (Damasio 2000; Palley 2000; Gerhardt 2004; Schore 2003a and b; Panksepp 2004, in press a and b; Carroll (in press)). Feelings, as expressed through the client/patient's movement, provide content and a framework which influences the direction of the therapy rather than direction being taken from the therapist's agenda. The therapist supports and challenges the client, engaging with their expressions. Movement is creative and improvisational, embodying the imagination whereby the body becomes the vehicle for self-expression and a bridge between emotion and motion for integration and healing. This form becomes the transitional space for the therapeutic relationship. DMT is embodiment in action.

Who is this book written for?

The book aims to present DMT accessibly to global readers from within the DMT profession (practitioners, students, clients) and to others such as those from arts therapies, counselling/psychotherapy, body psychotherapy, and arts for health practice. It is also edited with dancers, choreographers, dance teachers/students, community dance artists and other dance professionals in mind. It will be helpful to anyone who wishes to learn more about the use of creative movement and dance in psychotherapy and/or research methodologies appropriate to a number of therapeutic contexts. Worldwide audiences from within the disciplines of psychological therapies, groupwork, special education, arts in medicine, health and social care, psychology and other social sciences will find the book illustrative of the underlying background to DMT – a newly developing, innovative approach to psychological therapy. It is hoped that this new edition will stimulate a number of different practitioners from a range of professions, not solely DMT, in their thinking about theoretical issues, application of interventions and research processes and outcomes.

How is the book structured?

The approach taken for this book, as with the first edition, was collaborative, inviting participation from leading practitioner-researchers, new practitioner-researchers and previously published authors. This book is longer than the previous one with an additional two chapters, reflecting the increase in the volume of practice current in the UK. Each of the following 13 chapters have been designed with similar sections for ease of reference. The authors have usually introduced the topic, background and setting and reviewed the related literature followed by case material from practice, commentary and conclusions. Where appropriate, research methodology and analysis have been included, together with recommendations for further inquiry. The application of conclusions/findings to DMT theory and practice is normally provided. Any notes and references are given at the end of each chapter. Author and subject index are provided at the back of the book for reference. An Appendix gives the reader information on the professional associations, training programmes and relevant journals.

The chapters have been ordered in clusters from clinical interventions with those suffering dementia, enduring mental health problems, complex post traumatic stress disorder and Parkinson's disease at the beginning, to those with children and adolescents, transcultural practice, higher functioning populations such as pregnant women and private practice psychotherapy clients, training and student groups. At the end, there is an exploration of the interplay between choreographic and DMT skills and processes. The particular clusters of chapters are organised with an eye to their common elements such as children, cultural issues, mental health, theoretical matters, students and training.

What are the contributions?

All the authors in the book are practising dance movement therapists, registered with the professional association ADMTUK. Some are leaders in the field. The book includes some of those first generation authors who contributed to the first edition: Jeannette MacDonald, Bonnie Meekums, Helen Payne, Kedzie Penfield and Monika Steiner Celebi. They have offered to share their work again as it grows and develops. Unfortunately, not all of the previous authors were in a position to contribute again. Consequently there are several new authors writing on different populations/settings, others from similar settings/populations and those included the last time, whose chapters have a research emphasis. Due to the second aim of this new edition, that of documenting UK practice-led research in the field, most chapters do focus towards this end. No one model is stressed, encouraging practitioners to develop the most appropriate approach for their own context. For students and newly qualified practitioners it will stimulate thought about the various approaches, and for those changing settings there is a breadth and depth of considerations to reflect upon. In view of the new international programmes and the increasing research and academic interest, together with NHS recognition and career structure, this book is in step with the current pace of developments in the subject both globally and in the UK. The following section is an overview of the whole book, chapter by chapter.

In Chapter 2, 'Opening Doors', *Ute Kowarzik* reports on a study of dance movement therapy with people with dementia within the context of a continuing debate on how to improve quality of care. It is suggested that a DMT approach can provide an environment in which professionals and those responsible for care may observe and assess clients less intrusively than traditional clinical tools permit. This approach, which promotes and assesses well-being all in one, underlines the nature of DMT within a social care environment.

In Chapter 3, 'Dance Movement Therapy in the Community', *Vicky Karkou* demonstrates the role DMT continues to play in community care within the mental health service. Despite almost half the registered members of ADMTUK being recorded as practising in community environments such as charities, private practice, social services, community care and residential care, private hospitals or therapeutic communities, there is little in the literature, particularly the research-based publications. The chapter discusses major principles of DMT practice as described by practitioners themselves and gives clinical examples of such work with clients with enduring mental health problems who have recently moved into the community. Some findings from a larger nationwide study which surveyed arts therapists are used to ground the discussion. It is proposed that interactive principles, an empathic attitude and flexible ways of working are important principles of work in these settings. Debates in community work are identified where relevant to the practice of DMT in the community and major approaches to DMT are revisited in the light of this context.

In Chapter 4, 'Dancing with Demons', *Jeannette MacDonald* offers a retrospective single case study that describes DMT with a complex post-traumatic stress disordered client. Triangulation gives multiple perceptions of the same phenomena and grounded theory is employed to find some consonance between theory and clinical practice. The client's own experience of DMT, as reported in her journal and interview, is compared with the core data of the therapist's perception of the process of transformation. This gives a holistic account whereby metaphor and symbols are crucial to the integration of a fragmented sense of self. Creating dances, choreography, is seen as central to the approach whereby meaning from movement, with dance at its heart, renews and makes whole.

The following chapters emphasise inquiry from a pluralistic methodological approach. For example, in Chapter 5, 'Dance Movement Therapy with Patients with Parkinson's disease', *Jill Bunce* documents a project aimed at exploring the role of movement in a therapeutic relationship with patients suffering from the degenerative Parkinson's disease. Laban Movement Analysis observation tools are explicitly employed through the use of video with an inter-rater reliability method, together with her own subjective interpretation of the process of DMT and self-report questionnaires from patients. This research follows earlier studies of DMT with Parkinson's outpatients such as Westbrook and McKibben (1989). Findings included: an increase in body awareness; an improvement in self-confidence and communication skills; a lifting of depression; and improvement in specific motor abilities and balance. Future needs as expressed by patients concerned the need for support, communication and socialisation; the alleviation of depression and withdrawal; the need for strong boundaries and a safe place to discuss the experience of the disease.

The next author, *Sara Bannerman-Haig*, also presents research using movement observation as a basis for her practice in a special school with learning disabled adolescents and emotionally disturbed children. In Chapter 6, 'Stretching, Tensing and Kicking: Aspects of Infantile Movement in DMT with Children and Adolescents in Special Education', she aims to integrate DMT with children, psychoanalytical principles, and the experiential process of infant–mother observation, in order to begin to address what infantile modes of body communication represent. The study uses participant observation, reframing movement work with adolescents as observed in infants and toddlers. Laban Movement Analysis and the Kestenberg Movement Profiling systems are integrated into the research and practice to deduce meaning from the children's movements. The interdisciplinary approach to the research has developed the author's practice; for example, there is an increase in the use of words and verbalisations and greater depth in the consideration of interventions and interpretations which stem from interaction with clients.

Chapter 7, 'Hidden Treasures, Hidden Voices: An Ethnographic Study into the Use of Movement and Creativity in Psychosocial Work with War-affected Children in Serbia' by *Allison Jane Singer*, presents an inquiry using ethnography, which is now becoming more widely used in arts-based research. Her study demonstrates the importance of creativity and movement in an 'event' within the context of post-war international development work. Conclusions include the notion of exchange; the need for work to take account of context (particularly using 'ethno' or folk movement); the importance of multimedia accessibility and flexibility in the use of the term 'therapy' which is culture specific.

In Chapter 8, The Body of Culture: Transcultural Competences in Dance Movement Therapy, *Sara Boas* describes a study of DMT practice as cultural agency; a reciprocal process of self-making and world-making in which there are cultural bodies – people moving, not a 'body' of culture. Human movement and improvisation, it is claimed, are shaped by and do shape culture – from the social microcosm of the DMT group to larger social systems. The question is posed of how to transcend the contradiction between both body and a no body, culture and no culture. The term 'competence' in the chapter draws our attention to professional development, training and the need for active engagement, both academically and pragmatically, as a practitioner-researcher. This study calls on many aspects of the researchers' intelligence in a multimodal inquiry resulting in a multidimensional appreciation of the topic.

In Chapter 9, 'Another Royal Road: Freudian Thought Applied to Authentic Movement', based on her private practice in psychoanalytic psychotherapy, *Kedzie Penfield* elucidates how authentic movement can be integrated with psychoanalytic thinking. Propositions, illustrated by practice material, include reference to Freud, Klein and neuroscience in an exploration of transference, countertransference and projection within the two forms of the two free-floating languages of authentic movement and the practice of free association in psychoanalytic psychotherapy.

Chapter 10, 'Birth Moves: Dance Movement Therapy and Holistic Birth Preparation' by *Monika Steiner Celebi*, gives the reader an insight into how DMT, when combined with yoga within a psychoanalytic framework, can be beneficial to pregnant mums in antenatal care. A repertory grid (one with an in-depth interview) is used as a tool for eliciting concepts of what were the important and less important aspects of the holistic birth preparation classes from participants. Body-based experiences such as breath and body awareness, relaxation, practice of coping strategies and contact with other pregnant mothers were some of the most important elements. This is an example of how DMT appears to be on the move out into the community and demonstrates the importance of embodied knowledge being fostered in antenatal education.

Bonnie Meekums shares her thoughts on approaches suitable to therapeutic settings in Chapter 11, 'Embodiment in Dance Movement Therapy Training and Practice'. She makes links between what we can know about embodiment from multidisciplinary theoretical perspectives and what we know through our embodied practice, in order to develop innovative and integrated approaches to learning, training and practice (including supervision). A model is proposed for understanding the therapeutic process within DMT. The importance of the developing relationship between client and therapist is stressed within the framework of embodiment linked to a central concept of somatic intelligence as a cornerstone of DMT theory and practice.

Helen Payne offers an analysis of themes and processes from a research project exploring a personal development group during a two-year DMT training in Chapter 12, 'The Lived Experience of Students in a Dance Movement Therapy Group: Loss, Physical Contact and the DMT Approach'. It describes an in-depth, systematic, qualitative, participatory study, the first to involve trainee dance movement therapists within higher education reflecting on their own DMT experiences. The personal development module (the DMT group) of the postgraduate programme was the focus of the inquiry which aimed to investigate the nature of the DMT group experience for student clinical DMT practice, during and following their training. A number of themes emerged, including loss, physical contact and the approach towards DMT adopted for the group. The researcher immersed herself subjectively in the data to create the themes.

This was also the research method chosen by *Jill Hayes* in the Chapter 13, 'Dance Movement Therapy with Dance Students'. Here a focus is given to DMT in the context of choreography and performance with dance students in higher education. The study is an in-depth and highly detailed inquiry into a DMT process and subsequent memories and reflections. Recorded group reflections at the end of each of the DMT sessions and semi-structured interviews were analysed thematically. Findings included playfulness and play, necessarily re-evoking childhood and the freedom to enter imaginary worlds, leaving behind constraints and conventions of adult society which often require linear, rigid responses. A second key theme was self-confidence, that is, trust in the self which is fundamentally worthy of recognition as a creative being. Trust in self leads to participation, which in turn leads to a sense of solidarity building greater trust. Safety in this instance seemed to be intimately connected to the culture of acceptance (a non-oppressive relationship with others with no desire to control or change, where there is an absence of criticism – an allowing of each to tell their story and a validity of others' realities). Third, the theme entitled relationship is postulated as the possibility of 'depth relationship' and 'relational fluidity' and, it is claimed, this involves awareness of self in relationship as well as awareness of physical, emotional and mental states of others; connectedness, community and inner and outer awareness.

Rosa Shreeves provides a responsive final chapter, commissioned by the editor following an analysis of the contributions. In 'Full Circle' she offers an exploration of DMT in mainstream dance activities with respect to the following: *the craft of choreography* including fresh insights on how DMT theory and practice may facilitate a focus on the dancer's internal experience (such as her subjective relationship with her body in dance improvisation/choreography), the dancer's personal experience in choreography, her reflective capacities, play and the creative process; *healthier dancers*, for example, dance theory notions of dance as a transcendent experience, it is suggested, might be enhanced and expanded upon to foster dancer well-being. DMT could perhaps facilitate dancers to become congruent and self-aware, and, contentiously perhaps, giving them a greater understanding of the nature of personal transformation in making movement for dance.

What is the importance of research?

Those completed research projects represented give a definite flavour of the range of methodologies, topics and approaches to DMT research and practice generated by the authors' inquiring minds. Research though can be a difficult subject for therapists to embrace. However, without rigorous research DMT cannot develop further as a profession or discipline. For example, the HPC demanded as part of ADMT's application for state registration an overview of DMT research studies to date. Practice can be improved upon through the application of research findings and the clarification of theory.

Students and practitioners need to develop collaborative projects to inquire into issues and questions which are heartfelt to them, perhaps within the NHS or education services and/or together with other arts therapies practitioners-researcher. Increased co-operation with our colleagues in the other arts therapies (such as through the Arts Therapies Advisory Group, a subgroup to HPC), health and social care professions and counselling/psychotherapy may well provide the fertile soil for sowing the seeds and harvesting the fruits of research projects. These professions have more in common than differences when researching and can each learn from the other. Research using the emerging arts-based approaches such as those advocated by Wadsworth Hervey (2000) and McNiff (2000) may be another path towards documenting evidence of practice. These may appeal more to those in the field who feel distanced by the quasi-scientific methods. Authors in DMT such as Payne (1993b), Wadsworth Hervey (2000), Berrol (2000) and Cruz and Berrol (2004) provide overviews of a range of methodologies that could be considered depending on the research question/topic.

Can dance movement therapy offer something back to the world of dance?

One of the major themes to emerge from an analysis of the chapters in this edition has been the relevance of DMT to postmodern dance choreographic process. After all our struggles to differentiate DMT from dance (as performance/recreation/occupation or education), whilst acknowledging the strong roots it has in this art form, perhaps it can now reconnect in making an offering back to that discipline. By reconnecting with its origins in dance, DMT can give back to the processes, practice and performance in the art of dance. There do not appear to be publications which attempt to close the circle by examining the contribution DMT can make to the understanding of dance as an art form and of dancers' health. The chapter requested from *Rosa Shreeves* attempts to do just this in order to mirror the theme which materialised from the contributions.

In DMT, Schmais and White (1986), Stanton-Jones (1992) and Payne (2000) differentiate DMT from dance in psychiatry and groupwork respectively and Payne (1993b) offers a general overview of DMT research in various settings with different populations, the concepts drawn together through psychological therapies theory. Other books such as Behar-Horestein and Ganet-Segal (1999), Wadsworth Hervey (2000) and Cruz and Berrol (2004) present research on DMT theory and practice but do not link findings to dance. Neither does Levy (1995) who presents an edited book of chapters on DMT, embedded in an arts therapies context, with specific vulnerable populations or Chodorow (1992) who covers one view of Jungian thought and DMT, integrating dance aspects such as improvisation, emotional expression and dance steps. Pallaro (1999) overviews authentic movement and demonstrates the practice, history and connections with psychological therapies theory, followed by Adler (2002) on her teaching and discipline of authentic movement although explicit links to dance therapy and practice are limited.

Recently it has been shown that dance as a performing art might benefit from DMT and other therapies and more emphasis is placed on dancer well-being these days (International Association for Dance Medicine and Science, Dance.UK 2004). Buckroyd (2000) explores the student dancer's health, suggesting changes in teaching approaches and provision of therapy/ counselling. She maintains an emotionally mature dancer facilitates self-care and enhances creativity. Since affect is inherent in movement (Brooks and Stark 1989), DMT may help dancers become emotionally educated and improve well-being (Payne 2006).

Increasingly dance students study an introduction to DMT as part of undergraduate dance education and dancers/choreographers participate to develop team building/creativity. Dancers and choreographers are attracted to DMT as a way of enhancing team building and creativity. In community dance there is a growing awareness of DMT (for example, a community youth dance project flyer mentions dance as therapy alongside recreation and performance). DMT is increasingly applicable in high functioning communities such as student populations. Payne (2001, 2003) focuses on DMT as a personal development group with students and Hayes (1999, 2004) evaluates the role of DMT in the training of student dancers and choreographers.

Dance theorists (Tufnell and Crickmay 1990; Marranca and Dasgupta 1999; Cottom and Sager 2002; Koltai 2002; Tufnell and Crickmay 2004) have elucidated the need for choreography and performance to offset the externally targeted technique with a process which prizes inner experience, inviting the dancer's involvement with ideas in choreography. The authoritarian nature of dance education (Smith 1997) seems at odds with the notion of creativity which has an internal focus. Group experiences (where dance is normally created), exploration and self-reflection could enhance the creative process in dance. Beiswanger (1978) and Nadel (1978) describe dance creation as co-operative and empathic, emerging out of choreographic sensitivity to the quality and style of the dancer, and Dilley (1990) describes outer, inner and transcendent awareness as useful to choreographers.

Improvisation has been documented as essential to inspiration, creativity and choreography (Sheets Johnstone 1966; Paxton 1982; Fraleigh 1987; Blom and Chaplin 1988; Tufnell and Crickmay 1990, 2004; Nagrin 1994; Halprin 1995, 2003; Lycouris 1996) and as personal, inner transformation (Steinman 1986). Predock and Roll's (2000) research concludes personal themes would give choreographers rich stimulation and an authentic source of inspiration. Improvisation encourages free, playful experimentation with movement and imagination (Smith-Autard 2000). Lindquist (2001) claims play in DMT facilitates personal investment in the movement process with simultaneous occurrence of personal emotion and image. If dance is a personal experience needing to be authentically, kinaesthetically communicated to others, empathy between dancers and audience needs cultivating. Cottom and Sager (2002), Koltai (2002) and Nadel and Strauss (2003) suggest there is a place for intimacy, authenticity and empathy in choreography and performance.

Jill Hayes in her chapter shows how DMT can contribute to dancer training and education. Aspects might include DMT approaches to enhancing playfulness; relationships and self-confidence resulting in an increase in somatic intelligence for example. Her research suggests DMT techniques might be used for building relationships, stressing the importance of play to creativity and the implications of neglecting the 'inner' person in favour of the outer expression. Building relationships between dancers and choreographers (and perhaps audiences) requires embodied empathy (Cooper 2001), group relationship through movement, and an understanding of the nature of witness and mover, which, given the performance/audience aspect, may offer original observations in terms of dance theory and practice.

Further research questions that may highlight our understanding of dance from the DMT perspective concern:

- the relationship between mind, personality and body–movement–dance
- the theoretical significance of embodied metaphor/symbolism to creativity and the unconscious
- the nature of somatic intelligence and any insight this might provide into interdisciplinary research, teaching and learning
- the role of embodiment in our capacity for health, well-being and recovery.

DMT theory, research and practice have much to offer to dance as an art form.

This book provides discussion on the following related areas of dance: the nature of somatic intelligence, relationship building, intimacy, authenticity and embodiment, improvisation, the creative process, imagination, symbolism and the unconscious, emotional intelligence and well-being, and motivation/inspiration for moving and witnessing movement.

Writings from choreography and performance validate personal investment in the movement process (Lindquist 2001; Foster 2003), the importance of imagination (Tufnell and Crickmay 2004), the creative process (Green 1996) and consciousness through dance (Fraleigh 2000) where ordinary movement play is valued as a method of exploration. (Foster claims this is a rejection of the modernist expressive approach to choreography.)

Findings drawn from DMT, for example, the communication of movement, emotion and image arising simultaneously may assist the development of understanding in the related area of both dance training and performance. The emerging disciplines of body psychotherapy (Stanton 2002; Totton 1999, 2003, 2005), somatic psychology (Hartley 2004) and body therapies, or somatics (Bateson 1990, 1993; Fortin 1995; Green 1999) may also benefit from awareness and knowledge developed in DMT.

The challenges of interdisciplinary work not only with dance but across professions in health and social care will strengthen DMT. Practitioners need to seek out opportunities for research outside their discipline. Research methodologies outlined in these chapters may be suitable for interdisciplinary and collaborative research in DMT, dance and related areas such as body psychotherapy and counselling/psychotherapy. Dance is already exploring its practice as a form of research (Hetcht 2005) as with other arts disciplines which has been a recognised approach towards DMT and other arts therapies research as well.

Summary

This chapter has introduced the reader to this unique collection of chapters from DMT authors, all of whom are practitioner-researchers. The book reflects a breadth of the developing theory, research of and approaches to DMT in the UK. Of particular significance is the focus on connections between DMT and dance, choreographically and as a performing art. As well as providing practice-based evidence, the book endorses and disseminates original practice and research projects with varying methodologies and with differing populations in dance, health, education and the community. We hope you will enjoy reading these contributions. The editor welcomes contact with other practitioners.

References

Aposhyan, S. (2004) *Bodymind Psychotherapy: Principles, techniques and practical applications*. New York: Norton.

Adler, J. (2002) *Offering from the Conscious Body*. Vermont: Inner Traditions. Association for Dance Movement Therapy.UK (2004) Online. Available HTTP: <http://www.admt.org.uk.> (accessed 22 August 2004).

ADMTUK (2002) *Arts Therapy: Benchmark Statement*. Gloucester. Quality Assurance Agency for Higher Education. Online. Available <HTTP://www.qaa.ac.uk/academicinfrastructure/benchmark/health/ArtsTherapy.pdf> (accessed 23 September 2005).

Bartel, L. and Ne'eman, N. (1993) *The Metaphoric Body*. London: Jessica Kingsley.

Bateson, G. (1990) Dancing fully, safely and expressively – the role of the body therapies in dance training, *Journal of Physical Education, Recreation and Dance* 61, 9, 28–31.

—— (1993) Stretching technique: a somatic learning model – Part 1: Training sensory responsivity, *Impulse: The International Journal for Dance Science, Medicine and Education* 1, 2, 126–140.

Behar-Horenstein, L. and Ganet-Segal, J. (1999) *The Art and Practice of Dance Movement Therapy*. Needham Heights, MA: Pearson.

Berrol, C. (2000) The spectrum of research options in dance movement therapy, *American Journal of Dance Therapy* 22, 1, 29–46.

Beiswanger, G. (1978) Chance and design in choreography, in M.H. Nadel and C. Nadel Miller (eds) *The Dance Experience*. New York: Universe Books.

Blom, L.A. and Chaplin, L.T. (1988) *The Moment of Movement: Dance Improvisation*, London: Dance Books.

Brooks, D. and Stark, A. (1989) The effect of dance/movement therapy on affect: a pilot study, *American Journal of Dance Therapy* 11, 2, 101–111.

Buckroyd, J. (2000) *The Student Dancer*. London: Dance Books.

Carroll, R. (in press) A new era for psychotherapy: Panksepp's affect model in the context of neuroscience and its implications for contemporary psychotherapy practice, in J. Corrigall, H. Payne and H. Wilkinson (eds) *About a Body: Working with the embodied mind in psychotherapy*. London: Routledge.

Chodorow, J. (1992) *Dance Therapy and Depth Psychology*. London: Routledge.

Cooper, M. (2001) Embodied empathy, in S. Haugh and T. Merry (eds) *Roger's Therapeutic Conditions: Evolution, Theory and Practice*. Ross on Wye: PCCS.

Cottom, M. and Sager, P. (2002) Following the arc: an ongoing dialogue about performance and authentic movement, *Contact Quarterly* 27, 2.

Cruz, R. and Berrol, C. (2004) *Dance Movement Therapists in Action: A Working Guide to Research Options*. Springfield, IL: Charles Thomas.

Damasio, A.R. (2000) *The Feeling of What Happens: Body and Emotion in the Making of Consciousness*. New York: Harcourt Brace.

Dance.UK website. Online. Available: HTTP <http://www.danceuk.org> (accessed 23 December 2004).

Dilley, B. (1990) Creative process and meditation, *Contact Quarterly*, fall, 40–44.

Feder, B. and Feder, E. (1998) *Art and Science of Evaluation in the Arts Therapies: How Do You Know What's Working?* Springfield, IL: Charles Thomas.

Fortin, S. (1995) Towards a new generation: somatic dance education in academia,

Impulse: The International Journal for Dance Science, Medicine and Education 3, 253–262.

Foster, S.L. (2003) Improvisation in dance and mind, in A. Cooper Albright and D. Gere (eds) *Taken by Surprise – A Dance Improvisation Reader*. Middletown, CT: Wesleyan University Press.

Fraleigh, S.H. (1987) *Dance and the Lived Body*. Pittsburgh: University of Pittsburgh Press.

—— (2000) Consciousness matters, *Dance Research Journal* 32, 1, 12–15.

Gerhardt, S. (2004) *Why Love Matters: How Affection Shapes a Baby's Brain*. London: Brunner-Routledge.

Goodill, S.W. (2005) *An Introduction to Medical Dance/Movement Therapy. Health-care in motion*. London: Jessica Kingsley Publishers.

Green, J. (1996) Choreographing a postmodern turn: the creative process and somatics, *Impulse: The International Journal for Dance Science, Medicine and Education*, 4, 267–275.

—— (1999) Somatic authority and the myth of the ideal body in dance education. *Dance Research Journal* 31, 2, 80–100.

Halprin, A. (1995) *Moving Toward Life*. Hanover, NH: Wesleyan University Press.

—— (2003) *The Expressive Body in Life, Art and Therapy*. London: Jessica Kingsley.

Hartley, L. (2002) *Somatic Psychology: Body, Mind and Meaning*. London: Whurr.

Hayes, J. (1999) Movement linked to feeling and image: dance students' perceptions of an experiential group, *Journal of Contemporary Health* 8, 20–24.

—— (2004) Student dancers' perception of DMT in relation to performance and choreography, unpublished PhD thesis, University of Hertfordshire, UK.

Hetcht, T. (2005) Creativity in the development of a narrative in ballet: a danced-as–practice-as-research project, paper presented at PARIP International Conference, University of Bristol.

International Association for Dance Medicine and Science. Online. Available HTTP: <http://www.iadms.org> (accessed 23 December 2004).

Jones, P. (2004) *The Arts Therapies: A Revolution in Healthcare*. London: Brunner-Routledge.

Kashyap, T. (2005) *My body, my wisdom: A handbook of creative dance therapy*. New Delhi, India: Penguin Books India.

Koltai, J. (2002) Forms of feeling, frames of mind: authentic movement practice and an actor's process, *Contact Quarterly* 27, 2.

Laban, R. (1978) *Modern Educational Dance*. London: Macdonald and Evans.

Levy, F.J. (ed.) (1995) *Dance and Other Expressive Arts Therapies*. London: Routledge.

Lindquist, G. (2001) The relationship between play and dance, *Research in Dance Education* 2, 1, 41–52.

Lycouris, S. (1996) Destablishing dancing: tensions between the theory and practice of improvisational performance, unpublished PhD thesis, University of Surrey.

McNiff, S. (2000) *Art-based Research*. London: Jessica Kingsley.

Marranca, B. and Dasgupta, G. (1999) *Conversations on Art and Performance*. Baltimore: Johns Hopkins University Press.

Meekums, B. (2000) *Creative Group Therapy for Women Survivors of Child Sexual Abuse*. London: Jessica Kingsley.

—— (2003) *Dance Movement Therapy: A Psychotherapeutic Approach*. London: Sage.

Nadel, M.H. (1978) The process of creativity in dance, in M.H. Nadel and C. Nadel Miller (eds) *The Dance Experience*. New York: Universe Books.

Nadel, M.H. and Strauss, M.R. (eds) (2003) *The Dance Experience: Insights into History, Culture and Creativity*. Princeton, NJ. Princeton University Press.

Nagrin, D. (1994) *Dance and the Specific Image: Improvisation*. Pittsburgh: University of Pittsburgh Press.

Newman, P. (1998) *Voice and Movement Therapy*. London: Jessica Kingsley.

Palley, R. (2000) *The Mind–Brain Reality*. London: Karnac.

Pallaro, P. (ed.) (1999) *Authentic Movement*. London: Jessica Kingsley.

Panksepp, J. (2004) *Affective Neuroscience: The Foundations of Human and Animal Emotions*. London: Karnac.

Panksepp, J. (in press a) The Psychiatric and Clinical Implications of the Core Emotional Systems of the Mammalian Brain, in J. Corrigall, H. Payne and H. Wilkinson (eds) *About a Body: Working with the embodied mind in psychotherapy*. London: Routledge.

Panksepp, J. (in press b) Applications of the affective neuroscience strategy to clinical issues, in J. Corrigall, H. Payne and H. Wilkinson (eds) *About a Body: Working with the embodied mind in psychotherapy*. London: Routledge.

Paxton, S. (1982) *Contact Improvisation*. Theatre Papers 4th series. Dartington: Dartington College of Arts.

Payne, H.L. (ed) (1992) *Dance Movement Therapy: Theory and Practice, First Edition*. London: Routledge.

Payne, H.L. (ed.) (1993a) *A Handbook of Inquiry in the Arts Therapies: One River, Many Currents*. London: Jessica Kingsley.

—— (1993b) From practitioner to practitioner-researcher, in H.L. Payne (ed.) *Handbook of Inquiry in the Arts Therapies: One River, Many Currents*. London: Jessica Kingsley.

—— (2000) *Creative Movement and Dance in Groupwork*, Bicester: Speechmark.

—— (2001) Students' experiences of a DMT group: a question of safety, *European Journal of Psychotherapy, Counselling and Health* 4, 2, 167–292.

—— (2003) Authentic movement in groupwork, *Moving-On, Newsletter for the Australian Dance Therapy Association* 2, 2, 15–17.

Payne, H.L. (in press) Wellbeing and embodiment: authentic movement in mindbodyspirit connection, in J. Corrigall, H. Payne and H. Wilkinson (eds) *About a Body: Working with the embodied mind in psychotherapy*. London: Routledge.

Pearson, J. (1996) *Drama and Movement in Therapy*. London: Jessica Kingsley.

Predock, J. and Roll, S. (2000) An exploration of improvisational and psychological techniques to facilitate the use of personal themes in choreography, in *Dance: Current Selected Research*, vol. 4, New York: AMS Press.

Roth, G. (1990) *Maps to Ecstasy: Teachings of an Urban Shaman*. London: Mandala.

Schmais, C. and White, E. (1986) Introduction to dance therapy, *American Journal of Dance Therapy* 9, 23–30.

Schore, A. (2003a) *Affect Regulation and the Repair of the Self*. Hove: Lawrence Erlbaum Associates.

Schore, A. (2003b) *Affect Disregulation and the Disorders of the Self*. Hove: Lawrence Erlbaum Associates.

Shaw, R. (2003) *The Embodied Psychotherapist*, London: Routledge.

Sheets-Johnstone, M. (1966) *The Phenomenology of Dance*. Madison, WI: University of Wisconsin Press.

Smith, J. (1997) The conservatory as a greedy total institution, paper presented at the 30th the Annual Conference on Research in Dance, University of Arizona.

Smith-Autard, J.M. (2000) *Dance Composition*, 4th edn. New York: Routledge.

Stanton, T. (ed.) (2002) *Body Psychotherapy*. London: Brunner-Routledge.

Stanton-Jones, K. (1992) *Introduction to Dance Movement Therapy in Psychiatry*. London: Routledge.

Steinman, L. (1986) *The Knowing Body*. Boston and London: Shambola.

Totton, N. (1999) *The Water in the Glass: Body and Mind in Psychoanalysis*. London: Rebus Press.

—— (2003) *Body Psychotherapy: An Introduction*. Maidenhead: Open University Press.

—— (ed.) (2005) *New Dimensions in Body Psychotherapy*. Maidenhead: Open University Press.

Tufnell, M. and Crickmay, C. (1990) *Body, Space, Image*. London: Virago.

—— (2004) *A Widening Field: Journeys in Body and Imagination*. London: Dance Books.

Wadsworth Hervey, L. (2000) *Artistic Inquiry in Dance Movement Therapy: Creative Research Alternatives*. Chicago: Charles Thomas.

Westbrook, B.K. and McKibben, H. (1989) Dance/movement therapy with groups of outpatients with Parkinson's disease, *American Journal of Dance Therapy* 11, 1, 27–37.

Chapter 2

Opening doors

Dance movement therapy with people with dementia

Ute Kowarzik

Introduction

Promoting the well-being of, and caring for, people with dementia can be challenging as cognitive loss, changing behaviour and reduced possibilities of verbal communication makes assessing and responding to individual needs difficult. Kitwood (1995) first questioned the 'culture of dementia care' and the understanding of dementia on which it was based in the late 1980s. The 'standard paradigm' as Kitwood phrased it (cited in Bender 2003: 24) defines dementia as an organic, progressively degenerative disease. This view still prevails and ignores the social psychological environment to which the person with dementia is exposed post diagnosis. Kitwood argued that the 'malignant social psychology' (1997: 45) reinforces the negative beliefs associated with dementia such as a progressive loss of cognitive and psychological function. The 'new culture of dementia care', he suggested, creates a person-centred care environment in which 'personhood' (1997: 8) was maintained, offsetting and possibly even reversing neurological impairment (1997: 53). Since he shifted the focus away from a neuropathological to a person-centred approach, the debate on how best to assess care needs for those affected with dementia has intensified and, indeed, is ongoing (Holden 1995; Kitwood and Benson 1995; Perrin and May 2000; Bender 2003).

As dance movement therapists we are able to contribute to this debate. Our approach to working with older people focuses on activating individual resources and creating a supportive environment in which personal expression is encouraged, even where an individual's physical and/or cognitive function may be diminished (Stockley 1992; Sandel and Scott Hollander 1995). For a person with dementia a dance movement therapy (DMT) session can enhance well-being as the therapeutic environment provides a space where they can rediscover, and to some extent recover, aspects of themselves through movement.

This chapter presents observations made as part of an evaluation of the Links Movement and Communication (LMC) programme for the training of careworkers in movement and communication activities in a residential care home. The findings revealed that engaging people with dementia in a way that draws on past experiences, such as dance and songs they had once enjoyed, can open possibilities for communication to both people with dementia as well as residential careworkers. The enormous shift in perception of the care-workers involved in the LMC training, described below, opened new ways of relating to those they cared for. The potential for communication increased, for the carers because of changed perception and for the clients because they had an opportunity to show aspects of themselves that were often hidden amidst the daily routines of the care home.

Here I discuss this particular approach in the context of a continuing debate on how to improve quality of care, and go further by suggesting that a DMT approach can provide an environment in which professionals and those responsible for care may observe and assess clients less intrusively than tra-ditional clinical assessment tools permit. This approach promotes and assesses well-being all in one.

The links movement and communication (LMC) programme

The Links programme is a unique training programme developed by Marion Violets (2000, 2002, 2004), a senior UK dance movement therapist who has worked extensively with elders and will be referred to as the 'therapist' in the text below. The programme provides therapeutic support using elements from DMT to people with dementia while training residential careworkers along-side in movement and communication activities aimed at enhancing mobility and communication amongst clients. Thus, the purpose of the LMC sessions was twofold:

- providing movement and communication activities for clients with dementia
- providing practical training sessions to complement the theoretical aspects of the LMC programme taught on a weekly basis.

The programme was delivered in several public residential care homes across North London, UK in 2001. However, the independent evaluation was con-ducted[1] in only one of the care homes. The aims of the evaluation were: to identify the benefits that clients derived from participation in regular movement and communication activities; to describe trainee careworkers' experience of the training. The research team consisted of an experienced movement analyst[2] responsible for analysing the video material and myself, a dance movement therapist and researcher who observed and video recorded selected sessions as well as conducting the face-to-face interviews with trainee careworkers.

The LMC programme is based on a DMT approach that aims to further the integration of physical, psychological and spiritual aspects of the self and which has been successfully applied in working with older people (Stockley 1992; Sandel and Scott Hollander 1995). For people with dementia this means supporting the expression of a changing 'self' that may experience loss and activating the body's capability to recover memory lodged in the musculature of the body (Moore and Yamamoto 1994; Rothschild 2000; Caroll 2002). Violets, in developing the LMC programme, builds on this approach and makes use of neuroscience to underpin her work, drawing on the work of Hanniford (1995) and Damasio (2000) amongst others. This means stimulating the clients' skills that are retained even though cognitive function may be impaired.

The LMC sessions followed a set sequence and structure to provide familiarity for clients, although a client-centred approach ensured that individuals' needs were attended to. The use of props such as a soft ball, beanbags, colourful scarves and stretch clothes encouraged engagement and communication amongst participants. Clients and trainee careworkers sat on chairs arranged in a circle for each person to see other participants and to be seen (Sandel and Scott Hollander 1995), with the therapist moving in and out of the circle to support and encourage individual clients in the activity. The therapist's use of touch as a way of connecting with each client and to enhance bodily awareness formed an important element of the work (Violets 2000).

Methodology used in evaluating the LMC programme

The evaluation took a qualitative approach and drew on various tools for data collection trying to capture clients' experiences from multiple perspectives and included the following:

1   Three sessions were observed by the researcher, one at the beginning, one at the mid-point and at the end of the 12-week LMC programme, using an observational framework developed specifically for this research. This observational assessment tool (see Table 2.1) recorded the level of the client's engagement in activities, mobility, participation in songs, nonverbal and verbal communication, body posture and expression of moods. Observed interactions of the group as a whole, the group dynamics and expressions of individual clients were noted.
2   Video recordings of the three observed sessions allowed for a detailed analysis of the group process and emerging movement patterns, providing a record over time. It allowed for cross-referencing between the researcher's observations made during the sessions and those of the movement analyst independently viewing the video material.

Table 2.1 LMC assessment tool

| Setting | Observations | Observer's name | | | | Date | Session | | Video observation |
		Client A	Client B	Client C	Client D	Client E	Client F	Client G
Ball activity	Catches ball							
	Does not catch							
	Throws ball							
	Aims when throwing							
	Varies direction							
	Tracks ball							
	Kicks ball							
	Becomes inactive							
Stretch cloth	Grasps and holds							
	Looses grip							
	Able to regain grip							
	Synchronises rhythm							
	Becoming inactive							
Scarf	Takes and holds scarf							
	Follows mvt with scarf							
	Initiates movement							
	Folds scarf effectively							
	Becoming inactive							

Table 2.1 LMC assessment tool—Continued

Setting		Observer's name				Date		Session			Video observation
	Observations	Client A	Client B	Clien C		Client D		Client E		Client F	Client G
Song Music	Does not participate										
	Sings along										
	Gestures rhythmically										
Use of body	Describe posture										
	Postural change										
	Active through limbs										
	Active through trunk										
	Stands/moves about										
Mood	Most alert during										
	Describe general mood										
	Note mood changes										
Verbal Interaction	With other clients										
	With group										
	With therapist										
	With staff										
Other											

3   Narrative tape-recorded and transcribed interviews were conducted with the trainee care workers after they completed the LMC training, using a topic guide to elicit their experience of the training. The topics included questions on their reasons for undertaking the training, experience of the training, observations on clients and other benefits derived from the training. (In the event they also commented on clients' behaviour outside the group context).
4   Notes from trainee careworkers collated during the training.
5   The therapist's observations, including those recorded in an interview conducted by the movement analyst.

The clients themselves were not interviewed about their experience. This was thought to be difficult as it would have meant relying on verbal communication. In hindsight this is perhaps a shortcoming of the evaluation.

Participants in the LMC group

The clients were selected by the trainees on the basis of criteria agreed with the dance movement therapist. For example, clients needed to feel comfortable in a group situation and have some mobility. The LMC group consisted of six clients, three trainees, the dance movement therapist, and on three separate occasions the researcher. Two of the clients did not participate in the last session that was assessed and videorecorded. Consequently, the research is based on a small, selective sample that nevertheless confirmed the anecdotal evidence which had emerged from other LMC groups conducted by Violets (2000, 2002).

The clients were in their late seventies and early eighties, two men and four women, all but one diagnosed with varying degrees of dementia. One client was believed to have a learning disability and the diagnosis of dementia was unclear. Some clients had recently arrived in the home and were still in the settling-in phase, while others were longer term residents.

The three trainees came to participate in the programme more by chance than choice. The care home manager had suggested the training to them and initially they were unaware of the level of involvement required. Curiosity and a certain amount of anxiety were first responses to being asked to participate in the training, feelings which dissipated instantly after the therapist introduced the aim of the training programme and its content. All trainees were careworkers with several years' experience of working with people with dementia, some holding an NVQ[3] in care.

Observing clients' responses

Clients' responses to various activities were noted on the assessment sheet, enabling the research team to describe the clients' many resources. Some of these became more visible during the session and over time, including the way clients used the group activity for their own self-expression as the examples below illustrate (particularly the vignette about a resident named Bert in this text). Bert's engagement with other group members, and spontaneous responses to activities, provided evidence of the LMC programme's positive effects on clients. The video recordings supplemented observations made during the session and provided a precise record of the group dynamics and development over time.

Other evidence emerging from the evaluation suggests that the therapeutic environment created a space where clients were encouraged and supported in self-expression. Jean, for example, got up to dance to the music played in the background, a familiar song of the 1940s. She moved from side to side in synchrony with the therapist, sustaining rhythm and balance with grace until the music stopped. Her body had remembered the rhythm and she shifted her weight with ease from side to side while the music was playing. Yet when the music stopped and she walked to her seat, she briefly lost her balance and relapsed into her unsteady walk. For a 'significant' moment she was moving freely, unsupported by the walking stick she tended to use.

The LMC group provided clients with an environment where they could rediscover their skills of moving, singing and communicating with others. The format of the group session in itself offered a coherent structure repeated week by week, that is, the ball game, throwing beanbags, working with the stretch cloth. Through repetition of movement and activities clients seemed to regain confidence in their mobility. For example, initially Lucy had to be encouraged to throw the ball that had fallen into her lap, yet after a few sessions she could be observed tracking the ball, catching it and throwing it to the careworker, calling out to her from across the circle. In one of the later sessions Lucy spontaneously got out of the chair to recover the beanbag that had dropped behind her chair. By doing so she demonstrated full engagement in the activity, initiative and motivation. No one had asked her to pick up the object, she had decided this for herself, perhaps realising that the activity would have come to an end without her intervention. The fun generated through these playful activities promoted and facilitated interaction between participants of the group and laughter was common in the sessions.

Sustained activities over longer time spans, such as holding onto a stretch cloth and lifting it up and down to bounce the ball on the cloth, required synchronising the movement with others, strength in the hands and focus on the object. Most clients showed considerable determination in holding onto the cloth and moving with the group. Apart from the physical benefits this activity provided, it also offered a greater sense of together-ness and perhaps achievement in a task that required persistence and strength. On one occasion, however, Susan was feeling unwell and decided to remove herself from the group; sitting outside the circle on a chair she sipped her tea until she felt better and rejoined the group. This action of withdrawing from a group activity was evidence that Susan was able to make an independent decision about her needs, reflecting self-regulation and perhaps a degree of self-care.

Observing clients caring for others demonstrated that forming relationships was still a possibility. Bert noticed that Lucy, who was sitting next to him, had difficulty in folding the scarf at the end of the session and leaned over to help. His body shape expressed a willingness to communicate with her, albeit non-verbally. Ann and Susan were more demonstrative in their joint action while singing a duet, each taking a turn, waiting for the other to finish, finally joining together in song. Neither were 'told' to sing together, but it happened spontaneously because they felt inclined to do so. The space enabled clients to express themselves and sometimes their feelings for others. In one session Ann, without doubt the most accomplished singer in the group, turned to Bert who was sitting next to her. Opening her arms then placing one hand on her heart she sang, clearly remembering the lyrics of the song, while her body language and facial expression made her intention obvious – she sang for him!

These observations are only snapshots of clients' interaction in the sessions. Interestingly, clients' movement possibilities were already observable in the first session which was videoed. Clients merely needed the space and opportunity to express them. However, for some clients verbal communication and expression clearly increased over time. Like any group situation it took time for them to get to know each other and learn to trust. For example, initially Lucy was observed to be the most withdrawn member of the group, yet she emerged, bit by bit, as someone who wanted to tell her story. In the last session she talked about her past, mentioning the people to whom she had been close. She may not have been coherent throughout, but she had the confidence to 'take the floor' (for three minutes) to share something of herself with the group.

Bert 'opening the door'

> 'I was surprised that he opened the door; usually he keeps it locked, but when I came to collect him for the group, he opened it and came along without his usual grumbles.'
>
> (Interview with trainee careworker)

Bert was in his mid-eighties and had been diagnosed with dementia. He had recently been placed in the home and attended the group regularly. He showed some flexibility in limbs and torso during the activities, was able to bend down to pick up the ball or select a scarf laid out on the floor, although his movement was slow and cautious. At times it took a while before he co-ordinated his movements. In the sessions he demonstrated considerable strength and sustained engagement in activities (ball game, beanbag and stretch cloth). There were signs of spontaneity in action, such as clapping hands in response to another client's successful action of throwing a beanbag across the circle to another person. He revealed his humorous side when he took off his shoe in order to kick the ball, earning cheers from other group members. Then putting the shoe back on, he lifted his knee with ease, keeping an almost upright position, showing a surprising agility in the body that his often slow and cautious movement had disguised. He responded instantly by raising his elbow in a quick move to return the ball aimed at him. He was laughing and slapping his thigh in response to another client teasing him during the ball game by pretending to throw the ball and then holding it back. He talked about his Irishness and told with pride of the many Irish people who had found success in different parts of the world. Once he arrived late to the session and entered with a humorous body gesture, attracting the group's attention. This was the same person trainee careworkers had described as being aggressive and at times unco-operative outside the session.

Bert is an encouraging example of how participation in the LMC group enabled him to 'open the door', both metaphorically and in actual fact. One trainee careworker recalled that once, when she went to collect him for the group, he had locked the door, as was usual. While on most other occasions he would have refused to open his door, he unlocked it promptly when he realised that he was being collected for the LMC group; he got ready to join the group without his usual grumble. Participating in the group provided a space for him 'to be seen' and acknowledged by other members of the group, and 'seeing' or becoming aware of others himself. It enabled him to express himself physically in a more varied and perhaps challenging way, interact non-verbally and verbally with others, and present himself as a person with a history and cultural heritage of which he was proud. The careworkers, seeing Bert from a different perspective, facilitated new relationships between them as they discovered his qualities, rarely witnessed in the day-to-day events in the home. But he had opened the door to allow other people to relate to him and build friendships, reducing some of the aggressive behaviour he had shown.

Trainees' experiences

All three trainees were interviewed by the researcher towards the end of the LMC training. One trainee had conducted a movement activity session testing the newly learnt skills. Leading a session was the final assessment of their successful completion of the training for which they received a certificate of attendance, enabling them to run movement and communication activity groups with ongoing monthly supervision from a senior registered dance movement therapist.

The trainees were pleased to have had the opportunity of participating in the training. They all commented on how it had increased their ability to communicate with clients with dementia. They expressed surprise at seeing clients in this new context and commented on the clients' greater physical mobility and eagerness to join the group activity. They talked about discovering clients' ability to sing, dance and talk about past life experiences, complementing the knowledge that they had already acquired about clients through their work. They were able to see clients in a new light, gaining insight into the possibilities of expression that each client possessed, physically and emotionally. All commented that they were more able to see their client as a 'whole' person. The most significant points they made were:

- a greater understanding and knowledge of various aspects of dementia
- discovering clients' physical possibilities, in particular their strength revealed in the various movement activities
- an awareness of clients' increased communication skills, but also their own skills in relating to clients
- an experience of friendship between clients themselves, clients and careworkers and workers themselves
- an increase in observational skills enabling them to recognise and describe clients' changed behaviour and improved physical conditions
- an ability to apply the learnt skills outside the movement session enriching the communication with clients in their daily work
- the capacity to perceive each client as a 'whole person'.

All trainees commented on the greater job satisfaction they had experienced as a result of participating in the programme. While the purpose of the training was to provide trainees with the skills of conducting movement and communication sessions for people with dementia, these findings revealed that the training had more far-reaching outcomes. It had influenced the way trainees viewed and engaged with their care work. Having become sensitised to their clients' movement and communication possibilities in the sessions, their own observational capacities were much enhanced. The evaluation, therefore, was able to draw on these observations. In the interview they suggested that the benefits which clients had derived from participation in the LMC group were also noticeable outside the group context, for example:

- One trainee careworker described the aggressive behaviour of one of the clients whose usual response to suggestions or instructions was verbal abuse. The client's attitude and relationship to the careworker had changed dramatically. Since participating in the group she found him more approachable – they joked and teased each other. This, she thought, was due to him feeling more confident about himself and the fact that he was talking and interacting more frequently with others. This change in behaviour was confirmed independently by another trainee careworker.

- Trainees commented on clients' willingness, even eagerness, to come to the group. They contrasted this to clients' usual responses to other activities on offer, which often entailed resistance. They observed that after only a few LMC sessions clients' response to being collected for the group was one of excitement and they were happy to follow the invitation to the group promptly. Although there had been other activities on offer, it generally took some persuasion to engage clients in other activities, sometimes with little success. Trainee careworkers commented on this different response from their clients and concluded that there were some aspects in the LMC work which seemed to have a greater impact on clients without being able to define exactly what this was. It is possible that the integration of some of the movement and communication activities in the daily routines of care kept the clients' sense of excitement alive. Equally the carers' own enthusiasm for the LMC work may have shaped their positive perception.
- One trainee talked about the ease with which she was able to perform her care duties since both the client and herself had attended the group. For example, being able to engage and communicate with the client more meaningfully, she felt that the client she cared for had become more co-operative, which made the tasks of dressing and undressing easier. Also being able to engage through a song or a dance made the care of their clients a more varied and joyful task.

While each of the trainees had good communication skills prior to participating in the training, learning new skills and, in particular, different ways of relating to clients with dementia had opened new opportunities. More importantly, they were able to carry these ways of relating into the day-to-day contact with clients, potentially keeping awake the skills that clients had recovered or learnt in the group.

Discussion

This chapter has illustrated the benefits of dance movement therapy to people with dementia in a residential care setting, opening up possibilities for creating a stimulating care environment. While the aim of the LMC group was to support people with dementia in engaging in movement and communication activities, the sessions offered another kind of space, one in which a fuller and more varied expression emerged through interaction between therapist, careworkers and clients. Careworkers sensitised to the potential of those they cared for enabled them to build relationships which positively affected their care work and ultimately job satisfaction. It created the conditions for what Kitwood (1997: 53) termed a 'positive social psychology', an enabling environment where personhood was respected. This method of working also allowed for the drawing up of a profile of clients' physical abilities, emotional expressions and verbal as well as non-verbal communication skills. Such information might provide a valuable input into an assessment of well-being and care needs. Together with careworkers' improved observation and communication skills, it provides the potential for continual assessment and appropriate support for people with dementia.

However, the methodology used for this pilot study has to be examined more rigorously to evaluate its wider application for care planning purposes. The assessment tool used in this study was specifically designed for the purpose of this research and has not been tested in a wider clinical environment. Also, as pointed out above, the research presented here involved a small client sample. It could be criticised for not applying any clinical assessment tools commonly used in establishing levels of functioning and well-being of people with dementia. Yet, looking at the wider debate on the definition of dementia, range of assessment tools and how best to identify care needs for this population suggests that this is a field wide open to exploration and further development.

There remain serious questions about definition and characteristics of dementia as Bender (2003) points out. Building on Kitwood's work he systematically examines the assumptions made in defining dementia and its major clinical features and concludes that the clinical evidence presented is often poor, inconclusive or even contradictory (Bender 2003: 27). If there are weaknesses in defining dementia adequately, then perhaps the effectiveness of assessment tools used must be questioned too, in particular as they will determine the treatment and level of care the individual with dementia will receive. Ready and Ott (2003), in reviewing 'quality of life measures' for dementia, found that a wide range of definitions was employed in defining quality of life and suggest that the validity of these measures requires further investigation. Nevertheless, they conclude that assessment of well-being and quality of care may be more meaningful for planning interventions in care as improving quality of life was more feasible to undertake than intervention in other aspects of the dementia. Discussing ways of assessing quality of care, Perrin and May (2000: 136) suggest that often assessment is about 'capacity for doing' rather than 'capacity for being', and advocate dementia care mapping (DCM) alongside other measures (p. 127) in assessing well-being. This method has been widely applied to evaluate the quality of care in institutional care settings and aims to capture the quality of engagement experienced by people with dementia. Information is collected by 'mappers' who observe the interaction between carer and people with dementia in daily routines over a specified period of time, which can be intimidating for some care staff.

In contrast, this chapter has discussed an alternative approach which widens opportunity for a less intrusive kind of assessment of well-being: one that can be integrated into daily care work, and which can be an enriching experience for people with dementia and their careworkers alike. Perhaps DMT offers an 'holistic' approach combining engagement, assessment and care for people with dementia all in one. Yet, as suggested above, more in-depth research would be needed to validate the assessment tool used. Equally important, though, is for the DMT community to reflect on our practice in the light of government policies for older people and demonstrate the value of DMT in implementing policy. For example, the LMC programme promotes some of the standards set out in the National Service Framework for Older People (Department of Health 2001), in particular person-centred care, fall prevention, support with mental health and promoting an active healthy life in older age. DMT can play a unique role in assisting residential care homes to meet their obligations under the policy framework for older people.

Notes

1   With permission from the respective local authority, care home manager and staff involved.
2   Carol-Lynn Moore is a well-established movement analyst who teaches in the USA and UK; an insight into her work is reflected in Moore and Yamamoto (1994) *Beyond Words*.
3   National Vocational Qualification (NVQ) is the UK system of accreditation of vocational skill training.

References

Bender, M. (2003) *Explorations in Dementia: Theoretical and Research Studies into the Experience of Remediable and Enduring Cognitive Losses*. London: Jessica Kingsley.

Caroll, R. (2002) *Why Psychosomatisation is Complex: Going Beyond Cause–Effect*. Lecture given for Confer London, 6 February 2002. Online. Available HTTP <http://www.thinkbody.co.uk> (accessed 23 March 2004).

Damasio, A. (2000) *The Feeling of what Happens – Body, Emotion and the Making of Consciousness*. London: Vintage.

Department of Health (2001) *National Service Framework for Older People*. Online. Available HTTP: <http://www.dh.gov.uk/PolicyAndGuidance/HealthAndSocial CareTopics/OlderPeoplesServices/fs/en> (accessed 18 May 2005).

Hanniford, C. (1995) *Smart Moves – Why Learning is not all in your Head*. Virginia: Great Ocean Publishers.

Holden, U. (1995) *Ageing, Neuropsychology and the 'New' Dementias: Definitions, Explanations and Practical Approaches*. London: Chapman and Hall.

Kitwood, T. (1995) Cultures of care: tradition and change, in T. Kitwood and S. Benson (eds) *The New Culture of Dementia Care*. London: Hawker Publications.

Kitwood, T. (1997) *Dementia Reconsidered: The Person Comes First*. Maidenhead: Open University Press.

Kitwood, T. and Benson, S. (1995) *The New Culture of Dementia Care*. London: Hawker Publications.

Moore, C. and Yamamoto, K. (1994) *Beyond Words: Movement Observation and Analysis*, 3rd edn.: London: Gordon and Breach.

Perrin, T. and May, H. (2000) *Wellbeing in Dementia: An Occupational Approach for Therapists and Carers*. London: Churchill Livingstone.

Ready, R.E. and Ott, B.R. (2003) *Quality of Life Measures for Dementia*. Online. Available HTTP <http://www.hqlo.com/content/1/1/11> (accessed 23 March 2004).

Rothschild, B. (2000) *The Body Remembers: The Psychophysiology of Trauma and Trauma Treatment*. London: Norton.

Sandel, S.L. and Scott Hollander, A. (1995) Dance/movement therapy with aging populations, in F. J. Levy (ed.) *Dance and Other Expressive Dance Therapies*. London: Routledge.

Stockley, S. (1992) Older lives, older dances: dance movement therapy with older people, in H.L. Payne (ed.) *Dance Movement Therapy: Theory and Practice*. London: Tavistock/Routledge.

Violets, M. (2000) We'll survive, in D. Aldridge (ed.) *Music Therapy in Dementia Care*. London: Jessica Kingsley.

—— (2002) Re-awakening the language of the body, *Journal of Dementia Care* 10, 5.

—— (2004) Life after hope, in S. Evans and J. Garner (eds) *Talking over the Years – Psychotherapy with Older People*. London: Routledge.

Chapter 3

Dance movement therapy in the community

Group work with people with enduring mental health difficulties

Vicky Karkou

Introduction

Following the closure of the large institutions in the 1980s, community work has become an area under considerable expansion for a number of dance movement therapists. This chapter will discuss major principles of work as stated by the practitioners themselves and will present a clinical example of such work with clients with enduring mental health problems who have recently moved to the community. Some findings from a nationwide survey in arts therapies will be used as a basis for this chapter. The survey was informed by grounded theory and consisted of a combined methodology: interviews, survey, brief case studies. Findings suggest that interactive principles, an empathetic attitude and flexible ways of responding to client needs are important to dance movement therapists undertaking this kind of work. Further development of theory and practice is needed in order to address the diverse characteristics of dance movement therapy (DMT) in the community.

Background

Since the emergence of dance movement therapy (DMT) in the 1940s to the current date, the shape of DMT theory and practice has changed significantly. DMT has become a separate profession in its own right with a developed body of knowledge and outlined standards of practice (Quality Assurance Agency 2004). Perceptions about the treatment of mental health have also changed and the environments within which treatment is offered have diversified (Regel and Roberts 2002). Increasingly today, dance movement therapists are asked to practise in community settings with clients with a wide range of symptoms/diagnosis. For example, in the recent register of the DMT professional association register (ADMTUK 2004/2005) almost half of the registered members are recorded as practising in the community in environments such as charities, private practice, social services, community care, residential care, private hospitals or therapeutic communities.

However, community work is still an area very rarely addressed in the DMT literature. It is even less common to find research-based publications completed on this topic. Reasons for the limited written information available are not clear. Ansdell (2002) claims that, for the music therapy field, practitioners feel that their work in such environments does not readily fit within the current understanding of what music therapy is. They often find themselves doubting whether what they do is indeed music therapy. It is possible that there is a similar problem in DMT. Furthermore, in many community-based jobs dance movement therapists are employed on a free-lance basis and/or with short contracts. The lack of appropriate payment, conditions of work and a career structure may therefore create easier associations between this work and a less established, thus less valued, practice, that is, a practice not 'worthy' of reporting about.

Thus, while reviewing relevant literature for this chapter it became important to focus upon identifying relevant debates in community work that can be of value to dance movement therapists working in the community. It became equally important to revisit some major approaches to DMT work and consider their strengths and limitations within a community-based context.

Caring in the community

Contemporary community care seems to be an amalgamation of principles and practices, some of which can be traced back to early post-war Britain when the community care movement boomed considerably. For example, the need to care for the returning soldiers from the war in the late 1940s and 1950s, has led to the realisation that issues of mental health are recurrent amongst a large portion of the population. Today, the Royal College of Psychiatrists (2001) claims that one in four people might develop a mental health problem at some point in their lives. They campaign alongside voluntary organisations such as Rethink and Mind, and the active involvement of service users, for the removal of the stigma associated with mental health difficulties. Innovative treatment ideas in the 1950s and 1960s (for example, introduction of rehabilitation programmes, psychological therapies and psychotropic drugs) are now in common use, while services that began developing in the 1950s (such as day centres, outpatient clinics, hostels and social care services) are now regarded as part of regular mental health provision, especially for people with enduring mental health problems.

Over the years however, and particularly since the closure of the large institutions in the 1980s, community care has meant different things for different people (Barnes 1990; Yip 2001). For example, for some community care stands for care *in* the community in the form of statutory and non-statutory professional services. For others it stands for care *by* the community in terms of non-institutional provision; for example, from family, friends and members of the community as a whole. These different definitions of community care can be seen in governmental policies initiated by different political parties. For example, the Conservative government of 1990 prepared the *NHS and Community Care Act* that outlined the transfer of care from large institutions to the community. By allocating limited resources to support a smooth transfer of care, community care came to mean care by the community in the cheapest possible way. Community care became a dumping ground for chronic or long-term patients and left a number of vulnerable people with a questionable quality of care and in many cases a total lack of care. It soon became apparent that there were multiple limitations of discharging vulnerable people to a community that did not necessarily possess the sensitivity, knowledge, resources or ability to integrate people in need of specialised care and support.

Since then, a number of governmental initiatives have aimed to make community care for people with mental health problems more workable and combine structured interventions in the community with the informal care offered by the community. Mental health grants and specific accommodation arrangements for people discharged from hospitals, a care programme approach, community care plans and community care assessments have all been introduced. With the publication of the *National Service Framework for Mental Health* (Department of Health 1999) and the setting up of the *National Institute for Clinical Excellence* (NICE 2002) in the same year, current attention has turned towards developing national standards for mental health services and offering guidelines on best practice for patients, carers, health professionals and the public.

Despite the shortcomings of governmental policies regarding community care since the 1980s, the shift of care from the large institution to the community has opened up possibilities for a number of new treatment choices for the mental health service users. DMT is one such option.

DMT with people with enduring mental health difficulties

Within community settings, dance movement therapists are working with a diverse population. Possibly the most representative client group is people with enduring mental health difficulties, including people diagnosed with schizophrenia. According to the NICE guidelines for schizophrenia (2002) the aims of therapeutic interventions with this client group should be, amongst others, to improve overall quality of life, minimise symptoms, decrease distress and improve communication and coping skills. A strong social component is highlighted on these aims and reflected in recommendations for the value of family therapy as an effective intervention next to cognitive behavioural therapy. Although neither DMT nor any of the other arts therapies are mentioned in the guideline, certain DMT approaches seem also to be particularly relevant and of potential value (Ritter and Low 1996). Most of these approaches however have been developed and extensively described for hospitalised patients. One such example is the early work undertaken by Marian Chace.

Chace's DMT approach developed in response to attempting to engage institutionalised people with schizophrenia at the St Elizabeth's Hospital in the USA. Levy (1988) reports that Chace's work developed a strong relational and social character as a result of influences from Sullivan (1955), an American psychiatrist who is regarded as the founder of the interpersonal school of psychotherapy, and who was working at that time in the same hospital with Chace. Indeed one of the basic premises that has informed Chace's work is the belief that human beings have an innate desire to communicate and dance can become a form of communication.

Within a community environment and particularly when working with people with schizophrenia, the work of Chace remains pertinent. Principles such as the value of body action, symbolism, the therapeutic movement relationship and rhythmical activity, as articulated by Chace's protégées Chaiklin and Schmais (1986), suggest an acknowledgement of the value of both intra-psychic as well as interpsychic processes, the 'inwards' and 'outwards', the personal and the social. Symbolism enables people to access the unconscious and the personal. The therapeutic relationship enables issues to be worked through with another, while rhythmical activity binds the individual with more than one another, the group and even possibly the wider community. It is interesting that Chace's work often involved setting up performances with her clients which other members of staff and other patients could attend (Levy 1988); a way of working that contemporary DMT thinking rarely acknowledges as part of mainstream practice.

Since the time of Chace, a number of other approaches have emerged and developed and Chace's contribution, albeit still popular, became just one of the many ways of working with clients with enduring mental health problems. For example, several approaches are presented in key DMT texts (Payne 1992; Stanton-Jones 1992; Meekums 2002; Karkou and Sanderson 2006) and a number of assessment tools have been developed specifically for people with schizophrenia, such as Davis (1981). In the UK, Laban-based work became particularly popular (Payne 1983; Levy 1988; Karkou and Sanderson 2001). However, accelerated professionalisation within the last 20 years has also translated into a close affiliation with established psycho-therapeutic schools of thought and psychoanalytic thinking in particular. For example, in Stanton-Jones (1992), Payne (1992), Meekums (2002) and Karkou and Sanderson (2006) there are extensive references to psychoanalytic/ psychodynamic thinking next to other more humanistic-based ideas.

In a key article that refers specifically to DMT work with clients with schizophrenia, Sandel and Johnson (1983) use psychoanalytic language as a conceptual frame. They refer to the 'nascent group' and describe group processes that consist of an initial 'social facade' followed by the 'collapse' of the group, a 'gestation' period and the final stage of 'dissolution'. This type of group is seen as a type of 'life support system' rather than a therapeutic intervention. Sandel and Johnson (1983) believe that individuals with severe psychosis on the whole are unable to internalise an interpersonal structure if they move further away from the constant presence of a containing environment. As a result, the aim for DMT group work is not to eradicate problems or disease but to prevent atrophy and maintain functioning.

Contributions from Sandel and Johnson (1983), as well as theorists drawing upon the same pool of psychoanalytic understanding, highlight the need for a strong theoretical framework as an important support to the DMT work and the dance movement therapist. It seems that the more challenging the work, the stronger the need for theoretical explanations and practical guidance. For the therapist trying to make sense of/or cope with intense states of fragmentation and chaos, and retain a sense of hope that is essential for all different therapeutic approaches, contributions from psychoanalytic/ psychodynamic thinking can be invaluable.

Dance movement therapy and community work

However, how relevant is this body of knowledge for community work? Similarly to Chace's approach, most applications of psychoanalytically informed DMT have been developed and extensively documented as work undertaken in the large institution. The degree to which group processes such as the ones described by Sandel and Johnson (1983) are applicable to clients with schizophrenia who live in the community is worthy of further study.

Furthermore, psychoanalytic/psychodynamic thinking has been criticised by contemporary arts therapists (Byrne 1995) as a product of modernism that assumes universal application, general rules and norms, and holds a white, middle-class, western, male bias. Postmodern thinking that reflects current British society and is closely aligned to the diverse community work currently undertaken is not at ease with clear and comprehensive 'absolutes' and 'truths'. For example, within a DMT context it becomes questionable whether it is useful to look at the movement profiles of our clients who have been diagnosed with schizophrenia as arrested at an oral stage of development (Siegel 1984). Such conceptualisation becomes even more questionable when our clients come from diverse backgrounds, hold different ideas and understanding of their own condition and possibly have been brought up in a substantially different family and social structure. Fixed ways of looking at the meaning of movement assume a specific type of development and neglects biological and cultural factors. Similarly, it is worth considering whether the transferential relationship that is advocated within psychoanalytic/psychodynamic frameworks and is often characterised of unequal power dynamics (that of a mother and a child) is the only type of relationship that should be fostered when working with clients. At times this type of relationship can be at odds with ideas valued within community settings such as empowerment and social integration.

Since the 1960s, the community care movement, and voluntary organisations in particular, have advocated a humane culture towards mental health and placed a very strong emphasis upon service users' needs and rights. This is currently reflected on governmental policies such as the NHS Plan (Department of Health 2000) that supports service users in terms of their participation in the decision making of all aspects of their treatment. Historically, in settings such as voluntary organisations there has been a strong reaction to treatment approaches that pathologise or are seen as pathologising service users. Staff members of voluntary settings may pejoratively refer to psychiatric treatment as 'defensive medicine' and question excess prescription of drugs. They may also criticise psychoanalytic approaches as perpetuating the role of the unquestionable and sometime unapproachable professional, and consequently as disempowering and marginalising women, ethnic minorities and other socially oppressed groups including people with mental health issues. In contrast, 'real' relationships are valued, the service user's central role in treatment is advocated and choice and action (whether this is a political, social or psychological action) are celebrated (Llewellin 1994).

It remains unknown, however, whether the above principles are prevalent amongst dance movement therapists working in the community. Findings from the research study following will attempt to reveal overall consensus amongst community dance movement therapists, present an example of practice drawn from my own DMT work and offer a starting point for further discussion.

Research methodology

Data relating to community DMT work have been drawn from a nationwide survey (Karkou 1998; Karkou and Sanderson 2005). The study aimed to provide a general picture of the practice of arts therapies in the UK and was influenced by grounded theory (Glaser and Strauss 1967; Strauss and Corbin 1990). It consisted of three stages:

- interviews
- questionnaires
- brief case studies.

Stage I: interviews

Semi-structured interviews were conducted with leading arts therapists and served as an important step for 'grounding' the study in the field; five of them were dance movement therapists practising in the UK. The qualitative data collected was analysed using a subjective content analysis (Bliss *et al.* 1983) that allowed categories to emerge through scanning the data back and forth in a procedure that resembled what Strauss and Corbin (1990) call a 'comparison method'.

Stage 2: questionnaires

A questionnaire was devised in order to collect information regarding opinions and factual information about the therapists and their work. A large part of the questionnaire consisted of statements gathered from analysing the in-depth interview material. These statements referred to arts therapies theory and practice. Participants were asked to state their degree of agreement or disagreement on a scale of 1 to 5 in which 1 stood for strong disagreement and 5 strong agreement with each statement. The questionnaire was piloted and finally distributed to all registered members of the arts therapies professional associations. One hundred and fifty-five questionnaires were sent to all dance movement therapists found in the ADMTUK register. The collected data was analysed using SPSS. Both descriptive and inferential statistics were employed. Some descriptive results specifically referring to community DMT are included here.

Stage 3: brief case studies

At a later stage, a number of case vignettes were collected that aimed to illustrate some of the major findings from the questionnaires and show distinctive ways of working. One such example will be presented here.

Quantitative findings: the big picture

Sample

Participants in the second stage of the study (questionnaires) included 41 dance movement therapists. From these, ten dance movement therapists regarded community work as their main working environment (24.4 per cent) and offered their opinions regarding theoretical underpinnings and practical considerations surrounding their work. These ten dance movement therapists will be regarded as the sample of the study and data they provided regarding theoretical underpinnings and practical considerations surrounding their work will be looked at in more depth.

Comparing the proportion of community dance movement therapists of this study (undertaken in 1995) with the proportion of dance movement therapists who are currently working in community settings (ADMTUK, 2004/2005), it is apparent that there is an increase of community-based work amongst dance movement therapists of almost 25 per cent. Because of this increase, plus the small sample of this study, results presented should be treated with caution. Nonetheless, given the increased interest in the area and lack of any other nationwide study specifically addressing this topic, findings can be seen as valuable, albeit moderate, indicators of wider trends within the field.

Theoretical and clinical principles

In Table 3.1 some key theoretical principles are presented that have gained agreement amongst community dance movement therapists participating in the study. The principle with the least agreement is also presented. Strong agreement is apparent with the first three statements included in this table that referred to the body–mind connection, that is, agreement with some fundamental assumptions of DMT work. Also a high mean score is shown in statements that attempt to define the field as something that is neither about dance making alone, nor about teaching or about the therapists' artistic interests. It appears that participants were making a point of distinguishing DMT from therapeutic dance, dance education and dance as an art form, reflecting the years of effort spent towards establishing DMT as a distinctive discipline (Payne 1990, 1992; Karkou and Sanderson 2001, 2005; Meekums 2002; Karkou and Glasman 2004).

A number of positive statements are also made about what DMT is: it is about an 'active interaction', and concerned with developing a relationship either between the client–therapist or between the client and other members of a group. Faith in the containing function, and thus the healing potential, of a group is apparent: 'the group is a container'. Group work, a characteristic of DMT practice work in general (Karkou and Sanderson 2001, 2006), appears equally relevant to work undertaken with people with enduring mental health problems. Unsurprisingly, the two DMT approaches discussed earlier, the interactive model of Chace (Chaiklin and Schmais 1986) and the psychoanalytically informed DMT practice by Sandel and Johnson (1983), also refer to groups.

It is also interesting that Principles directly aligned to humanistic/ interpersonal psychotherapy are included in Table 3.1: 'I respect that clients are their own experts' and 'The clients I have worked with have taught me most of what I know'. At the same time, there is scepticism towards a pure analytic approach as a potentially 'tough' way of working.

Two more types of work that emerge from the theoretical principles included in this table refers to developmental and eclectic/integrative perspectives. Concerning the former, the following statements receive agreement amongst community dance movement therapists: 'Movement/dance is found at a pre-verbal level of development' and 'I am aware of developmental stages my clients are at'. The specific nature of these developmental models is not revealed from the study. It is suspected that the work of Laban

Table 3.1 List of theoretical principles

Principle*	Mean[1]	Standard deviation[2]
Strong agreement		
One of my fundamental hypotheses is that there is a strong body–mind relationship	4.8	0.4
Dance making reflects the state of mind	4.6	0.5
Changes in moving facilitate changes in the state of mind	4.6	0.5
Agreement		
Dance making alone is not the therapeutic process	4.3	0.8
I am not teaching anyone how to move	4.3	1.1
Active interaction between two people is a key element for DMT	4.2	0.9
The group is a container	4.2	0.4
I respect that clients are their own experts	4.2	0.8
Movement/dance is found at a pre-verbal level of development	4.1	1.0
The development of relationships between the members of the group is a key factor	4.0	0.7
The most important thing is the relationship between client/s and therapist	3.9	0.9
To work purely in an analytic way can be very tough	3.9	0.7
It depends which population I am working with, what sort of theoretical approach I am adopting	3.9	0.7
I am aware of developmental stages my clients are at	3.7	0.5
I use a number of different approaches for each client	3.7	0.5
I do not think that I have one model that I follow	3.7	1.1
I am not trying to reflect the particular area I am interested in as an artist	3.6	0.9
The clients I work with have taught me most of what I know	3.5	0.7
Middle level (neither agree/nor disagree)		
None of the existing theoretical models are right	2.9	1.0

* A scale 1–5 was used: 1 = strongly disagree, 2 = disagree, 3 = neither agree/nor disagree, 4 = agree, 5 = strongly agree.

1 The mean score shows the average score. The higher the mean score, the stronger the agreement with the specific statement.

2 Standard deviation shows the average distance from the mean. High scores indicate wider distribution of responses.

(1975), Sherborne (1990), Kestenberg (1975) or Siegel (1984) is referred to here.

Eclectic/integrative principles with which community dance movement therapists present an agreement include: 'It depends which population I am working with, what sort of theoretical approach I am adopting', 'I use a number of different approaches for each client' and 'I do not think that I have one model that I follow'. The need for a flexible way of working is apparent in these statements. Although flexible practices are valued amongst dance movement therapists working in all settings (Karkou and Sanderson 2001, 2005), the diverse and often unpredictable nature of community work makes the need for flexibility even more pertinent. At the same time the danger from an amorphous, a-theoretical practice is also raised and apparent in the statement with the least agreement presented in Table 3.1: 'None of the existing theoretical models are right'.

A number of different clinical principles are revealed and presented in Table 3.2. Ideas of how to enable the therapeutic process to begin are included in the first three statements: feeling comfortable with the therapist and with movement work and establishing clear boundaries, especially when vulnerable clients are concerned. Metaphor and projection are important concepts relevant to DMT in the community as well as DMT in other settings (Karkou and Sanderson 2001, 2005).

Table 3.2 List of clinical principles

Principle*	Mean[1]	Standard deviation[2]
Agreement		
A lot of the initial work is about enabling clients to feel comfortable enough with you	4.3	0.7
With a client who is fragile, I have clear boundaries within the session	4.2	0.8
A lot of the initial work is about enabling clients to feel comfortable enough with the artistic process	4.1	0.6
Metaphor enables profound change to take place	4.0	0.9
Projection into dance/movement is a process lying at the heart of DMT	4.0	0.5
I am much more focused on the here and now	4.0	0.7
Within a session you do not necessarily have some form of action	3.9	0.6
I bring to the session my own personality	3.9	0.6
I do have certain techniques that I bring out when it is appropriate	3.8	0.6
Individually you have to follow what happens with the client	3.8	0.8
I am trying to respond with my whole self	3.8	0.7
I encourage clients to be as spontaneous as they possibly could be	3.7	0.8
I tend to work with the group as a whole	3.7	0.7
I am describing the behaviour back to my clients	3.6	0.8
Disagreement		
I would not actively do any dance/movement myself, ever	2.0	0.7

* A scale 1–5 was used: 1 = strongly disagree, 2 = disagree, 3 = neither agree/nor disagree, 4 = agree, 5 = strongly agree.
1 The mean score shows the average score. The higher the mean score, the stronger the agreement with the specific statement.
2 Standard deviation shows the average distance from the mean. High scores indicate wider distribution of responses.

Most of the other statements included in Table 3.2 fall under a broad humanistic/interpersonal framework: working on the here and now, bringing in the therapist's own personality, the therapist responding with his or her whole self and following the client when working one to one, but at the same time bringing in certain techniques, especially when the work takes place in groups. The therapist is seen as actively involved in the session, an idea that is closer connected with the interactive model of Chace than with psychoanalytic/psychodynamic thinking. This set of statements implies that, in general, 'real' relationships are valued, that is, relationships that advocate an equal power dynamic between the therapist and the client. At the same time, action is not the only thing happening in sessions: 'Within a session you do not necessarily have some form of action'. Inactivity, stillness and reflection are expected and maybe at times encouraged. This can also be the time when psychoanalytic/psychodynamic methodology becomes particularly relevant in terms of reflecting upon the relationship with the therapist or the dance and making links with one's past or current life.

Some of the theoretical and methodological principles highlighted above seem to be in accordance with principles adopted from the community care movement such as, questioning the 'authority' of the professional and empowering the service user (Department of Health 2000; Llewellin 1994). Community dance movement therapists seem to value psychoanalytic/ psychodynamic ideas, especially regarding the theoretical conceptualisation of the work. In practice, however, and without totally disregarding psychoanalytic methodology, they tend to operate primarily in an empathetic and flexible way to the client's needs, especially when face-to-face contact with clients is concerned.

Qualitative findings: An example of practice

Some of the above principles are apparent in the following example of DMT work.

Context of the work

The work had taken place in a voluntary organisation that valued community principles such as autonomy, self-determination, user participation and community-led initiatives, alongside more recent ideas about performance, hierarchy, cost effectiveness, monitoring, evaluation, public accountability and public relations (Llewellin 1994; Baggott 1998).

DMT was a new service in this organisation, it was run by a colleague (co-therapist) and me. It was informed by Chacian principles such as the value of body action, symbolism, the therapeutic movement relationship and group rhythmical activity. Linked with these principles was an overall interpersonal underpinning with Yalom (1985) being the strongest psychotherapeutic influence. Session structure included: (a) verbal and physical warm-up; (b) shared leadership and theme development; (c) movement and/or verbal closure. Given the frequent changes in the setting, we decided to introduce blocks of 12 sessions which members in the group were encouraged to commit to after attending a few open-taster sessions. Those members who wanted to continue for longer were encouraged to do so by attending more than one block. Over time a core membership was established with some new members being introduced gradually at the beginning of each new block. Extracts from sessions I describe here come from the last block in a day centre before we moved to an alternative location run by the same organisation. Some sessions from this block were videotaped as part of a small evaluation project.[1] Extracts from these recordings were shown to the clients during the review session of this block (session 11 out of 12) as a way of reminding people what we had done. It was also an opportunity for some of them to see themselves moving for the first time: a way of seeing themselves and knowing that they have been 'seen' in a more concrete manner. The need for feedback from group members and therapist/s is highlighted within the interpersonal group psychotherapy literature. Playing video extracts back to the group resembles the written feedback that Yalom (1985), for example, talks about: the therapist prepares and sends out to group members brief descriptions of each session.

Group members

There were five members in the group with a wide age range (34 to 75); all had a diagnosis of some form of schizophrenia. Most group members shared a preference for using the periphery of their bodies, that is, hands or feet rather than engaging in whole body actions. Their movement often looked disconnected from the rest of the body and lacked continuity with the other activities in the session. They often engaged in repetitive movements that lacked clarity of 'inner attitude' (Davis 1981). It appeared easier for them to follow than initiate movement.

Most of the group members had moved from lengthy institutionalisation to the community. The move into the community was a major cause of disruption to their lives. Still, they were seen as unsuitable for counselling or other verbal therapeutic interventions due to the severity of their mental health problems. Two of them, for example, had limited ability to communicate verbally. The remainder, although quite verbal, often talked in a very incoherent manner. They therefore lacked opportunities to express loss of the familiar environment, fear, anger or find opportunities for intimate interactions. Furthermore, life in the community required a much wider range of social skills than their previous hospital-based environments. It was possible that they found themselves insufficiently equipped to deal with this change. DMT was offered to them as a 'life support system' (Sandel and Johnson

1983) rather than as a treatment of their underlying mental health problem. DMT also aimed to improve well-being and contribute towards a better quality of life.

Group development

Two new group members, Lucie and Tony,[2] were introduced to the group that consisted of three core people: Jeanne, Roger and John. Tony, one of the newcomers, attended the open sessions with a strong confrontational attitude towards the other members and the therapists; verbally he was bringing into the group images of murder, suicide, disaster and sex. In Laban's terms (1975), he presented frequent outbursts of free flow movement on the sagittal plane. John, one of the older members of the group, reacted to this behaviour with sharp reproofs of Tony's attitude, language and overall presentation. In my notes I wrote:

> I need to be 'big' (i.e. expand my kinesphere) in order to contain the overall sense of fragmentation and disruption. Tony seems to be threatened by entering a new group but at the same time his arrival signifies a threat to the others.
>
> (Author's clinical notes, first open session)

By the third session the newcomers had become familiar with the group activities and ground rules (for example, Tony's threatened/ing and sexualised behaviour had lessened). They had also developed a sufficient degree of initial rapport either with the therapists and/or other members of the group. In the middle of a shared leadership task (Chacian circle) the work started to evolve around conflict and confrontation. When it was the turn of Jeanne, a quiet and frail woman in her seventies, to initiate movement, she stopped moving altogether. She then brought her arms in front of her chest with tight fists and a lot of binding resembling a fighting/boxing position. Her involuntary shaking completely disappeared, there was no sign of the confusion that she normally presented, making this gesture a very clear body statement. This developed into a movement theme for the whole group of binding and release with our arms. When I asked group members to give a name to what we were doing, Roger responded immediately with the word 'boxing'. While we continued moving I reminded them of ground rules of safety and encouraged the group to explore further the idea of 'fighting' (I asked them: 'What are we fighting against?' 'How else can we fight?'). Most of the group members took this idea on board, especially Tony. He introduced a 'karate' movement, which we all tried together in different variations. For the remaining time in the session, the group continued discussing the theme of fighting through references to scenes of violence and disaster from television soaps, personal experiences of fighting and feelings of anger and guilt.

During the following weeks, a number of changes took place. Members of staff reported that Jeanne was asserting herself outside the group, refusing to give cigarettes to other service users who normally found her an easy target for repetitive begging. Tony became particularly respectful towards other group members and much more settled than in previous sessions. In general he seemed to be more at ease with attending the centre, while his inappropriate behaviour and language were minimised. The fact that he had the chance to share his fears with the DMT group and experience new and safe ways of dealing with his fears could have played a role in this change. At session 11, when we reviewed the whole group work by playing back selected video recordings from some of the sessions, Tony remembered his 'karate' movements and briefly repeated them. Introducing negative emotions into the group did not have disastrous consequences for him, the group or the therapists. My own fears about the group collapsing into fragmentation and chaos, as warned by Sandel and Johnson (1983), became less intense.

In the weeks following the third session, the group seemed to be dealing with difficulties associated with the use of the body. Food and eating was a theme which was discussed repetitively and moved in a number of different ways. During session eight, medication became the main group topic. Discussion about ill bodies evoked a lot of sadness in the group. Movement was minimal and when not actively supported by the therapists did not last for long.

In session nine, the co-therapist introduced the theme of going for an imaginary picnic, which developed into what I perceived as a deep interpersonal experience. Members seemed particularly engaged in eating and drinking imaginary food and drinks that they had brought with them. Exaggerated mimicking of biting, drinking and swallowing were the main movement themes. This was accompanied by a lot of laughter, an apparent sense of joy and a spirit of sharing. For the first time Lucie seemed fully engaged in this group task, offering imaginary food to others and tidying up. When it was time for the picnic to finish, the group united into a lengthy silence that felt intensely sad. In the review of the group (session 11), Tony seemed very disappointed that the picnic session was not included in the video extracts shown (the picnic session had not been videotaped).

The goal for the remaining sessions was to facilitate an ending and allow for relevant feelings to be shared. In session ten we reminded members about the forthcoming ending of the group and informed them that this would be the last block of sessions. Members talked a lot about families and relatives, making references to death, loss and separation. In the movement section, soon after a physical warm-up, Jeanne initiated an outward movement with her arms that originated from the chest and was directed towards the centre of the group. Roger called this movement the 'broken heart'. The group developed a dance that started from holding hands in a circle which incorporated Jeanne's 'broken heart' movement and finished with individuals standing very close to each other. A clear, unifying rhythm was adopted that kept all members in movement synchrony. They called it the 'ring dance', a name that seemed very relevant to the proximity between members and the circular formation adopted throughout the dance. Despite repetitive encouragement from the therapists to finish with the dance, group members seemed reluctant to stop. They were repeating the same movement sequence again and again until an agreement was reached to repeat it two more times and stop. The session ended with all participants applauding each other and shaking hands. It felt as if group members were giving their last intimate performance as a celebratory ritual for the forthcoming ending. In the review session, when clips from the 'ring' dance were shown, Jeanne kept repeating in a soft gentle manner: 'We are all there together, we are all there together . . .'

In the remaining two sessions (the review in session 11 and session 12), people seemed able to recall the 'fighting' session, the 'picnic' and the 'ring' dance and were able to make some comments about them but did not attempt to reconnect in the same way. The end of the group had come.

Conclusions

In the above clinical example, group development is presented in a way that loosely resembles Sandel and Johnson's (1983) description of the nascent group. However, a more positive development is apparent. Although there was obvious fragmentation and disruption, especially with the arrival of Tony, the group managed to move quickly after the 'fighting' session to the gestation phase. Furthermore, unlike the negative prediction by Sandel and Johnson (1983), the gestation phase of sessions four to eight gave birth to intimacy, for example, in the 'picnic' and 'ring' sessions. In the 'ring' session, group members took advantage of the opportunity to discuss losses and separation and prepare for the forthcoming ending. Differences between the development of this group and the 'nascent' group described by Sandel and Johnson (1983) can be explained as the result of different conceptualisations of the work. For example, the above group was facilitated through an interactive/interpersonal DMT perspective. In contrast, the 'nascent' group was primarily rooted in psychodynamic thinking. Differences can also be explained as the result of working with relatively higher functioning clients living in the community rather than with hospital patients.

Tony continued working with us in the new setting we moved to and integrated into a group with much higher functioning clients. Every time I visited the day centre Roger would recognise me and run to shake my hand. With a big grin on his face he would tell me: 'Long time, long time' and 'When is dance due?' Although no attempts were made to establish any long-term effects of DMT for the group as a whole, the interactive nature of the work, empathetic responses to group members and flexibility were key therapeutic elements in my view. Findings from the survey suggest that similar principles of practice are also shared amongst other dance movement therapists. For example, valuing active interaction and humanistic principles, acknowledging psychodynamic ideas but using them in a modified way and adopting an overall eclectic/integrative rationale depending on the needs of the clients were some principles revealed from the nationwide survey. The loose application of Chacian work with this client group was particularly relevant as it offered opportunities for vitalisation, exploration of feelings and development of social skills that often are not readily available to people who have moved from lengthy institutionalisation to the community.

However, this example is just one way of working in community settings. Unlike other types of community work, it has largely remained within the confines of current definitions of DMT in the UK and very close to what could be regarded as 'typical' practice. When dance movement therapists are asked to carry out additional tasks such as act as advocates, offer dance lessons, participate in community events and organise performances, it becomes particularly difficult to retain a 'typical' practice. In some cases and with some colleagues the 'non-typical' might constitute the main type of service offered. In these cases, it becomes pertinent to reconsider whether certain types of dance teaching, community or therapeutic dance, when facilitated by a dance movement therapist, fall by default outside DMT remits or not. It is also worth thinking about how DMT can actively contribute towards challenging mental health stigma and actively enable service users to integrate in the wider society. Community dance movement therapists are increasingly faced with the challenge to expand beyond the confines of the closed doors and the private therapeutic space and move towards working with the community setting as a whole and/or the neighbourhood. The Chacian approach, sufficiently adapted, might address group work outside the typical DMT space. Psychodynamic underpinnings can enable conceptual understanding of broader group dynamics and guide practice. However, other theoretical frameworks and practical ways of working may also become relevant as more useful ways of working with certain clients and in certain environments. If this is the case, which ones are indeed relevant and which ones are not still remains unclear.

In order to address the above challenges, further discussion and extensive research are needed that specifically address community work. Ansdell (2002), for example, advocates the need for a paradigm shift in music therapy that will accommodate work undertaken outside the statutory sector. He claims that currently there is discrepancy between the conceptual understanding of what music therapy is and what actually takes place in daily practice. If this is not already a pertinent need for the DMT field, there is definitely an urgent need to take a closer look at community work to develop appropriate ways of working that embrace current trends and are sensitive to community principles and values.

Notes

1   Permission from the manager of the setting and client consent (in the presence of another member of staff) was gained prior to the commencement of this block of sessions. Every time the camera was brought in, clients were reminded about the project again and verbal consent was renewed. It was made clear that the recording could stop any time if they felt uncomfortable and/or erase parts of it if requested. With the exception of the first time, whenever the camera was brought into the session people did not seem to pay much, if any, attention to it.
2   All names have been changed in order to protect confidentiality.

References

ADMTUK (2004/2005) *Register of Members 2004/2005*. Torquay: ADMTUK.

Ansdell, G. (2002) Community music therapy and the winds of change: a discussion paper. *Voices: A World Forum For Music Therapy*, 2, 2, 1–37. Online. Available HTTP: <http://www.voices.no/mainissues/Voices2(2)ansdell.html> (accessed 26 December 2004).

Baggott, R. (1998) *Health and Health Care in Britain*. Basingstoke: Macmillan.

Barnes, C. (1990) *The Cabbage Syndrome: The Social Construction of Dependence*. Basingstoke: Falmer Press.

Bliss, J., Monk, M. and Ogborn, J. (1983) *Qualitative Data Analysis for Educational Research*. Beckenham: Croom Helm.

Byrne, P. (1995) From the depths to the surface: art therapy as a discursive practice in the post-modern era, *The Arts in Psychotherapy* 22, 3, 235–239.

Chaiklin, S. and Schmais, D. (1986) The Chace approach to dance therapy, in P. Lewis (ed.) *Theoretical Approaches in Dance/Movement Therapy*, vol. 1. Iowa: Kendall/Hunt.

Davis, M. (1981) Movement characteristics of hospitalised patients, *American Journal of Dance Therapy*, 4, 1, 52–71.

Department of Health (DH) (1999) *National Framework (NSF) for Mental Health: Modern Standards and Service Models*. Online. Available HTTP: <http://www.dh.gov.uk/assetRoot/04/07/72/09/04077209.pdf> (accessed 26 December 2004).

—— (2000) *The NHS Plan: A Plan for Investment, A Plan for Reform*. Online. Available. HTTP: <http://www.dh.gov.uk/assetRoot/04/05/57/83/04055783.pdf> (accessed 15 January 2005).

Glaser, B. G. and Strauss, A. L. (1967) *The Discovery of Grounded Theory: Strategies for Qualitative Research*. Chicago: Aldine.

Karkou, V. (1998) A descriptive evaluation of the practice of arts therapies, unpublished PhD. thesis, University of Manchester, School of Education.

Karkou, V. and Glasman, J. (2004) Arts, education and society: the role of the arts in promoting the emotional wellbeing and social inclusion of young people, *Support for Learning* 19, 2, 56–64.

Karkou, V. and Sanderson, P. (2001) Dance movement therapy (DMT) in the UK: issues of theory and assessment, *The Arts in Psychotherapy* 28, 197–204.

—— (2006) *Arts Therapies: A Research-based Map of the Field*. Edinburgh: Elsevier.

Kestenberg, J. (1975) *Children and Parents: Psychoanalytic Studies in Development.* New York: Jason Aronson.

Laban, R. (1975) *Modern Educational Dance.* London: MacDonald and Evans.

Levy, F. (1988) *Dance Movement Therapy: A Healing Art.* Reston: American Alliance for Health, Physical Education, Recreation and Dance.

Llewellin, S. (1994) Psychotherapy in the voluntary and independent sector, in P. Clarkson and M. Pokorny (eds) *The Handbook of Psychotherapy.* London: Routledge.

Meekums, B. (2002) *Dance Movement Therapy: A creative psychotherapeutic approach.* London: Sage.

National Institute for Clinical Excellence (NICE) (2002) *Schizophrenia: Core Interventions in the Treatment and Management of Primary and Secondary Care.* London: NICE. Online. Available HTTP:<http://www.nice.org.uk/pdf/CG1NICEguidelineoster.pdf.> (accessed 15 January 2005).

Payne, H. (1983) The development of the Association for Dance Movement Therapy, *New Dance,* winter, 27.

—— (1990) *Creative Movement and Dance in Groupwork.* Oxford: Winslow. Reprinted 2000.

—— (ed.) (1992) *Dance Movement Therapy: Theory and Practice.* London and New York: Tavistock/Routledge.

Quality Assurance Agency (QAA) (2004) *Benchmark Statement: Healthcare Programme – Arts Therapies.* Gloucester: QAA.

Regel, S. and Roberts, D. (2002) *Mental Health Liaison: A Handbook for Nurses and Health Professionals.* Edinburgh: Baillière Tindall Royal College of Nursing.

Ritter, M. and Low, K. (1996) Effects of dance/movement therapy: a meta-analysis, *The Arts in Psychotherapy* 23, 3, 249–260.

Royal College of Psychiatrists (2001) Press release: Changing Minds Anti-Stigma Campaign Film '1 in 4' Adopted by World Health Organisation's 'Stop Exclusion: Dare to Care' Campaign. Online. Available. HTTP: <http://www.rcpsych.ac.uk/press/preleases/pr/pr_191.htm> (accessed 27 December 2004).

Sandel, S. and Johnson, D. (1983) Structure and process of the nascent group: dance/movement therapy with chronic patients, *The Arts in Psychotherapy*, *10*, 131–140.

Sherborne, V. (1990) *Developmental Movement for Children.* Cambridge: Cambridge University Press.

Siegel, E. V. (1984) *Dance Movement Therapy: Mirrors of Ourselves. The Psychoanalytic Approach.* New York: Human Sciences Press.

Stanton-Jones, K. (1992) *An Introduction to Dance Movement Therapy in Psychiatry.* London: Tavistock/Routledge.

Strauss, A. and Corbin, J. (1990) *Basics of Qualitative Research: Grounded Theory Procedures and Techniques.* London: Sage.

Sullivan, H. S. (1955) *The Interpersonal Theory of Psychiatry.* New York: Norton.

Yalom, I. (1985) *The Theory and Practice of Group Psychotherapy*, 3rd edn. New York: Basic Books.

Yip, K. (2001) The community care movement in mental health services: implications for social work practice, *International Social Work* 43, 1, 33–48.

Chapter 4

Dancing with demons

Dance movement therapy and complex post-traumatic stress disorder

Jeanette MacDonald

We are bound to our bodies like an oyster is to its shell.

Plato

Introduction

A thin, wraith-like figure drifted into the therapy room, feet barely touching the ground. She reached out a bony hand, tentatively, towards me. 'I'm Alice,' she said. This was my first introduction to the person whose story we will hear in this chapter. Excavating my papers and notes whilst preparing to write this piece has been personally revelatory. It was very difficult to choose one small area of work to focus upon when I was invited to write this chapter. At the time of writing it is over 30 years since I began working with dance movement therapy (DMT) techniques in the UK National Health Service (NHS). Initially I worked with learning disabled clients (MacDonald 1992). During the last 20 years I have been privileged to broaden my practice, working privately whilst continuing to work within the NHS, developing mental health work, teaching students, supervising colleagues, teaching with and supporting European colleagues to develop training and professional regulatory bodies for DMT. Suffice here to set Alice's story in context.

Methodology

This study is a retrospective review of the DMT case notes of a client presenting with symptoms of complex post-traumatic stress disorder (PTSD). I chose to study this case in an attempt to make visible that which is invisible; the process in ameliorating her distressing symptoms through DMT interventions. When I contacted Alice to obtain permission to use her story she not only agreed but also gave me full access to her own journal[1] and a copy of an interview she had completed with her then care manager. I will therefore rely upon three data sources, the interview, Alice's journal and my own clinical case notes and reflections from supervision. The core data is my own clinical case notes and the peripheral data will come from the journal and the interview. This process helps in the refinement of concepts so that 'the interconnected data within the core setting are strengthened through the triangulation with the periphery, but equally with interconnected data collected in the wider setting' (Holliday 2002: 43). Triangulation is normally thought of as increasing the validity of qualitative research by getting and comparing 'multiple perceptions' of the same phenomenon (Stake 1994: 241). Using grounded theory (Pidgeon and Henwood 1996) my aim is to find some consonance between theory and clinical practice. My principal research question is: Does DMT help to reintegrate the cognitive, emotional and physical disconnection, which is often a feature of PTSD? I finished working with Alice several years ago and she has now moved to another part of the country. Several identifying features have been changed and Alice is a pseudonym to protect her identity. Use of the first person throughout will provide continuity and flow of text. Holliday (2002) asserts that the use of the first person is a major device for separating the different voices in the text, thus increasing the transparency and accountability of the research.

This is a heuristic (Moustakas 1990) account of a traumatic childhood and its consequent embodied distress. Evaluation of treatment through single case study research both enhances clinical accountability and contributes to the existing clinical database (Acierno *et al.* 1996). I have reviewed all the data retrospectively and I shall use a constant comparative method of analysis (Snyder 1992) throughout the text.

Diagnostic features of PTSD

The American Psychological Association (1994) defines simple PTSD (DSM IV) as follows:

A. Exposure to life threatening experience
   Intense subjective distress upon exposure
B. Re-experiencing the trauma
   Recurrent intrusive recollections, or repetitive play
   Recurrent dreams
   Suddenly acting or feeling as if the traumatic event were recurring
   Intense distress upon re-exposure to events reminiscent of trauma
   Physiological reactivity upon re-exposure
C. Persistent avoidance or numbing of general responsiveness
   Efforts to avoid thoughts or feelings associated with trauma
   Efforts to avoid activities
   Psychogenic amnesia
   Diminished interest in significant activities
   Feelings of detachment of estrangement
   Sense of foreshortened future

D. Persistent symptoms of increased arousal
   Difficulty falling or staying asleep
   Irritability or outbursts of anger
   Difficulty concentrating
   Hypervigilance
   Exaggerated startle

In addition:

* Drug and/or alcohol abuse are commonly associated with this condition.
* Significant functional impairment.

There is growing recognition that PTSD can result from an accumulation of shocking events both life threatening and non-life threatening and the resultant PTSD is referred to as complex PTSD (Kinchin 2001). Complex PTSD is defined by the following factors:

I.   Alteration in Regulation of Affect and Impulses
   Affect Regulation
   Modulation of Anger
   Self-Destructive
   Suicidal Preoccupation
   Difficulty Modulating Sexual involvement
   Excessive Risk taking
II.   Alterations in Attention or Consciousness
   Amnesia
   Transient Dissociative Episodes and Depersonalisation
III.   Somatization
   Digestive System
   Chronic Pain
   Cardiopulmonary Symptoms
   Conversion Symptoms
   Sexual Symptoms
IV.   Alterations in Self-Perception
   Ineffectiveness
   Permanent Damage
   Guilt and Responsibility
   Shame
   Nobody Can Understand
   Minimising
V.   Alterations in Perception of the Perpetrator
   Adopting Distorted Beliefs
   Idealisation of the Perpetrator
   Preoccupation with Hurting Perpetrator

VI.   **Alterations in Relations with Others**
       Inability to Trust
       Re-victimisation
       Victimising Others
VII.   **Alterations in Systems of Meaning**
       Despair and Hopelessness
       Loss of Previously Sustaining Beliefs

Literature review

A comprehensive search of Amed, Medline, PsychLIT and PsychINFO for the keywords dance movement therapy and post-traumatic stress disorder revealed references for general DMT research articles but a review of these offered nothing relating specifically to DMT and complex PTSD. The range of problems arising from PTSD is very wide and there is a correspondingly wide range of PTSD research literature, which it is beyond the scope of this chapter to review. Surprisingly, there is relatively little emphasis upon the mind–body, body–mind continuum. Callaghan (1993) underlines the central-ity of this continuum in her work with victims of torture, as does Rothschild (2000). Van der Kolk (1994), an eminent and controversial PTSD researcher, has written extensively on the psychobiology of PTSD. The very early work of Marian Chace (Chaiklin *et al.* 1993) in the USA, was essentially with the effects of PTSD as she danced on the back wards with men suffering from the traumatic effects of war. According to Peterson *et al.* (1992) there is increasing evidence that avoidance of painful material is a central mechanism in PTSD. I wish to question whether creative and transformational DMT interventions can help to access and integrate this painful material effectively.

Foa *et al.* (2000) present a range of current evidence-based treatments for PTSD which include the creative arts therapies, that is, dance movement therapy, music therapy, dramatherapy and art therapy as the major modalities. David Read Johnson states:

> The mean effect size of dance movement therapy for core psychiatric symptoms, based on meta-analyses, has been estimated as 0.37 (range = 0.15 to 0.54; Cruz and Sabers, 1998). However, no estimates are available with specifically PTSD populations.
>
> (Read Johnson cited in Foa *et al.* 2000: 308)

He proceeds to recommend the design of arts therapy treatments specific to PTSD.

The story

Alice was referred to me at the Creative Therapy Service – a unique, community-based NHS resource offering the four arts therapies, dance, art, music and drama. It is housed in a large country house in beautiful grounds surrounded by trees and shrubs. It is within the city boundary and accessible by public transport. Alice had recently completed a ten-session group for 'survivors of sexual abuse' facilitated by a community psychiatric nurse. This experience had re-opened many psychological wounds for her, wounds and memories which she had tried to avoid throughout her life. She was starting to write about this traumatic material in a journal when her care manager referred her to me to help her work through the emergent stories. From our very first meeting it was clear that Alice was 'disembodied'. Here is an observation from her care manager: 'When I first met Alice she was physically thin almost ethereal and gave the impression of being almost all spiritual rather than physical presence.'

Alice had a long history of terrible physical, emotional and sexual abuse, both at the hands of her own parents and subsequently from her foster parents. She told me that she had stopped developing around the age of 13 and that her physique had changed little since then apart from having grown taller. Here is a short extract from her journal:

> My brother tells of this incident. Apparently I wouldn't use the pot, so my father picked me up by my legs and repeatedly banged my head against the cooker. I must have passed out. I remember them wrapping towels and scarves around my head, there was blood everywhere. My father took me to the hospital; I was walking off the edge of the pavement. I reached out my hand for him to hold and he pushed me away. Blank until I came to in hospital. I had been unconscious for three days. Fractured skull. My mother and father told them I'd fallen down the stairs and banged my head of each step. The Dr. didn't believe them. They tried to make me a ward of court but it didn't go through, my mother told me. Next I remember going home in an ambulance. I had been given a rag doll. My brother and some of my sisters remember the next bit; as soon as I got in the house I had started screaming again and the rag doll was taken away from me. I was put in the cellar again . . . I remember a huge rolling pin, my sister being battered with it, she screaming and I was too. Sister was in hospital for weeks. Both of us taken away from them . . . I remember the sexual abuse that my real father did to me also.

Alice's journal is very shocking and painful to read and relates to a catalogue of violation and torment, which we confronted in our DMT sessions over a period of two years. She began her journal towards the end of the previous survivors' group and continued following our individual DMT sessions. I was not aware of, nor had access to, her journal until I began this review process.

Although Alice had begun the healing process by confronting her painful memories within the survivors' group, she was still far from any physical remembering as evidenced by her arrested physical development, persistent shallow breathing, rigid posture and high chin. Stromstead (1994) talks about how, following trauma, the individual might engage in a 'spiritual bypass' of the body's experience. Here is another extract from her journal:

> As a child I developed an ability to separate myself as a physical being into a place of infinite light, warmth and loving understanding. Away from my inward fearful struggle to fight against my abusers aggression and darkness against me. I did not realise the full significance of this then. Now I identify this place as a higher spiritual dimension of great wisdom that kept my spirit if not my body safe and whole.

We can hear another account of this phenomenon in the interview with her care manager:

Care manager: What helped you to survive? How did you cope?
Alice: I can remember a number of occasions when I was being beaten just going right out of my body and sort of floating . . . that kept me going.
Care manager: Your spiritual self?
Alice: Yes.

Clearly, leaving her body was Alice's way of living through her appalling childhood. This characterological use of dissociation underlies the description offered by Allen and Coyne:

> Although initially they may have used dissociation to cope with traumatic events, they subsequently dissociate to defend against a broad range of daily stressors, including their own posttraumatic symptoms, pervasively undermining the continuity of their experience.
>
> (Allen and Coyne 1995: 620)

When she was 18, Alice reported going to live with a kind and gentle elderly lady whom she refers to in her journal as Aunt B. She describes this as her first experience of any sort of loving empathetic relationship. She trained as a nurse and went to work overseas for a short while before returning to the UK to continue nursing. Although she found it physically and emotionally stressful and difficult she enjoyed nursing and after a few years she gave birth to her daughter. She maintained no contact with the child's father. Alice concentrated her efforts in denying her own pain and creating a loving home for her daughter. She relates in her journal that being responsible for this small child saved her many times when, because of her emotional pain, she contemplated taking her life. The crisis came when one of her brothers took his life. This was the catalyst that compelled Alice to seek help.

The dance movement therapy sessions

As Alice had disconnected so completely from her body I felt that it was essential to approach this work very gently to avoid a complete flight from reality and to give context to her story text. When discussing her work with survivors of political torture and organised violence, Callaghan (1993) talks about how the process of reintegrating body and mind may be profoundly disturbing. I recalled a training intensive with Babette Rothschild, a body psychotherapist specialising in PTSD, where she stressed the importance of first creating a 'safe' physical place within the therapy space. The body is no longer a safe place for someone who has experienced physical shock or abusive physical treatment. I believe that because the body has experienced a normal shock reaction to an abnormal event, the neuorobiological effects may be compounded and held within the body structure. This body defence against feeling was described in the work of Reich (1945). In complex PTSD these abnormal events are repeated so the body's shock reaction is repeated. Almost like learning to dance, the repeated body actions and reactions become unconscious acts. These defence reactions are coping mechanisms for continuing to live in the world and therefore extreme caution is essential when attempting bodywork with a body holding and defending the psyche against overwhelming shock and disintegration.

For Alice, the safe place was a huge green floor cushion. A number of the early sessions were spent inhabiting the green cushion and as I sat beside her she reached out to hold my hand and, looking into my eyes, she told me her story. Stories are an important element of the therapeutic journey. Since the core problem in PTSD consists of a failure to integrate upsetting experiences into autobiographical memory, the goal of treatment is to find a way in which people can acknowledge the reality of what has happened, without having to re-experience the trauma all over again. For this to occur, merely uncovering memories is not enough: they need to be modified and transformed: placed in their proper context and reconstructed into neutral or meaningful narratives. Thus, in therapy, memory paradoxically becomes an act of creation, rather than the static recording of events which is characteristic of trauma-based memories.

In her novel *The Stone Diaries* Carol Shields (1995) talks about how we need important others to listen to our life stories: 'Life is an endless recruitment of witnesses' (Shields 1995: 36). This and other modern novels attest to the importance of having someone to listen to our experiences. This sort of relationship requires the development of an affective bond (Bowlby 1982). The most important new information is probably the fact that the patient is able to confront the traumatic memory with a trusted therapist in a safe environment (van der Hart and Spiegel 1993). In order to help the patient regulate emotional arousal, secure attachment may be even more important than evoking the traumatic memories. Therefore, it is important for the patient to establish and maintain an emotional connection with the therapist. A rapidly expanding body of research (Schore 1994; Perry *et al.* 1995) has shown that disturbances of childhood attachment bonds can have long-term neurobiological consequences. In addition to the disturbances in affect regulation, van der Kolk (1995) identifies studies which show that childhood abuse, neglect and separation have far-reaching biopsychosocial effects, including lasting biological changes which affect the capacity to modulate emotions, difficulty in learning new coping skills, alterations in immune competency and impairment in the capacity to engage in meaningful social affiliation (van der Kolk 1995). Listening to the client's narrative whilst maintaining physical contact helps to develop a trusting therapeutic relationship. Any sort of physical contact with sufferers of PTSD must be approached with great care and sensitivity as the body is the container of so many of their painful and abusive past experiences. Working with survivors of torture (Callaghan 1993) describes the body as the physical and psychological site of destruction. This is illustrated in the following extract from my case notes:

> Today Alice explained that if she could just 'get it all out, without running away' it would be a first! When she related particularly distressing events her whole body tensed, her breathing became very shallow and the pitch of her voice became very high. She squeezed my hand with great intensity, hunched her shoulders and screwed her eyes tightly shut! When she had finished speaking she let out an enormous sigh, released her grip on my hand, opened her eyes and looked at me hard. 'What do you think about that?' she said. I told her that I felt very shocked and amazed that she had survived all her ordeals. She smiled ruefully; my response appeared to ease her tension. She continued her story and this 40-year-old woman reached out to hold my hand again.
>
> (Session 8 of 67)

We took short breaks from the narrative to focus on her body, naming and affirming body parts, discovering numb and frozen parts and breathing into every part of the body. When distressing or uncomfortable sensations emerged we would try to relate them to her story, to put them in their place, to reconnect with their source. Alice created metaphorical 'pockets' in the green cushion and when she was able to connect a physical sensation to her story she would put it into her pocket, 'For later,' she said. I kept details of her pockets and their contents in my clinical notes.

Stromstead (1994) describes this descent back into the body as critical to the healing and transformative process. Movement was restricted to the green cushion until Alice felt secure in her body boundaries and ready to step into the larger space. This took the best part of a year. Alice wrote in her journal:

In my childhood I came to know a different level of physical linear time, I give my heart's thanks to this higher dimension that has held me secure within its infinite love throughout my life.

Now reflected within mother earth, her seas, sky, carpets of hills and valleys and all her profuse nature, is a gentle though awesome care and strength, that has drawn me ever close. Balancing and nurturing my physical senses within the depths of her living beauty and hope. I have been twice blessed.

I can see now from this entry in her journal that for Alice the big green cushion symbolised the earth and all its nurturing qualities. My notes speak of the physical softening and relaxation of Alice's body when she came to sit or lie on her cushion. My supervision notes speak of my own need to move quickly through some of the very heavy material we were processing. I began to set aside a 15-minute debriefing session for myself following our DMT sessions, so that I could 'dance out' the narrative that I had embodied in the transference:

> The goal of working with transference is the main goal of much of psychotherapy and body-psychotherapy: separating the past from the present so that the ghosts and imprints of the past no longer interfere with life in the present freeing the individual to develop new and more effective resources and tools to further his life.
>
> (Rothschild 1993)

The body of the therapist is an important tool, the most basic one. It is the therapist's body that will resonate to many of the subtle tensions and emotional states in the client. Reich (1945) called this process 'vegetative identification'. It means to feel in your own body a sense of the client's struggle, rhythm and quality of pulsation. Following our sessions Alice not only kept a journal but also began to paint and draw. She told me that she needed to record the physical experiences of our sessions. This raised the question for me of how the primacy of movement might act as a catalyst for further creative expression. Indeed, Sheets-Johnstone is eloquent in her argument:

> Behaviours evolve only because behaviours are essentially complex dynamic patternings of movement, and movement being the mother tongue of all animate forms, thinking in movement is both a primary fact and a perpetual possibility of animate life.
>
> (Sheets-Johnstone 2000: 11)

It may be argued that freeing Alice's body to move without fear and with emergent new patterns perhaps helped to create new multimodal pathways for expression of her internal state. Alice was beginning to make sense of her experiences and to integrate them physically, mentally and emotionally. There is a need to address the effects of the trauma on people's perceptions of themselves and the world around them. People are meaning-making creatures. As we develop we organise our world according to a personal theory of reality, some of which may be conscious, but much of which is an unconscious integration of accumulated experience. These mental schemas organise psychological experience via the process of assimilation and accommodation and assure continuity of one's identity (Horowitz 1991). Although most people cannot clearly articulate the content of their mental schemes, they nonetheless determine what sensory input is selected for further coding and categorisation. Adaptive resolution to a stressful experience consists of the modification or accommodation of one's view of self, and others, which permits adaptive action and continued attention to the exigencies of daily life. In order to deal successfully with a distressing experience, it is necessary to refrain from generalising from that experience to the totality of existence, but to view it merely as one terrible event that has taken place at a particular place at a particular time (Epstein 1991). Here is another extract from Alice's journal:

> *Today I felt angry, sad, angry*
>   And tired
>   Not a physical tiredness
>   Just an inner tiredness
>   Of living torn apart emotionally
> *Always trying to find a way*
>   Of dealing with the effects of past memories
>   Still trying to heal the pain
>   That makes me feel so sad.

From this and the following extract from the interview it can be seen that she appears now to be able to differentiate her angry and sad feelings and that she was learning to recognise her physical responses to her memories.

Care manager: How do you manage to express your rage and anger without it spilling out and hurting others?

Alice: What I used to do when I was a child, I bit my finger. You can see the scars there. In temper.

Care manager: Did you bite it to the bone?

Alice: I bit it. Part of it was hanging and I had to have it stitched! I used to bite my arms a lot when I was a child. Not when I was growing up, because I didn't want to be angry – I recognised I had a lot of anger inside me that I needed to deal with. I started dealing with it when I was having individual DMT with J and I learned that I didn't have to keep it all inside. It does more damage to me so I've got an anger cushion[2] I really thrash hell out of. I don't think it's anger. I know there is still a lot of pain. It's sadness. I do cry now and I find I can cry more but it still gets stuck sometimes. If I'm really angry (it's wonderful because it makes a terrific amount of noise) I screw the *Radio Times* up and whack the table and just scream and shout but I don't do it very often.

It is interesting to note that I did not have access to either Alice's journal or the interview during the therapy period. The dates of these documents add weight to my decision that because Alice was beginning to recognise her physical responses and attribute them correctly to events in the past it was timely to move from the relative safety of the green cushion and into the larger therapy space. The larger therapy space seems to serve as a metaphor for the world. Bartenieff and Lewis (1980) speak of the immediate kinesphere – the space around the body serving as an individual's bridge into the world. My notes from this first session away from the green cushion are an example of this.

Alice stepped slowly and reluctantly into the far corner of the space and wrapped her arms tightly around her fragile body. 'I feel so cold and exposed,' she said. She described feeling the same as she had when anticipating a physical attack. I sank to the ground in front of her and slowly she followed me. Then she stretched out full length on her front and began to snake along the ground, tracing a diagonal path from the upper right corner towards the lower left corner of the space. As she approached the centre she curled into a tight ball. 'Help me, help me!' she said, not looking but stretching out her hand towards me. Keeping low on the ground I moved slowly towards her and took her hand. She related memories of being punished and physically beaten as a young child; she related feeling pain and soreness at the base of her spine.

(Session 33 of 67)

I felt at the time that we were at a very critical stage in the therapy as Alice was re-experiencing her early distress both physically and emotionally. I can see now from her journal written after this session that it was, indeed, the case. It is so important in this work not to retraumatise the client and to keep all conscious physical activity firmly placed and attributed to the here and now or contained and identified as past events that have been survived and left behind. This is what she wrote at the time:

I had done something wrong and the punishment you and my foster mother decided I should have was a smacked bottom for a week before I went to bed. It hurt daddy and what hurt more was the look of delight on your face as you made me strip, then put me over your knee. Whilst you and my foster mother laughed together. I had been a bad girl you said, though I still can't remember what I had done. Then I went to bed crying, thinking why do they hate me so.

It is little wonder that she felt such pain and soreness at the base of her spine! We identified Alice's diagonal pathway across the space as a timeline and she related particular traumatic events in her childhood to particular places along this physical and spatial diagonal. She started to choreograph her personal story with very clear symbolic movements along this line. I reflected these movements back to her and, when she chose, we would stop and talk about the experience. Emphasis was made upon the fact that although we were quite firmly here in the present, the dance that she was creating along the diagonal belonged to events that had happened in the past. She danced her diagonal dance many times, sometimes alone, a frail and poignant figure. Sometimes she asked me to join her and occasionally she stepped away asking to see, 'what it looked like'. I suggested that she could create another pathway in the space that might symbolise the present and future. From my case notes:

Alice was very excited today about the prospect of creating another pathway in the space and I was surprised to witness her clarity of purpose in placing the large green cushion along the centre of the back wall and standing very firmly in its centre. She then proceeded to run, quite fast, very lightly on her feet, all around the edge of the room, right hand touching the wall. Avoiding the corners she made a complete circle, returning to the green cushion and throwing herself down upon it with a huge 'Haaaaa!', head thrown back, arms and legs outstretched with a smiling face. She related feeling a sense of freedom and release. I reflected back to her the run along her pathway. She observed that it looked as free as it had felt. We talked about the possibility of incorporating the two pathways, her past timeline with all of its symbolic, tortured and painful movements and this new circular pathway. Alice expressed some resistance to repeating or returning to the diagonal. We will have to approach this essential symbolic integration very gently and slowly. I believe that if she can physically integrate her past traumatic experiences into her present body – felt experience of freedom from pain and rigidity, she may move some way towards healing her pain.

(Session 41 of 67)

At our next session Alice reports a reduction in her nightmares and flashbacks. She also relates to this in her interview:

Care manager: Have you had fewer dreams following therapy?
Alice: Oh I still dream, but not that kind of dream.

Care manager: When was the last one?
Alice: That was when I was seeing J because I remember telling her about it. Last time I saw her was a couple of months ago but previous to that I was actually seeing her every week so it could have been then.

Papadopoulos (2001) claims that dance, in a structured creative context, allows for dialogue between the conscious and unconscious and the possibility for interaction between the two. I would suggest that this interaction could facilitate the psyche-soma integration so necessary in healing past traumas. Rather than an expression of healing and freedom from pain (a facile interpretation), Alice's fast, free-flowing circular movement pathway could be regarded as a defence against addressing her painful feelings (Boas 1952) – a literal flight from pain. In her interview Alice speaks about a recurring dream:

> The dreams are not necessarily recurring dreams – I haven't had one of those for months and months, the one of my foster mother and would always be her and I would always be in either some corridors, running round corridors or in a maze. I don't get them any more.

It is for this reason that the therapist needs to approach this stage of the work with thought and caution. We are aware of the neurophysiological effect of movement upon the body, the release of endorphins producing the 'feel good factor' (Stephens 1988: 41–42). If this is contained in a purely body-felt experience we risk compounding the dissociation that the traumatised client has effected, further removing them from the source of their pain. It is only through confronting this pain that there can be a prospect of real, holistic healing. The client therefore needs to integrate all the movement experiences witnessed and expressed within the therapy space. We may need to revisit and refine certain movement sections before they may be woven into the finished piece. When working with symptoms of PTSD, the dance that our clients create needs to become a seamless piece of movement. It may express hidden and unconscious aspects of their lives, which have previously seeped out in nightmares, flashbacks, panic attacks and phobias and other physical, emotional and psychological symptoms. From my case notes:

> Alice was very resistant to revisiting her diagonal timeline today. She expressed the fear that she might get stuck there – be overwhelmed by painful memories – be unable to escape – to move! She repeated her circular, wall-touching run two or three times until she collapsed exhausted upon the green cushion. I did not press her to return to the diagonal but sat beside her whilst she told me some more of her painful memories. She said that she felt safe on the green cushion and that to her

it represented mother earth. I commented upon the fact that she had placed the green cushion at the starting point of her circular pathway and that it might help her to slow down her run and enjoy exploring this new pathway and its difference in relation to the old diagonal. I reminded her also of the symbolic pockets she had created in the cushion and how we might need to look at some of the things she had placed inside. I hoped that by making these tenuous links to persuade her to acknowledge the horrors of the diagonal and to begin to integrate the two pathways. Alice has brought me some wonderful, colourful drawings, which she has done following our sessions. They are stunning!

(Session 43 of 67)

The following extract from Alice's journal was written after this session:

Last night before sleeping I asked for help in this work I am doing to release the fear, hurt and deep sadness I feel. Feeling a safe, slow, quiet, seeping energy through my body whilst lying there. Thinking to myself that I have always felt safer outside and this safety amongst nature has become very precious to me. For I am not a victim of mother earth, whatever my experiences from human kind have been. In nature I can be a whole like everyone, a part of her is for me also, and I am accepted on the earth for the me that is now.

Having felt so very tired for so long, relaxed and was able to sleep. On waking up much later than usual I felt a light brightness.

This integration and healing is also reflected in this extract from the interview:

Care manager: You have remembered, worked through and owned your pain. Are you now able, like grief, to let it go?
Alice: That is how I feel now. Whereas as before I did all that work I was running away from it. I control it now. Sometimes things come up but I can honestly say that the last three or four months, it is almost as though my head has been freer.

We have heard from her journal that Alice was symbolising and experiencing the green cushion as the earth. In fact, in the journal she talks about 'mother earth'. As she had been unable to internalise a 'good mother' in her development we were able to use the cushion as a 'holding place' and also a transitional object (Winnicott 1995). I suggested that she could take the green cushion with her to revisit the diagonal time line. It is important that avoidance patterns do not become embedded in the therapy space, so we needed to find a satisfactory way to overcome this fear whilst not overwhelming the ego with too much raw and primitive material. To embrace the necessity of returning, as part of the process, to the very painful events that therapy is supposed to 'overcome' sounds manageable in the abstract, but is, of course, over and over again, deeply painful for both client and therapist in the intricate emotional detail which is their particular relationship. The client needs us to lose whatever we identify as our 'therapeutic position' sufficiently so that we are available for re-enactment. Only in externalising and re-experiencing in the therapeutic relationship what was unbearable in the past, and uncontainable by the client's ego in the present, is the full extent of the client's pain sufficiently accessible to transform itself. Here, the transformative character of dance acts as a container for feelings that might have been unmanageable in the past. Placing the disturbing feelings of anger, hostility, shame, disgust and so on within the dance form allows the psychic distance necessary to process these feelings and to give them a suitable place: a place not only within the narrative but within the therapeutic space which, through dance, comes to symbolise the life space and patterns. Here is another extract from Alice's journal:

> Somewhere along the way my emotions of heart and mind separated, travelling in different directions. Each along isolated lines, broken pieces drifted occasionally into the same route, surprising me with their rare clarity of view. More often shifting back to such heaviness of heart and confusion of mind.
>
> It happened a long time ago; my feeling became disconnected from the logic of my thinking.
>
> A warm stability of being in this world and trusting another soul, I couldn't know. Only what I saw 'to be' cruelty, harshness seemed 'all that was' a long time ago. When I learnt not everything was like the experiences I had, the routes my heart and mind were travelling realised with shattering hurt, pieces needed healing, a love to bring them back together along the same line.

It is interesting to hear the linear pattern created in the therapy space echoed in her narrative. We can see that Alice was beginning to locate her traumatic experiences in the past – 'a long time ago' – and to recognise the need to reintegrate thought and feeling – 'pieces needed healing'. I suggested some of her story connected to some classic fairy tales, and perhaps we could use the tales to weave a dance between her light-hearted circular pathway and the intensity of the diagonal. In his compelling work, Early (1993) examines the archetypal nature of psychological trauma, particularly as it applies to combat veterans. By examining the fairy tales, fables and folklore that have been handed down through the ages, this author is able to argue persuasively that much classic literature has elements of trauma survival woven through it, indicative of the timeless, collective struggle humankind has with trauma. Early finds elements of PTSD in fairy tales such as *Cinderella, Little Red*

Riding Hood, *Snow White*, *Blue Beard*, and *Beauty and the Beast*, as well as in modern-day fables such as *Superman* and *Batman*. The characters in these stories are often abused and abandoned and bent on avenging the evil forces that traumatise them. They dichotomise the world into good and evil and seek situations that replay the trauma experience. The author shows how these same feelings and behaviours are found in PTSD sufferers such as war veterans and rape victims. Early asserts that these tales are so popular across cultures precisely because they express fundamental human problems created by psychological trauma and provide an emotional outlet for people struggling with traumatic memories. Jungian psychologist Birgitte Brun (Brun *et al.* 1993) advocates the power of fairy tales to offer rich symbolism and therapeutic distance to difficult themes. Our discussion around themes from fairy tales appeared to touch Alice profoundly and she rose from the ground and walked to the corner of the room with clear firm steps, head bowed in thought. Here are some notes from this session:

> Today Alice dragged the green cushion over to the far corner of her diagonal. She reached into the metaphorical pockets in the cushion, drew out some of her symbolic experiences – those that were 'for later'. A ritual emerged where she lay each 'traumatic experience' along her diagonal and addressed each one with a movement piece, eventually she symbolically stamped two or three flat into the ground, others she symbolically tore into tiny pieces and tossed the pieces all around the space, moving gently but firmly between her diagonal and circular pathways. Her movements were clear and deliberate.
>
> (Session 47 of 67)

I made no attempt to interpret her dance but I did suggest that, providing she was satisfied with the result, she could repeat and rehearse it. Dance is the only time–space art form (De Mille 1963) and as such is a most valuable container for immediate experience. It is truly 'of the moment'. Following this session Alice wrote in her journal:

> I can only be responsible for the moment I am in.
> This moment is perfect, it is whole.
> I will be its completeness, not being a past or a future.
> For 'all' is contained within this moment's pure freedom.
> I will be its all.
> If only for a moment.

And an extract from the interview:

Care manager: What do you think has helped you to overcome your traumas?

Answer: Since a child, colour has been especially important to me but
                   my heartfelt thanks really to my work with J who encour-
                   aged the development of my creative ability, the use of
                   which helped me to heal the broken pieces within me.

The last extract is from Alice's care manager:

Alice's healing journey and process is powerfully reflected in the complete contents of her journal and in her drawings. The work she did on
reconnecting with her body shows in the change from clear, sharp, angu-
lar shapes and vivid colours using felt tips to the use of pastels and the
introduction of more earth tones. Alice's journey is a testament to the
indestructibility of the human spirit against all the odds and as such is a
message of hope to others working in the field.

Alice produced over 50 stunning drawings, which she had completed outside
of the therapeutic space but in parallel with the therapy sessions. Photographs of just two follow. The first was produced at the very beginning of our
work together. The second was towards the end (see pages 66 and 67).

Discussion

A summary account of individual DMT work over a period of two years, one
of weekly therapy and one of monthly sessions, underlines the need for careful and sensitive approaches to traumatic material. There is clear evidence
from three separate sources that supports the hypothesis that dance movement interventions can help a traumatised individual to re-inhabit their body
and to create new, healthy life meanings and pathways. It can be argued that
the human condition is inherently one of embodiment and, whilst listening to
the narrative is important, unless past experiences are consciously integrated
on a body-felt level they remain poised to inhabit the body in unconscious
and unhealthy ways. This is evidenced in the numerous somatic problems
experienced by sufferers of PTSD. The creative quality of dance as an art
form offers the opportunity to utilise physicality, symbolism, metaphor and
story within a structured context; one in which the body is the principal tool
of expression. Weaving together past and present pathways appeared to be
instrumental in affording the possibility to confront painful memories and
consequently to dissolve or transform them. It was of paramount importance
to create a safe, holding environment and from this to rebuild the capacity to
form a trusting relationship. The nature of the trauma might inform the basis
of the therapeutic relationship. A female having experienced rape, sexual
abuse and or physical and emotional violence from a male perpetrator might
have difficulty forming a sound therapeutic relationship with a male therapist
and vice versa. As I reviewed my notes I recognised the difficulties that we

Figure 4.1   Alice's picture made at the start of DMT

Figure 4.2   Alice's picture made at the end of DMT

encountered in the transference as Alice recalled terrible abuse at the hands of her father and foster mother and father. It was an intensely emotional experience forcing me to explore the darkest corners of the mind. Arbitrary convenience ruled the choice of participant for this study and such a small sample does not allow for generalised reporting in the traditional sense. The findings do, however, appear to provide a legitimate link to theory and a stepping stone to further research. The usefulness of this study will be considered by those who read it through their personal interpretation of the findings of Coffey and Atkinson:

> Establishing the trustworthiness of the insights generated through exploratory research is the job of those who are consumers of the research not the job of social science researchers.
>
> (Coffey and Atkinson 1996: 163)

Conclusion

Individual DMT is a powerful tool in reintegrating a fragmented self suffering from complex PTSD, particularly focusing upon the quality of the relationship. More research is needed into the place of DMT as an effective treatment modality for sufferers of complex PTSD. The traditional verbal psychotherapies do not pay enough attention to helping people recognise and understand bodily sensations (van der Kolk 1994). Choreography (creating dances), the essence of the art form, is central to my DMT practice with this population. This fundamental approach requires a therapist to have a broad and extensive range of dance skills underpinned by sound psychological theory. Whilst physical relaxation exercises are helpful and play a part in body awareness, the body is designed to move and it is through movement that real integration takes place. Movement with dance at its heart, the art form that encompasses all the senses, creates meaning from movement and the possibility for renewal and transformation. It is an honest reflection of the mover. In Alice's own words:

> Let us dream awhile
> And go to a wide space
> Where we can be a light
> Airy and free
> From our sad lonely pain of hearts darkness
> And fear.
> This space within our mind's soul
> Is real, full and makes us feel a
> Completeness
> Dancing a freedom of joy slipped past the heaviness of suffering.

Notes

1 Alice issued a caveat with her journal in that any material used was not to be edited.
2 The cushion she speaks of here was not our large green cushion but another small cushion that she kept at home.

References

Acierno, R., Hersen, M. and Van Hasselt, V.B. (1996) *Accountability in Psychological Treatment*. New York/London: Plenum Press.

Allen, J.G. and Coyne, L. (1995) Dissociation and vulnerability to psychotic experience. The Dissociative Experiences Scale and the MMPI-2, *Journal of Nervous and Mental Disease* 183, 615–622.

American Psychiatric Association (1994) *The Diagnostic and Statistical Manual of Mental Disorders (DSM-IV)*. Washington, DC, American Psychiatric Association.

Bartenieff, I. and Lewis, D. (1980) *Body Movement: Coping with the Environment*. London: Gordon and Breach.

Boas, F. (1952) Creative dance, in L. Bender (ed.) *Child Psychiatric Techniques*. Illinois: C.C. Thomas.

Bowlby, J. (1982) *Attachment and Loss, vol. 1, Attachment*, 2nd edn. New York, Basic Books.

Brun, B., Pedersen, E.W. and Runberg, M. (1993) *Symbols of the Soul: Therapy and Guidance through Fairy Tales*. London: Jessica Kingsley.

Callaghan, K. (1993) Movement psychotherapy with adult survivors of political torture and organised violence, *The Arts in Psychotherapy* 20, 411–421.

Chaiklen, S., Lohn, A. and Sandel, S. (1993) *Foundations of Dance/Movement Therapy: The Life and Work of Marian Chace*. Columbia, MD: Marian Chace Memorial Fund of the American Dance Therapy Association.

Coffey, A. and Atkinson, P. (1996) *Making Sense of Qualitative Data*. Thousand Oaks, CA: Sage.

De Mille, A. (1963) *The Book of the Dance*. London: Paul Hamlyn.

Early, E. (1993) *The Raven's Return: The Influence of Psychological Trauma on Individuals and Culture*. New York: Chiron.

Epstein, S. (1991) The self-concept, the traumatic neurosis, and the structure of personality. In D. Ozer, J.M. Healy, Jr and A.J. Stewart (eds) *Perspectives in Personality, vol. 3*. London: Jessica Kingsley, pp. 63–98.

Foa, E.B., Friedman, M.J. and Keane, T.M. (eds) (2000) *Effective Treatments for PTSD*. New York: Guilford Press.

Holliday, A. (2002) *Doing and Writing Qualitative Research*. London: Sage.

Horowitz, M.J. (1991) *Person Schemas and Maladaptive Interpersonal Patterns*. Chicago: University of Chicago Press.

Kinchin, D. (2001) *Post Traumatic Stress Disorder: The Invisible Injury*. Didcot: Success Unlimited Publications.

MacDonald, J. (1992) Dance movement therapy for people with learning difficulties, in H. Payne (ed.) *Dance Movement Therapy: Theory and Practice*. London: Tavistock/Routledge.

Moustakas, C. (1990) *Heuristic Research: Design, Methodology and Applications.* Newbury Park: Sage.

Papadopoulos, N. (2001) The dynamics of the dance movement experience: combining Jung and Winnicott, *E-motion, ADMT Quarterly*, Spring.

Perry, B., Pollard, R., Blakely, T., Baker, W. and Vigilante, D. (1995) Childhood trauma, the neurobiology of adaptation and 'use-dependent' developments of the brain: how 'states' become 'traits', *Infant Mental Health Journal* 16, 4, 271–291.

Peterson, K.C., Prout, M.F. and Schwartz, R. A. (1992) *Post-Traumatic Stress Disorder: A Clinician's Guide.* New York/London: Plenum Press.

Pidgeon, N. and Henwood, K. (1996) Grounded theory: practical implementation, in N.K. Denzin and Y.S. Lincoln (eds) *Handbook of Qualitative Research Methods.* London: SPS, pp. 86–101.

Read Johnson, D. (2000) Creative therapies, in E.B. Foa, T.M. Keane and M.J. Friedman (eds) *Effective Treatments for PTSD.* New York: Guilford Press.

Reich, W. (1945) *Character Analysis.* New York: Simon and Schuster.

Rothschild, B. (1993) *Publishing on the Internet.* Online. Available HTTP: <http: www.trauma.cc/> (accessed 4 December 2003).

—— *The Body Remembers: The Psychophysiology of Trauma and Trauma Treatment.* New York: Norton.

Schore, A.N. (1994) *Affect Regulation and the Origin of the Self: The Neurobiology of Emotional Development.* Mahwah, NJ: Lawrence Erlbaum Associates Inc.

Sheets-Johnstone M. (2000) The primacy of movement, *Psycholoquy*, 11(098) Movement Primacy (1) Publishing on the Internet. Online. Available HTTP: http:// www.cogsci.ecs.soton.ac.uk/cgi/psyc/newpsy?11.098> (accessed 18 May 2005).

Shields, C. (1995) *The Stone Diaries.* New York: Penguin.

Snyder, S. (1992) Interviewing college students about their constructions of love, in J.F. Gilgan, K. Daly and G. Handel (eds) *Qualitative Methods in Family Research.* Newbury Park, CA: Sage, pp. 43–65.

Stake, R.E. (1994) Case studies, in N.K. Denzin and Y.S. Lincoln (eds) *A Handbook of Qualitative Research.* Thousand Oaks, CA: Sage, pp. 236–247.

Stephens, T. (1988) Physical activity and mental health in the United States and Canada: evidence from four population surveys, *Preventative Medicine* 17, 1, 35–47.

Stromstead T. (1994) Reinhabiting the female body, *Somatics: Journal of the Bodily Arts and Sciences* 1, 18–27.

Winnicott, D.W. (1965) *Maturational Processes and the Facilitating Environment.* London: Hogarth Press.

van der Hart, O. and Spiegel, D. (1993) Hypnotic assessment and treatment of trauma induced psychoses: the early psychotherapy of H. Breukink and modern views, *International Journal of Clinical and Experimental Hypnosis* 41, 191–209.

van der Kolk, B.A. (1994). The body keeps the score: memory and the evolving psychobiology of post traumatic stress, *Harvard Review of Psychiatry*, 1, 253–265.

Chapter 5

Dance movement therapy with patients with Parkinson's disease

Jill Bunce

Introduction

Dance movement therapy (DMT) has been part of my life, as a practitioner, for twelve years. This chapter is a sharing of part of that practice which has involved the integration of research, theory and practice, much soul searching and thought. Yet, I feel that I am still at the beginning, and see my work with progressive neurological illness with new insights as the field progresses. Different viewpoints shift my practice to the relationship between body and mind, and to the unconscious landscape that both therapist and client inhabit within the creative expression of dance and movement.

I met people with Parkinson's disease (PD) for the first time on a student placement (Bunce 1996) and I have worked with PD patients since then. I have worked with other populations but, through understanding and discovering the complexities of this syndrome, I have acquired a general understanding for using DMT with their group. In earlier days I was fortunate to study with a neurologist. At that time DMT was a new field and neurological concepts were divorced from psychotherapy theory. It was difficult to find a theoretical base for the practice in which I was involved. I decided to research the effects of DMT and its benefits to patients with PD. I wanted to try and find a rationale for DMT to give a basis and understanding for working with progressive disease such as PD. There is a growing field of awareness in psychotherapy and its neurological connections (Palley 2003) and my practice has grown to encompass these new ideas. I have observed some interesting links between early attachment and body responses to stress; the development of emotional relationships and their neurological significance and the role of movement as an integrative part of these.

Palley suggests that conscious awareness comes after the 'doing'. She cites Libet *et al.*'s (1983) experiments that subjects are consciously aware of their decision to act after it has occurred. The implication for DMT practice is that the non-verbal act is primary, before the awareness of it occurs. This is due to the brain's need for a sensory fine-tuning to rapid and complex changes in the environment and involves the feedback of information to and from the brain.

In PD the feedback system is impaired and so there is a lack of response to the environment and a delay in emotional response to behaviour. I have observed this in my practice with PD patients who have attachment problems and those who have suffered abuse. There seems to be a disruption in feedback from the behaviour to their conscious awareness of it. The ability to feel what the body experiences is crucial. DMT is particularly suitable for making what is pre-verbal into consciousness (including into speech) and requires further research. According to Palley, the self also develops within the intensity of an interpersonal relationship and that development plays a part in the synchronicity of body and central nervous system (CNS) growth with the attunement of the mother. DMT provides an environment for the synchronous attuning and mirroring process and for the sensory reworking of experience in order for the non-verbal body memory to become conscious and verbal.

The research

The primary purpose of my research was to establish the relevance of DMT as a regular part of therapeutic treatment for PD patients. It was also to fulfil my desire to document a process in which my own personal involvement grew and developed. The aim for this study was to establish that some changes had been made in particular areas, both physical and psychological and to indicate what particular changes had occurred from the patients' and carers' perspective.

The aim of the research was to investigate the nature of the pathology of the disease, which can cause anxiety, depression, fear and a loss of confidence as well as physical disability. The role and psychological state of carers were also documented. The significance of the role of non-verbal communication in the disease was analysed. For this recordings were made that showed a lack of facial expression and body language which indicated that communication between patients, carers and the therapist was reduced. Lamb's (1965) analysis of posture and gesture was used in the observation of the videos. The research only refers to groupwork. There are three areas of understanding that inform the DMT practice:

- the body and the relevance of posture to neurological physiology and development
- movement analysis and its relationship to attachment
- the use of imagery and metaphor, which relates the unconscious process to the creative process in DMT.

In this population, there are psychological and physical symptoms and DMT seeks to address them both. It is necessary when working with this population to understand the relationship between the body and the mind. DMT needs a safe environment in which to explore psychological issues at the same time as paying attention to physical skills and body function. It is necessary to work with the family and carers as the patient is part of a family system where the illness often becomes a metaphor of dysfunction within the family. This assumes that the self is one that exists within a context of relationship, and that DMT provides an appropriate resolution.

During the DMT process there is integration between feeling states and the kinaesthetic experience. The verbal processing enables the patient to understand the bodily reactions to the emotions, and the way that feelings are expressed through image in language or in movement. The Parkinson's tremor becomes more prominent when people become anxious, and freezing occurs when they become frightened. Both of these reactions are a normal reaction to fear and anxiety but in PD the symptoms are more obvious and severe.

Features of Parkinson's disease

The psychological symptoms of PD are caused by deficiencies of neuro-transmitters in the brain. Some Parkinson's patients do not respond well to drug treatment and some of their psychological symptoms, such as depression and withdrawal, seem to influence the effectiveness of drugs. The blunting of drive, perception and a lack of response to the outside world is caused by a psychological state, rather than by ineffective medication therapy. The patient feels the lack of response and disorganisation in the mind. The therapist experiences the patient as a person without a sense of human presence. This is not a transferred feeling or reaction to the patient's feelings but an interpersonal feeling of the 'living dead' or an empty shell. There is a growing apathy (abulia), slowness of thought, blunting of drive and response to the outside world and an impairment of short-term memory. The curious mix of psychological and motor features has to be taken into account in any clinical DMT work, as motor symptoms can indicate psychological disturbance and psychological symptoms can affect motor performance. It is important not to differentiate, but to appreciate that the illness is not easily understood and that the relationship between the brain, body and consciousness is clearly connected. Todes (1990: 51), a psychoanalyst who has PD states:

> There is no mysterious leap or mind–body gap between the physiological-chemical psychological description and the underlying process. The gap or leap exists only between the subjective experience and the underlying process.

There are disturbances in motor function, marked by tremor, bradykinesia (slowness of movement), rigidity and impairment of posture. The most common symptom is a progressive slowing of everyday movement and a decrease in spontaneous movement. At the beginning of movement akinesis (loss of movement) takes place and the patient 'freezes'. Falls are common and balance is impaired, although gait disturbance and falling are not prominent early symptoms of idiopathic PD. (Charcot 1880), a mentor of Freud, concluded that the rigidity and the akinesia were the outcome of an inner struggle. This inner tension is followed by extreme tiredness. The akinesia causes exhaustion and results from a sense of agitation and alarm (Parkinson 1817). Parkinson also noticed that patients had little power to move even though motivated. There is a dullness of facial expression, lack of energy and an overall feeling of tiredness together with a lack of expression of emotion, focus and attention (Sacks 1991). This can be seen in a type of 'up-and-down' behaviour, a swing from an aroused and excited state to one of profound exhaustion and an almost catatonic state. If patients become involved in a movement, the motor symptoms disappear for a short time, or the disabilities can lessen. These concepts were emphasised by Charcot (1880) who compared the 'phases' of PD to those of neurosis. He named the phases as the (a) compliant-preservative, (b) obstructive-restive, (c) explosive-precipitate, and compared them with the (a) plastic, (b) rigid and (c) frenzied forms of catatonia and hysteria. There are several reports of abnormal personality features such as apathy and depression which antecede the onset of PD as described by Todes (1990). Since there is no evidence of a premorbid personality, there is no personality type that develops the illness. There does appear to be a genetic disposition towards the illness, a presence of early attachment difficulties and a reaction to loss, separation and bereavement (Todes 1990).

Dance movement therapy practice

I want to express the feelings I have experienced and incorporated into my current practice. The following words are illustrative of my experience of my sessions with an elderly patient who has had PD for ten years and who attended one of the research groups. After a five-year gap, she has returned for one-hour weekly group DMT, after an eye operation which emotionally upset her.

It was spring and H arrived. I remembered her from a few years back and recalled the small dainty figure and the pert hat with the feather and the sharp, slightly angry expression. I looked at her and saw the distant look of eyes that seemed to have no pupils. They looked beyond me as if they understood some distant landscape where I did not belong. As I looked at her, I thought how she had changed in the five-year gap, where I had lost sight of her.

The initial group had come to an end because of a lack of funding. We had to separate. She had sent me a card from South East Asia. I kept it. It was as if it was a way of me keeping her in mind. She was 80 years old when she first came to my groups with mild PD. She was active and played golf and was honest and broad minded in many aspects. Through those six years she suffered many setbacks and family traumas and yet she remained courageous and retained her sense of humour. She was physically fit and active considering that she was elderly and had PD. I had received some funding and had been able to start another PD DMT group with the possibility of doing further research. She arrived a few weeks later. I was pleased to see her as I had thought of her often. I wondered how she had coped with the separation when the previous group ended, although I had taken time to discuss the previous group drawing to a close.

Her hair was thin and she had a neglected appearance. She seemed lifeless and followed her husband as if she had no separate entity. He whispered to me that she needed psychological help. She turned to me and said, 'This did me more good than anything.' I felt the stirrings of loss and wondered what had happened to her. These were words that I wrote in my notes later about the feelings that I experienced as I moved with her. It felt as if she was like a baby searching through movement. She needed attention and focus through connection and relationship:

Loss
Displacement
The distant horizon
I fix my attention
And stare
Into your eyes
I search and meet your gaze
Motionless
We begin to move
You lift your arms to meet the sky
Life stirs and the stars begin to weep

My reflections continued:

She moved her fingers and her bony hands shaped the space with grace and precision. She began to stir with the movement. She took up the weights and lifted them vigorously. The power came to lift her arms and push as if to move some effort of birth. She showed continuing strength and repeated the movement. She appeared to be unaware of the rest of the group but I felt that she was beginning to be more responsive. She seemed less traumatised and able to respond to the rest of the group. H told me that she has had an eye operation and that she was having problems with her sight. She often sounded like a child who needed comfort and her voice was subdued and quivery.

Every week she began to say more and she told the group about not being able to see. She seemed to spend time alone in the session as if she was emerging from some shock. One week, she told the group that the operation had taken her sight. However, at times, it is as if she can see and she follows me as she mirrors the movement. As time goes on, I realise that her sight fluctuates and that sometimes she tracks the light. I am led to believe by her husband that her lack of vision is in her imagination and that she is having delusions and suffering from confusion. I reflect on her behaviour and conclude that the problem is due to the fact that she is experiencing double vision, which is a common symptom of PD. The cataract operation has interfered with the muscles in her eyes. I introduced some tracking exercises so that she could watch her fingers as she moved them. In my notes I wrote:

> She arrived the next week and her eyes were focusing. She had been practising the tracking exercises. She looked up at me and asked if I thought that I would rear her. I felt that I was connecting to her and that she was beginning to look at me and use facial expressions. There seemed to be a dialogue and relationship growing. I answered that I could sense her progress and that she was growing in confidence. She smiled in return. I felt the old H returning.

I further recalled in my notes:

> I write as I experience her. I sense that she is transferring her feelings to me. I am moved to write as if I can experience her loneliness.
> I am
> Pay attention to me
> I still exist
> My loneliness
> Is real
> I hold you in my gaze
> I hold you
> It is as if she fixes me as is she gains control. She can have a fixed point as a secure base. She talked of her son, of birthdays and anniversaries, of friends and said she was grateful that she could still read.

She brought in her golf clubs and other members brought in balls and a putting set. The group gained benefit from the swing and rhythm of using the golf equipment and when it was her turn to aim at the ball, I realised that she had double vision when the ball was a certain distance from her. The rest of the group played at moving the ball and she stopped at a certain distance and saw only one ball. She would repeat the slow steady strokes as she putted the ball. She began to develop an easy rhythmic swing with impulse and a concentrated and controlled stroke. The sound of the movement had the timing of a well-oiled and regular clock.

I wrote: 'It was important as a therapist to hold the person in mind. In the movement, I experienced her and I could hold her in my mind and body. I became the container for her and allowed her a mental space. The movement allowed H to experience the moment of the here and now and I had provided the mental space as a container.'

Emanuel speaks of object relations in the therapeutic encounter:

> One is challenged to experience terror without fear and without attachment. Perhaps a more accessible way of understanding this is to be able to take an interest . . . and trying to interest the patient in the minutiae of the moment to moment experience in the room requires that the anxiety involved is understood and contained by the object. It attempts to cultivate in the observer a non-reactive attitude to what is present.
>
> (Emanuel 2003: 22, 23)

He implies that this is only possible when the patient has experienced a sense of containment and self-identification with the therapist. This process takes time and will only be facilitated when the influence of the superego is reduced. By working through the transference, the patient can identify with the non-judgemental attitude of the therapist to mental thoughts.

I decided to bring in a large blue ball for the group, as the strong weight used in throwing the ball gives weight and purpose, expressed in strong and direct movement. I thought that it would add a different dynamic to the session. The group seemed to be flat and depressed and not expressing unresolved anger about their lives and the effects of the disease. The group liked the ball because it was big and they expressed how they had found they could throw it forcefully. One member, G, threw it with a force towards me and to each member of the group in turn. He described the frustration he felt about the treatment of his wife and of her suffering and death from cancer, a few years before. He felt that hope had been taken from her. Another member of the group told the group that his first wife had died also and that he had found it difficult to adjust. I felt the pain of the group. There was silence. It felt important to listen to their stories and hold the silence:

> Any loss which fundamentally disrupts the central purposes of our lives will normally provoke long and everlasting grief. To integrate those purposes, so that they can once again inform life, the bereaved have at once to retrieve and consolidate the meaning of what they have lost, detach that meaning from their retrievable past.
>
> (Parkes *et al.* 1991: 81)

I think that this statement could apply to my work with the PD group. The group has gone on to try more effective ways of treatment and the members have found more confidence to engage with life. I feel that we have worked through some of their loss, anger and frustration. H has joined in with the group. She listens intently and speaks if she is spoken to but remains shy. Her balance and physical ability are good and the group do not patronise her. She is slowly becoming part of a group again and is beginning to be sociable.

Methodology

Patients who had experienced DMT had expressed how valuable it had been for them. I had noticed that during group sessions movement qualities changed and abilities altered and psychological states affected motor performance. Permission from the patients and carers to use interviews, questionnaires and case vignettes was gained. Qualitative methods were selected that made the researcher central to the sense made from the interpretations and observations from the patients. I was therapist and researcher and made conclusions from the patients' views and my own observations. The problems in the collection of data were that there was an emphasis on meaning and not on accurate measurement of physical progress. This could have resulted in wishful thinking on my part, or making false claims. However, there was support from the neurologist in that she had seen patients maintaining a sense of well-being as well as remaining active, or at least not withdrawing from their family and friends. Since then, having worked with these patients for several years, they have maintained this sense of affirmation, controlled their depression and worked on maintaining the movement function. They have also connected their emotional states to this movement function and can observe when the physical symptoms are due to medication or due to the progressive deterioration. The aims for the groups were:

- to observe and note the interaction and communication between group members
- to extend the movement range of group members
- to use the metaphors from the movement process to reach unconscious feelings and understand their significance
- to increase body awareness so that psychosomatic reactions can be understood as reactions to feeling states and brain activity.

Movements were analysed by a trained movement observer and me and used to assist in the feeling of security and well-being in the patient and carer. The analysis provided an understanding of the movement. The movement quality was used by the therapist in the sessions: for example, when the quality of the movements was strong and quick or slow and sustained. This provided an insight into the patients' emotional state as there was a reduced sense of weight and time which corresponded to a disassociation from the body and loss of a sense of time. The engagement with strong weight would enable the patients to express their anger and frustration and the use of quick time would engage the use of impulse and improve movement phrasing. The PD movement quality is reduced and small in the use of space and can be identified as slow in the use of time. The fine and light touch feels like an absence of weight and this is often accompanied by a shuffling gait and lack of balance. The awareness of weight in the body stabilises the body and gives the patient more self-control and a conscious ability to gain a sense of balance. The engagement with strong weight in the movement process is accompanied by, in the verbal process, an emotional engagement and release. The body loses tension and the person is able to control the movement. The use of impulse and impact become part of the movement dynamics again, where the illness had reduced them. The movement phrasing improves so that precision and intention improve.

The consultant neurologist referred the patients. Patients with dementia were not selected, neither were those using a wheelchair, owing to transport problems. Three groups were formed:

- couples (carers and patients who were late onset patients)
- late onset patients only
- young onset patients only.

They attended on a weekly basis except for the holidays which lasted for two weeks in the winter and spring, and for four weeks in the summer. The sessions, of an hour's duration, took place over one year. There were six patients in each of the 'singles' group and eight in the 'patients and carers' group. These numbers of participants in each group were chosen as they seemed, from my past experience in running the groups, to be the most effective in ensuring attendance, safety and the provision of a sense of containment. This observation was made from my practice experience and not from any research evidence.

Data collection tools

Patients and carers were given a questionnaire, inquiring about their thoughts and feelings towards DMT and any perceived benefits. Patient and carers were interviewed and these were audiotaped. I transcribed the case vignettes from the tapes. I interviewed the patients in their homes and the hospital. Case study vignettes from five patients and one carer were documented from my observations and their comments. I did not feel any role conflict as together the participants I had discussed the use of the research for the benefit of the groups. They had all agreed to participate by completing a consent form prior to their participation and had the freedom to withdraw at any time. The members of the group felt it was important to co-operate with the questionnaires and interviews because it gave them a voice to express their personal views. They felt that their opinions counted and that answering the questionnaires might provide more information about the disease. They think there is a lack of knowledge about the disease and feel dismissed, or that there is not enough done to alleviate their suffering.

Carers in particular appear frustrated at the lack of knowledge about the disease and consequently feel a lack of support for the responsibility of caring. They often express sadness and anger at the loss of the person they married because they are no longer able to relate to them as adults. Clearly, there is a great need for work with groups of carers as well as patients. There is also a need for 'couples' groups, which may provide a place for the discussion of marital and family issues.

The dance movement therapy groups

In the early stages attendance fluctuated and the therapist's regular attendance became the constant container for the groups' lack of commitment. It took a long time for trust to develop and patients did not open up to each other easily at first. After eight sessions the groups began to enjoy being together and sharing their problems. This occurred at the same time as the therapist grew in confidence in her ability to elicit feelings and encourage their will to persist. As they were open groups, new patients referred by the neurologist would join but only stay for a few weeks and then leave. The problem of absence and a lack of ability to commit to a group, possibly through fear of and a denial of the illness, is still a feature of these DMT groups today. During the life of the groups, members were conscious of their trembling or lack of skills and were embarrassed at moving in front of others. Many patients had become isolated and the thought of joining a group caused symptoms to be exacerbated. Therefore it was decided that separate groups for young onset and the elderly would be formed.

The therapist insisted on confidentiality in all the groups. This developed a feeling of trust and outsiders such as occupational therapists and physiotherapists, who were there as assistants, were more easily accepted as a result. Information could be shared and an increase in awareness seemed to develop trust and ability to cope. Fears were dealt with and questions answered. The group members began to voice how valuable the positive regard was to them. Colour and different sensory stimulation was introduced by the use of props. A positive attitude to learning difficulties was emphasised. Many patients felt devalued and experienced a loss of self-worth at home.

The therapist joined in the movement process and initiated imaginative ways of using the movement, including images and movements arising from the patients' verbalisation: for example, saying 'I feel like a shrinking violet' or 'I feel that I have been possessed by this illness. My body does not feel like mine.' The patients' kinespheres were extended by the use of large movements with the arms, as group members reached out and stretched. The use of weight in punching and pressing encouraged the expression of frustration and strong feeling. An increased sensitivity with light weight suggested that they could express themselves and respond to fine touch. The patients were beginning to feel less restricted by their chairs. The group moved to a larger room and was given permission (through adequate insurance) to come out of the chairs and move freely. It had relieved the therapist as one patient had expressed discomfort at sitting down and drew attention to himself in the group by standing up. This caused anxiety, which the patient had used to manipulate the group. The therapist had contained their anxiety by allowing him to stand and stretch, after which he would join in with the rest of the group.

The sessions began with a warm-up which included movements from the patients' own repertoires, dependent on their bodies and their structural and anatomical states at the time. This was done slowly to prevent freezing and falling. The therapist initiated the movement so that they would extend their movements, mirroring her stretching and reaching. They gained confidence and ability in their movement as they realised that they could also extend and increase their movement range. Sessions were recorded on videotape in order to observe the movement. Subsequently this enabled the therapist to pay attention to the movement so that she was not relying on a need to believe that there had been a change or improvement in movement ability. A separate trained movement observer was consulted and assisted in analysing the movement and the emotional significance of the phrasing and effort qualities.

After a few months, patients and carers took turns to lead in the movement process. The warm-up was based on the anatomical structure of the muscles and joints, using the effort qualities of direct space, sustained time and strong weight. These elements introduced the movement qualities that were reduced by the illness. It was observed by the movement observer and therapist that these elements provided a structure for action and introduced drive and inner purpose. The initiation (the preparation and beginning of the movement) improved as each patient took turns. There was also time for free movement which was incorporated into the group process.

Feelings of competition were utilised by the therapist to encourage a sense of will and determination. Feelings of anger began to be expressed as the movements grew stronger and more defined. The group began to move and work together. Patients and carers began to express themselves verbally, which built up their confidence, no matter how quiet they had previously been.

The use of rhythm enabled the patients to use primitive ways of communication (Chaiklin 1975), which broke through the dysfunction and body 'armour' (Reich 1949) of the PD. These rhythms echoed the rocking of the child or the sensual rotating motion of an evocative dance. The Kestenburg (1975) developmental rhythms were used to assess where the patient or carer had a need to integrate emotional traumas, or past failed relationships. They assisted in reworking past movement stages, which had not yet been internalised. This was done by reflecting the movement or introducing an appropriate rhythm that related to a stage of development. This could be rocking, swaying or clapping to develop more energised movement.

It was important to set time boundaries and to keep to the same room. Time seemed to be a particular issue. The disease had given patient and carer a feeling of not belonging to life in the fast lane. They seemed to have no sense of time. The DMT group gave a constancy of time and space and this gave them a sense of security. One patient declared, as she stood to move, that 'standing on her feet' gave her independence. Many patients had lost touch with their feelings and their bodies. It was important for this population to work in a person-centred way (Rogers 1961). The patients and carers who had suffered emotional abuse or psychological rejection benefited from the core condition of unconditional positive regard. Standal (1954) defined 'positive regard' as the need to feel good about ourselves, which comes from significant others in early childhood. Positive regard from others develops self-regard. Patients require, at some level, to feel good about themselves despite having a debilitating illness. If this requirement is not met, the patient, who is surrounded by criticism and disapproval, or by confusing and ambiguous messages from the carer, becomes confused and depressed. The carer who is over-self-critical becomes overburdened. Both patient and carer will be anxious and as a result each demands or manipulates attention or affection from the other. It may be that the positive regard which the patients and carers experience in DMT is the first time they feel valued. They become less self-punishing and lose the guilty sense that the illness was a 'punishment' for their 'sins' of the past. Once group members let go of these ideas, they relax and their movements become less inhibited. Patients often say that they lack motivation because the future is bleak and hopeless. When they become more active and can maintain functional abilities, group attendance improves and members become physically active outside the group. This is often followed by an increase in physical and mental control which enables them to take up hobbies and maintain an active lifestyle.

Findings

The questionnaires indicated that patients and carers thought the benefits were:

- an increase in body awareness
- an improvement in self-confidence and communication
- a lifting of depression

- an improvement in specific motor abilities and balance, use of limbs and walking, the ability to do handwork and driving.

It was observed by the therapist that the opportunity to use the patients' movements in free creative movement influenced their motor abilities. The verbal process provided a safe container and a means of understanding the problems in coping with a progressive illness, through a mastery of movement and a sense of control. The exchange of ideas and the expression of emotions, such as the frustrations encountered with freezing and the everyday problems of coping with daily living, assisted with an overall sense of control.

These outcomes expressed as 'need' were recorded as part of the therapist's notes at the end of each session as well as from the interviews with patients. The needs that were most commonly expressed included (in my words):

- the need for support for patients, particularly from their family members
- the need for communication and socialisation, which enabled them to have more satisfying relationships
- the need to alleviate depression and withdrawal
- the need for strong boundaries so that past traumas can be reworked in an atmosphere of safety and security
- the need for reworking of defence mechanisms so that inappropriate defences could be removed and more appropriate ways of coping established
- the need for a safe place where experiences about the disease could be shared, where feelings of embarrassment, self-consciousness, loss and bereavement could be explored.

The perceptions of patients and carers also focused on the benefits of DMT. Analysis of findings from the questionnaires showed that they thought they had benefited from DMT group work which can be reframed as follows:

- an increased bodily awareness, which can assist in creating confidence in the mastery and development of movement range
- psychological balance and stability and the removal of inappropriate defences which can be seen to remove the psychological hindrances to functioning
- the ability to understand non-verbal communication which can be used to improve the social inter-reaction
- the alleviation of emotional stress which could assist in developing ways of coping with the disease.

Two patients had not shown any significant change where there were difficult family dynamics. In one case the patient was suffering from Lewy body dementia, in the other case the disease was too developed and the physical symptoms too severe. The questionnaire was designed and conducted by the therapist, with the co-operation and supervision of the neurologist, and it was given to the members of the group to complete individually.

Case vignettes

These two case vignettes include material from the unstructured interviews with patients.

K was 56 years old and had been diagnosed with PD for three years, although she felt she had the symptoms three years prior to the diagnosis. When she first came to the young onset group she was remote, did not mix readily and had lost a sense of time. She always arrived late. She moved, tottering on her toes, and could not run or jump. She had a tremor on the right side of her body, would sit on her hands and deny any symptoms of PD. She used to be a music teacher and had played the guitar well. She spoke of the loss of this ability and sadness at having to give up her job.

In the DMT sessions she could move in phrases and expressed a wish to take part in folk dancing. She was keen on rhythmic music and brought a sense of purpose and order to the group. She began to ride a bike again and seemed to be coping well and not suffering from depression. She had lost a baby at birth and brought to the group issues of grief and bereavement. As she started to support others in the group and gained in confidence, she started to give talks to groups in the town and to play the keyboard. She was less often late and attended regularly, taking the role of the 'wise woman' in the group and an active part in the local PD support group. Since participating in the DMT sessions over two years, she can now run, has taken up riding her bike again, still drives and can jump.

N belonged to the late onset group for nine months. At first he seemed quiet and shy but was prepared to participate. His communication seemed to have been affected so that he would talk at the same time as others and seemed to lack an awareness of 'give and take'. He had symptoms of PD for 20 years but it had remained undiagnosed until two years ago. He also had angina. He walked and participated well but was hindered by a short-term memory. He disclosed to the group that he had lost a son many years ago and also a second son who died in a car crash. He said that he could not remember anything after this crash and that his mind felt blank. He described how there are no entries in his own diary during this time. He had worked as a butcher in his own shop, and was still quick thinking and could understand complex ideas. He had a wide range of movements and introduced complex and well co-ordinated movements when he took leadership of the group in the movement process. He enjoyed coming to the group, became its comedian and was positive in his attitude. He said in his interview that when he got to Sunday he thought 'Good, it is nearly Tuesday, the day of the dance therapy group'. This patient left the group due to angina and died some time later.

Discussion and recommendations for future research

Patients' opinion empowers patients and carers. However, the therapists' observations and interpretations are also a valuable insight into the therapy process (Bunce 1996). It is important to place this qualitative assessment alongside the measurement tools to give some specific information on the relationship between movement performance and emotional response. As a piece of research this study has been descriptive. There needs to be more long-term research work to assess the effects of DMT on PD patients.

PD is a field where a considerable amount of help, care and support is needed. This research could indicate a way of working with other clients. For example, the finding that there is a relationship between feeling states, emotion, cognition, movement and body response could be generalised to the ways we conduct DMT with other populations. It is working with the integration of these states that makes DMT an effective intervention in mental and physical health. In the safe environment that DMT provides, PD patients and carers can relieve feelings and re-establish positive ways of interacting. The DMT groups, according to both PD patients and their carers, enabled both patients and carers to extend movement patterns and strategies and to re-live past experiences and traumas. In re-living past memories, they could relate their past experiences to their body experience, which in turn connects to their attitude towards others. The relationship of the body and mind and the neurological significance of this relationship is vital to an understanding of the use of movement (Palley 2003) in therapy. It is the unique integration of the body and mind in DMT that becomes the instrument of healing.

DMT has much to offer as a therapy alongside other therapies for PD patients and their carers. It is the hope that this research will extend the application of the DMT field and the development of movement observation for PD patients and their carers. It might open the field for future research, such as an in-depth single case study over five years, using video material of sessions taken over regular intervals of three months, alongside the use of a patient and carer diary to see if there were lifestyle changes or how the movement sessions related to emotional states.

An experimental approach could be used, such as the use of a control group as well as the DMT group. For example, movement performance could be measured (walking for a set time, measuring the time taken for a set task or measuring through a postural assessment Kestenberg's tension flow assessment or Lamb's posture and gesture analysis). A base line measurement to see if there had been any positive improvement or change from DMT experience over several years might be provided. Psychological changes relating to postural change, and the changes in shape flow could be measured using the Kestenberg Movement Profile (Davis 1992). Videotape could be used to assess small changes in posture. The measurements would ensure objectivity and accuracy of assessment for those factors that can be measured.

References

Bunce, J.M (1996) Dance movement therapy with groups of Parkinson's disease patients and their carers, unpublished MA dissertation, Laban Centre, London.

Chaiklin, H. (ed.) (1975) *Marion Chace: Her Papers*, Columbia, MD: American Dance Therapy Association.

Charcot, J.M. (1880) *De La Paralysie Agitans: Leçons sur les Maladies du Systems Nerveux.* [Descriptions of Parkinson's Disease]. Paris: Adrian Delahaye, pp. 439–467.

Davis, M. (1992) A description of the Kestenberg movement profile, in S. Loman, with R. Brandt (eds) *The Body Mind Connection in Human Movement Analysis.* Antioch: New England Graduate School.

Emanuel, R. (2003) A-void. An exploration of defences against sensing nothingness, *Journal of the Caspari Foundation* 12, 22–23.

Kestenberg, J. (1975) *Children and Parents: Psychoanalytic Studies in Development.* New York: Jason Aronson.

Laban, R. and Lawrence, F.C. (1974) *Effort*, 2nd edn. London: MacDonald and Evans.

Lamb, W. (1965) *Posture and Gesture*. London: Duckworth.

Libet, B., Gleason, C.A., Pearl, D.K. and Wright, E.W. (1983) Time of conscious intention to act in relation to onset of cerebral activity (readiness potential): the unconscious initiation of a freely voluntary act, *Brain* 106, 623–642.

Palley, R. (2003) *The Mind–Brain Relationship*. London: Karnac.

Parkes, C.M., Stevenson-Hinde, J. and Marris, P. (eds) (1991) *Attachment Across the Life Cycle*. London: Routledge.

Parkinson, J. (ed.) (1817) *An Essay on the Shaking Palsy.* London: Macmillan.

Reich, W. (1949) *Character Analysis*. New York: Farrer, Straus and Giroux.

Rogers, C. R. (1961) *On Becoming a Person*. Boston: Houghton Mifflin.

Sacks, O. (1991) *Awakenings*. London: Pan.

Sossin, K.M. (1987) Reliability of the Kestenberg movement profile, *Movement Studies* 2, 23–28.

Standal, S. (1954) The need for positive regard: a contribution to client-centered theory, unpublished partial PhD, University of Chicago.

Todes, C. (1990) *Shadow Over My Brain: A Battle Against Parkinson's Disease.* London: Class Publishing.

Chapter 6

Stretching, tensing, kicking

Aspects of infantile movement in dance movement therapy with children and adolescents in special education

Sara Bannerman-Haig

Introduction

This chapter is devoted to thinking about dance movement therapy (DMT) with children and adolescents, particularly those who have learning and/or emotional difficulties. The intention is to explore selected elements of spontaneous unconscious dance, movement and play that emerges in DMT sessions with these client groups in special school settings. However, my DMT practice during this research was significantly informed and influenced by the findings from my experience of observing a baby for two years once a week, within a psychoanalytic framework. In this chapter, therefore, I present reflections on and developments in my own understanding of my practice drawing on both the DMT and psychoanalytical traditions.

Central to this will be the consideration of the ways in which aspects of infantile movement can be identified and analysed in the DMT relationship from a psychoanalytical perspective with the clients. The term 'analyse' in this context will mean to reflect upon and to consider possible meanings underlying the movement, dance or dance play. Certain questions will be considered such as:

- Has the client retained an early infantile mode of movement?
- What could these infantile modes of body communication mean or represent when considered from a psychoanalytical perspective?
- What is the nature of the communication, for example, is it a communication about the baby part of the self?
- What is the client's possible state of mind as exhibited through movement or dance?

These questions will be considered through the weaving of strands of my DMT practice with psychoanalytical principles, drawn from the infant–mother observation, and my own DMT work with learning disabled clients.

I have selected two aspects from the research that relate to the infant's body and movement which featured in my psychoanalytic observations: these are agitated body states and muscular tensing. In this context the term agitated body states refer to extreme restlessness and muscular tensing, to moments when the infant tenses and strains all its muscles. Links will be made to the psychoanalytical concepts of containment, 'reverie' (Bion 1962) and the notion of a 'second skin' (Bick 1968).

Evidence will be presented in the form of vignettes drawn from work with two clients. A detailed discussion follows, including relevant child development, psychoanalytical, and DMT theory. Reflections on my practice arise throughout the chapter, interspersed, perhaps inevitably, by moments of doubt and confusion which arose during the process of applying the strategies of the two different disciplines.

My approach to dance movement therapy

My approach to DMT is firmly rooted in the belief that it is primarily concerned with personal growth through body–mind interaction, integration and expression. It is based upon a fundamental notion that changes in the body can effect changes in the psyche, and vice versa. As the dance movement therapy pioneer from the United States, Mary Whitehouse stated:

> Our movement is our behaviour, there is direct connection between what we are like and how we move. Distortion, tension and deadness in our movement is distortion, tension and deadness in ourselves.
>
> (Whitehouse 1969: 274)

This statement reflects the interdependence of the processes of the body and the psyche. The dance movement therapist uses movement and dance as the primary tools for communication, and it is the medium through which the therapeutic relationship develops. It is through the body that the therapist facilitates the conscious and unconscious processes that enable the recognition and expression of feelings and emotions (Bannerman-Haig 2001). DMT aims to further the emotional and physical integration of the individual (Payne 1992).

Whilst we are all 'observers' of life and of movement at some level, dance movement therapists work within a structure and framework in which their observations can be located. There are two systems which will be referred to periodically in this chapter: those of Laban Movement Analysis (Laban 1960) and Kestenberg Movement Profiling (Kestenberg 1975). Laban Movement Analysis provides a structure in which we can think about what the body is doing; how a movement is being done: for example, the quality or dynamic of the movement; where the person is in space, how they might use the space around them and how they might relate to others and the world around them.

Kestenberg attempts to relate movement to personality through developmental psychology. 'Kestenberg was interested in non-verbal communication and she created a system of not only describing and assessing movement, but also a means of interpreting it' (Loman 1992: 2). This is a well-developed, complex system. However, here only one aspect is referred to, that of tension flow rhythms. Kestenberg defined this as 'a change in the tension of a muscle, for example while one child crunches on a piece of candy, another one might languidly lick it, and each creates distinct patterns of muscle change' (Kestenberg *et al.* 1999: 23). Interesting parallels could be drawn between this system and psychoanalytical infant observation. In both systems the observer is concerned with possibly minute, subtle changes in the body and the corresponding psychological and emotional state which accompanies the physical change.

For the DMT practitioner movement observation can play a vital role. It is an integral part of my approach in my work with children and adolescents and makes a significant contribution to the initial and ongoing assessment of a client. It contributes to building a movement profile which subsequently informs the setting of appropriate movement and psychological goals. It is also an invaluable tool for monitoring change and development in the therapy process. North (1972) focused on personality assessment through movement and stressed how 'a human being reveals through the accumulation and variety of his movement, his own personality' (North 1972: 8). Others have noted that 'movement has the potential to reveal a host of non verbalised feeling states' (Kestenberg *et al.* 1999: 1). These comments reflect the significance of our body language and non-verbal communication. It can be useful to remember that movement is at the core of our development, and that changes in a person's movement might inevitably reflect a corresponding psychological change which can signal a change to a different state of mind. This was something that became most apparent in my infant observations, as well as more generally in my DMT practice.

My approach when working with children and adolescents varies, depending on my assessment of the needs of the client. In the case studies referred to later, the approach has been primarily non-directive, although some aspects such as the warm-up might be more directed. This is in order to prepare the body physically as well as psychologically for the session. When the approach is more directive, I might try to incorporate and suggest movements that are absent from the client's movement repertoire. This can be a subtle but effective way of increasing a client's repertoire of movement. More importantly, it can offer the opportunity for the client to experience a different feeling state in the body which is associated with moving in a different way. This can then provide the catalyst for a shift in the psychic state.

Other dance movement therapists who have contributed to research in the child and adolescent field are Payne (1987, 1992), Melville-Thomas (1987) and Meekums (1988, 1991). Movement with children tends to be natural, less organised and less stylised. The dance movement therapist has a wide range of tools for eliciting client movement material. Amongst the tools available are aspects of formalised dance as well as improvisation, games, play, developmental movement and the use of a variety of props. 'Like in dreams the material in movement improvisation may be raw, disguised, or seemingly unrelated' (Chodorow 1991). When a child begins to improvise in dance it can indicate development in the therapeutic relationship and also provide an insight into unconscious and conscious material that is emerging, even if not yet processed.

In DMT, emotions and feelings need to be expressed, acknowledged, understood and processed. In my practice, a central concern is to hold the client's mental state in order to help contain, then recognise the meaning inherent in the communication or expression, and finally work towards processing it. Hopefully this facilitates a shift to another state of mind, thus enabling growth.

Methodology

The research focus was on an idiographic, interpretative, qualitative approach. As Robson points out:

> It is only qualitative methodology that explicitly values the personal experience of the researcher and acknowledges and uses subjectivity as an inherent component of the research process.
>
> (Robson 1993: 5)

Qualitative research enables an examination of the process of the research as well as the development of the client. Through the use of a case study involving the infant observation and subsequently individual DMT clients, I have adopted an exploratory model, attempting to evaluate and understand the significance of the client material, as well as some of the processes and changes that have taken place in my practice. Within the case study I have employed participant observation, simple observation, 'a system of passive unobtrusive observation' (Robson 1993: 159), and movement observation as evaluative tools. Participant observation enables the researcher to access a real-life situation. The primary data are the interpretations by the observer of what is going on around and within them, Robson (1993). This is followed by the interpretations which should also allow one to monitor one's own experiences and thought processes (Woods 1986). Movement observation informed by Laban (1966) and Kestenberg et al. (1999) offered an evaluative framework. Issues such as what the body is doing, how a movement is being done, the quality or dynamic of the movement, where the person is in space, how they might use the space around them, and how they might relate to others and the world around them were all considered.

In thinking about my practice, I was aided by: (a) in-depth process notes based on the psychoanalytic infant observation model; (b) regular individual supervision with both a dance movement therapist and a child psycho-therapist; (c) group seminars with professional colleagues led by a child psychotherapist; (d) formal and informal meetings with other professionals. These structures framed my personal reflective processes and enabled me to consider new developments in my practice.

The longitudinal aspect (four years) of the research also assisted the reconsideration of my practice. The weekly sessions for both the infant observation and the DMT clients extended over two years and this allowed the development of a safe catalytic space in which both parties felt secure, enabling new approaches in my practice.

Agitated body movement and intense muscular tensing

Containment and reverie: a second skin

Out of the material that emerged over the two years, I would like to focus on two body states that are primarily located in early development and which could be linked to infantile states. One is agitated body movement, which occurs when an infant becomes very restless in its body. The other is severe body tension or rigidity, when an infant tenses and holds their body in a very strained and tense way. I will illustrate how infant observation in the psycho-analytic tradition has contributed to informing and expanding an analysis of what might be taking place and relate this to DMT practice. This will be followed by a discussion considering possible interpretations or meanings drawing upon a psychoanalytical framework. The first part of the discussion will focus on agitation in the body and what this could represent. The second will be more concerned with muscular holding and tensing and the idea that the body in this state can be used as a defence. Below are two examples from infant observation and an example from my DMT practice. I would like to remind the reader that the format of this section will consist of the presenta-tion of the infant observations and extracts of DMT practice, followed by discussion.

Carol

In the first observation the infant was 10.5 weeks, in the second, she was 6 months. Throughout this piece of work, in order to provide confidentiality, pseudonyms will be used for the infant and for the DMT clients. The infant will be referred to as Carol.

10.5 weeks
Carol began to cry for the second time. Mum picked her up and held her while she walked around the room. Mum was holding Carol so she was

facing outwards, but she continued to cry. I had a sense that Mum was trying really hard to understand and soothe her. Mum then looked at me and said, 'I'm going to try putting her in her pram as she might be tired.' Mum carried Carol to her pram and gently placed her in her pram in a half-sitting position. She immediately stopped crying and looked at Mum. Mum looked at her and said, 'That's what you wanted isn't it?' There was a huge smile on Carol's face. Mum had finally understood what she wanted and Carol seemed so pleased and grateful that Mum had understood her communication

6 months

Mum had been gone for 10–15 minutes, talking on telephone. Mum's voice became louder as she returned to the kitchen. Carol's eyes opened very wide and she had a fixed stare upwards. Then her eyes began to close. Carol became restless, her upper body began to twist, she turned her head from side to side, her mouth was screwing up with a twitch beginning on the left side. Carol's knees moved, she pulled them towards her torso. Her eyes closed and I wondered if she was preparing to cry. Mum came in talking. Carol half-opened her eyes and Mum bent forwards taking her face very close to hers. Carol made direct eye contact with Mum, looking intently into Mum's face. Mum spoke a few words to her, 'Well, how are you?' and Carol smiled as she continued to look directly at Mum.

David

The next extract is from a DMT session with a learning disabled adolescent, referred to as David, who had been diagnosed as having severe learning disabilities and was 13 years old when this session took place.

David took the ball and began to pat it hard and fast – there was a manic feel to his actions. He then kicked it very fiercely. He ran after it and kicked it randomly into the big space in which we were working. I commented on how he seemed angry about something, and how he might be letting me know by his actions that he was angry with me for not being there last week (it was the school half-term break). I was struck by his response. He stood still, made direct eye contact with me and changed the quality of his movements completely. Very gently and softly he pushed the ball to me. He used his fingertips, a great contrast to the previous strong kicking action I had witnessed. He looked at me maintaining a sustained and focused eye contact. We managed to have a long game of ball with this more gentle and contained movement quality. David then began to reduce the physical space between us. Initially we had been spaced quite far apart. Gradually he came closer so the space between us diminished greatly. I was struck by his overall body symmetry, with his arms, torso and knees bending simultaneously to produce a whole, gross, co-ordinated body movement.

Discussion

Several things struck me from these observations: first of all, the increasingly restless movement in Carol's body until Mum appeared. In the observations of Carol it can be seen how she appeared to have heard Mum coming after an absence, and Mum seemed to understand and acknowledge Carol's communications. This could have given Carol a sense of being understood at an emotional level. Carol had been 'contained' (Bion 1962). Mum appeared to be emotionally available to her infant on both occasions and had the capacity to hold her baby's anxiety or fear of abandonment, through proximity, gaze and the tone of her voice. The observation also illustrated Mum's capacity to process what had been going on through her use of words. On a physical or body level this could illustrate how the emotional holding changes the physical agitation in the infant clearly reflected through a stiller, quieter and contented body, leading to a different state of mind. Here we witness Bion's (1962) idea of the 'container' and the 'contained'. As Waddell highlighted when referring to Klein's concepts of love and hate and integration and disintegration, that 'with the nipple in the mouth, surrounded by loving arms . . . s/he will have a sense of coherence, of having a centre' (Waddell 1998: 27). In this example it is possible to get a sense of this in Carol. It is not just the emotional holding from the mother but the physical holding that goes with it.

Perhaps a similar process was taking place for David. He was in a lively excitable state, perhaps a little manic. He too was exhibiting a restlessness through his body actions. He was having difficulty getting close to the therapist. His fragmented body actions could suggest his emotional state was one of being 'all over the place' or one of feeling 'unheld' or 'uncontained'. It seemed as if this feeling was being communicated in how the ball was being randomly and unthinkingly kicked into different parts of the room with great strength. Britton (1992) cites Bion (1962) in his reference to beta elements:

> If the elements of a potential experience are left unprocessed, if they remain beta elements – they can not be treated like ordinary thoughts, but neither can they be treated as ordinary perceptions of the material world . . . there are three spheres where these precursors of thought might go out of mind.
>
> (Britton 1992: 39)

The sphere which could be relevant to David is that of 'going into the body'. His emotional experience had not been processed and was therefore being diverted into the 'sphere' of the body. This could have been what I was witnessing in the initial ball play mentioned above.

However, there had just been a school break and it was possible that David was also angry with the therapist for not being available to him the week before. David had really struggled to manage the gap of the school holiday. Carol was able to manage when her mother left her for 15 minutes; she only became anxious upon hearing her mother's voice. Perhaps Carol had been able to internalise her mother well enough to manage being left, whereas David was still struggling with separations and was not able to keep the therapist in mind for the duration of the break. Interestingly, when these thoughts were verbalised to him, David's physical behaviour altered a lot. As the extract described, David's movement behaviour changed along with a corresponding change in his state of mind. The body became more symmetrical, he slowed down becoming more focused and centred. He was able to make eye contact with the therapist and relate more closely to her; they had each other's attention. There could be a connection between Carol and David's emotional responses to absence of a significant other in these observations. They were both reflecting some state of anxiety or restlessness which was evident from their bodily non-verbal communications: 'Any one state of mind in the present, however fleeting, is founded in the past, and at the same time it encompasses a possible future' (Waddell 1998: 5).

It seemed possible that David's initial communications could have been linked to an earlier infantile state of mind in which he felt uncontained and misunderstood. Had the break aroused early infantile feelings of being left or abandoned, leaving David with feelings that could have felt unmanageable on his own? In their different ways, David and Carol had an experience of being understood, by the therapist or the mother respectively. Both David and Carol managed to find a place in which they felt emotionally comfortable. They had attained a different state of mind, one in which their difficult feelings had been processed which then enabled them to feel emotionally 'held' or 'contained'. This was confirmed by the visible changes that were reflected through their bodies. Bion (1962) talks about this emotional state as 'reverie', the state after the emotions have been understood and processed:

Reverie is that state of mind which is open to the reception of any 'objects' from the loved object and is therefore capable of reception of the infant's projective identifications whether they are good or bad.

(Bion 1962: 36)

It is the mother's ability to hold her baby's distress without being overwhelmed and her ability to feed back an experience to the baby which can then aid in the process of integration. David and Carol had their mental state understood and held, which as Bion stipulates 'constitutes a containment of fragmented aspects of the psychic experience' (Bion 1962: 25–27).

In Laban Movement Analysis the use of space can be linked to 'attention'. If a child is unfocused, using space in a very indirect, haphazard way, it is thought there is little attention to the relationship; in fact there may be no relationship. Again this was illustrated in the early part of my observation of David. However, when there was a shift from this physical state to being able to use the space more directly, there was a more sustained gaze and direct eye contact, and more focused, controlled use of space, with David being able to pass a ball to another. There was a sense that a relationship with the therapist was developing to become closer; another aspect from David's observation which could connect to an infantile state. Waddell refers to 'the shift in states of mind from what psychoanalytical theory describes in terms of paranoid schizoid to depressive or of primarily narcissistic to object related' (Waddell 1998: 7). It is possible that David shifted from a narcissistic state to a state in which he was able to relate to the object, the therapist, therefore allowing the relationship to become object related. The evidence which could have supported this was David's use of more gross, symmetrical and whole body movements together with his sustained eye contact. These were quite different to the sharp, fragmented actions witnessed earlier in the ball play. He was able to engage in a game with another, with the therapist, and there was a sense of two people relating more closely together.

Through being understood, it appeared that David was able to become more contained, which then allowed him to have a sense of self that helped him relate in a positive way to another. In this instance the other was the dance movement therapist. David was helped to move from one state of mind to another, from a fragmented state to a contained state in which some integration could begin to take place.

Next I would like to consider the muscular tensing and rigidity that can be seen in the body. Consideration will be given to the links of Ester Bick's (1968) notion of 'a second skin'. This will be highlighted with another observation of Carol and an extract from my DMT practice with Susan, a 15-year-old girl who had been diagnosed as having severe developmental delay with some autistic tendencies. The first observation is of Carol when she was three months old.

Carol

3 months

Carol followed Mum's movements around the room with her eyes, as Mum moved from one place to another. Mother then turned her back on Carol in order to peel some potatoes. Carol's gaze went towards the window. Carol then began to get restless and began to half cry. Her half cry was interrupted by a yawn and she rubbed her eyes. She continued to half cry, her body became more restless, her head began to turn from side to side, her arms and legs became very tense and contracted as she pulled them towards her centre. The volume of Carol's cry began to increase and then the mother turned around and picked her up out of her seat. She held Carol up in front of her face and Carol's body relaxed at once, her cry stopped. The mother made direct eye contact with Carol and she began to smile.

Susan

The following extract is from a DMT session with Susan:

> As Susan arrived in the space today she seemed delicate and completely out of touch with her body. When I looked at her, her body tension was painful to witness. We stood opposite each other, there was no eye contact between us at this stage and Susan was grinding her teeth. Her torso was held and her shoulders felt clenched, being held high up towards her ears. It felt as if the acute body tension was being directed upwards. It was all in her upper body, especially shoulders, face and mouth. I commented on her tension and she nodded a 'yes'. I began by asking her to lift her shoulders and let them go with the intention of trying to reduce some of the held body tension. She was able to follow my suggestions and after four or five times I witnessed some of the tension beginning to release. She stopped grinding her teeth, her shoulders relaxed down and her arms became less stiff. I introduced some breathing exercises and encouraged her to make sounds with me. This was in order to help her get in touch with her torso area, which seemed so rigid. Susan began to make eye contact with me as we moved together. I then asked Susan to lift her arm, she followed me as I demonstrated lifting my arm and letting go. However Susan was unable to 'let go' in the physical sense – leaving her held arm in the air. There was no release of her arm, no free flow, no ability to let go safely and allow her arm to fall by her side.

Discussion

It is the tension in the body witnessed in these observations and extracts which will be the focus of the following discussion. In Carol we see a young baby becoming distressed when her communication is not immediately received, at which point she applied her own coping mechanisms. This could be an example of Carol beginning to fall apart, she was trying hard to hold onto her object. In order to cope with the situation she applied her own strategies: first of all her focus was drawn to the window, the next strategy was to tense her muscles. Bick (1968) had a notion of the containing object experienced as 'a second skin' postulating that 'disturbance in the primal skin function can lead to the development of a "second skin" formation through which dependence on the object is replaced by a "pseudo-independence skin" (Bick 1968: 484). If the primary object is unavailable, a baby might try and hold itself together in a variety of ways. This could be done through searching for a replacement object such as a light, a voice, a smell or perhaps by tensing muscles – using the body as a way of psychically holding the self together:

> The 'second skin' phenomenon which replaces first skin integration manifests itself as either a partial or total type of muscular shell or a corresponding verbal muscularity.
>
> (Bick 1968: 486)

Babies can be seen to manifest this phenomenon, as if threatened they may fall apart. The observation of Carol could be illustrating this phenomenon and is an example of Carol applying her own mechanisms of holding herself together. However, she does not have to do this for long as mother responds to her needs. 'If the good object is felt to be possessed it gives a strong support and confidence when the subject is under stress' (Hinshelwood 1994: 79).

It was from having observed Carol using her body as a defence (second skin) which encouraged me to think in a different way about some of the acute body tension witnessed in my adolescent clients. In particular, Susan came to mind. She appeared to be someone who seemed painfully locked in her body. Her external armoury (Reich 1949) was severe. It seemed that Susan may have been someone who had had to apply a second skin early on in life, and this was what was being witnessed in her adolescent body. It was a defence that had its roots in infancy. It could have been a mechanism which she applied to hold herself together emotionally. As Kestenberg stresses: 'physical experiences leave long term traces upon the way people hold themselves and move' (Kestenberg *et al.* 1999: 2).

More significantly, it could have been an emotional experience which had manifested itself in Susan's body. In DMT the element of flow is associated to emotional feeling (North 1972: 241) and 'bound' flow is associated with control of feelings (Costinous 1978). From a DMT perspective, Susan was exhibiting very bound and held flow, which is located at an extreme end of the 'flow' continuum. Susan appeared very restrained and restricted in her body flow, unable to connect with her feelings. This could suggest that Susan had learned to hold onto her feelings through her body in the same way the infant Carol had, for a brief moment. Susan could be seen to have created a 'second skin' replacing her primary object 'by a pseudo-independence'. This strategy can protect the inner self and cuts off meaning to the internal world. Unfortunately with Susan the 'pseudo' holding could have been long lasting and might now be a part of her character (Reich 1949) as seen in adolescence.

It has been useful to clarify that muscular rigidity and tensing the body in such an acute way may well have its roots in infancy. This interdisciplinary research which resulted from applying infant movement observations and psychoanalytical understanding within my practice has proved effective in Susan's DMT work.

Summary and conclusion

This writing has represented a journey in which I have been able to begin to research and integrate aspects of psychoanalytical theory and infant observation into my practice as a dance movement therapist. It has provided an opportunity to present some themes which have emerged in my recent work. This process has stimulated a period of reflection, evaluation and reconsideration, thus allowing my practice of DMT to be viewed from a wider, more informed perspective. The result has been an increased awareness and greater depth in the consideration of interventions and interpretations which stem from my interaction with clients.

The exploration of these themes became part of a process in which psychoanalytical ideas and the strategies of dance movement were combined in an interdisciplinary approach in my work with the clients. This has given me a deeper understanding and has offered greater meaning to the therapist when considering what had taken place within the therapeutic process.

The experience of observing Carol was a turning point of paramount importance in my practice as a dance movement therapist, since it provided access to a greater range of therapeutic material and understanding, enhancing the efficacy of the therapist–client relationship.

The interdisciplinary approach to the research has developed my DMT practice in a number of ways; for example there is an increase in the use of words and verbalisations. As witnessed in the relationship between Carol and her mother, the words were of great significance, adding understanding to the child's experience of being physically held. This has influenced how words, sounds and vocalisations have featured far more in my own work.

Within a society in which intellectual processes are privileged, DMT as a discipline rooted in the body, has much to offer. Equally the analytical and theoretical underpinning which is offered by the psychoanalytical perspective provides a balance, enriching the work and enhancing the therapeutic process.

During the research process there were of course moments of doubt and insecurity which stemmed from combining the two disciplines. At times this imposed conflicting ideologies such as in the two different understanding of muscular tensing. Largely, however, there were positive resonances between the taxonomies and the strategies employed were complementary.

The work has reached a certain phase and I hope that I will be able to continue to develop my research, reflection and practice in order to further ideas and links between the two disciplines. A possibility for future research could be examining the game of hide and seek, trying to show how this game can be used to deal with fears and anxieties arising from separations, endings and loss. This is a game I have frequently witnessed both in infant observation and DMT childwork. Another theme in which interesting connections could be made is early conversations, attunement and synchrony. There is great opportunity for future synergies between psychoanalytical infant observation and DMT.

References

Bannerman-Haig, S. (2001) Primary tool, *Animated: Making Dance Matter*, autumn, 13–16.

Bick, E. (1968) The experience of the skin in early object-relations, *International Journal of Psychotherapy* 49, 484.

Bion, W. (1962) *Learning From Experience*. London: Karnac.

—— (1988) A theory of thinking, in E.B. Spillius (ed.) *Melanie Klein Today*, Vol. 1. London: Routledge.

Britton, R. (1992) Keeping things in mind, in R. Anderson (ed.) *Clinical Lectures on Klein and Bion*. London: Routledge.

Chodorow, J. (1991) *Dance Therapy and Depth Psychology: The Moving Imagination*. London: Routledge.

Costinos, C. (1978) *Therapy in Motion*. Chicago: University of Illinois Press. London.

Hinshelwood, R.D. (1994) *Clinical Klein*. London: Free Association Books.

Kestenberg, J. (1975) *Children and Parents: Psychoanalytical Studies in Development*. New York: Jason Aronson.

Kestenberg, J., Loman, S., Sossin, M. and Lewis, P. (1999) *The Meaning of Movement: Developmental and Clinical Perspectives of the Kestenberg Movement Profile*. London: Gordon and Breach.

Klein, M. (1997) Our adult world and its roots in infancy, in M. Klein *Envy and Gratitude and Other Works 1946–1963*. London: Vintage.

Laban, R. (1975) *The Mastery of Movement*. London: MacDonald and Evans.

—— (1960) *The Mastery of Movement*, 2nd edn. London: MacDonald and Evans.

—— (1966) *The Language of Movement: A Guide to Choeutics*. Boston: Plays Inc.

Loman, S. (1992) Fetal movement notation: A method of attuning to the fetus, in S. Loman (ed.) *The Body Mind Connection in Human Movement Analysis*. Keene, NH: Antioch New England Graduate School.

Meekums, B. (1988) *Dance Therapy in Family and Social Work*. Leeds: East Leeds Family Service Unit.

—— (1991) Dance movement therapy with mothers and young children at risk of abuse, *The Arts in Psychotherapy* 18, 3, 223–230.

Melville-Thomas, R. (1987) Focus on therapy, dancing the blues away, *Dance Theatre Journal* 5, 2, 15–16.

North, M. (1972) *Personality Assessment Through Movement*. London: MacDonald and Evans.

Payne, H. (1987) The perceptions of young people labelled delinquent towards a DMT programme, unpublished MPhil, University of Manchester.

—— (1992) Shut in, shut out, in H. Payne (ed.) *Dance Movement Therapy: Theory and Practice*. London: Routledge.

Reich, W. (1949) *Character Analysis*. New York: Noonday Press.

Robson, C. (1993) *Real World Research*. Oxford: Blackwell.

Segal, H. (1973) *Introduction to the Work of Melanie Klein*. London: Karnac.

Waddell, M. (1998) *Inside Lives: Psychoanalysis and the Growth of the Personality*. London: Duckworth.

Whitehouse, M. (1979) Jung and dance therapy: two major principles, in P. Bernstein (ed.) *Eight Theoretical Approaches to Dance Movement Therapy*. Iowa: Kendall-Hunt.

Woods, P. (1986) *Inside Schools: Ethnography in Educational Research*. London: Routledge.

Chapter 7

Hidden treasures, hidden voices

An ethnographic study into the use of movement and creativity in psychosocial work with war-affected refugee children in Serbia

Allison Jane Singer

Introduction

This chapter is drawn from PhD research in dance ethnography that examines the use of movement and creativity in psychosocial work with war-affected refugee children. It is based on one year's fieldwork in Serbia and draws on my experience, skills and training as a performance artist, dance movement therapist, ethnomusicologist and dance ethnographer. At the time of my fieldwork, dance movement therapy (DMT) as an independent and recognised profession and training did not exist in Serbia, and access to training opportunities were very limited. Two central questions formed the basis of the research:

1 How effective are movement and creativity as a source of development in psychosocial work with war-affected refugee children?
2 How effective are movement and creativity as a source and medium for integration and understanding between different communities, specifically refugee and host communities?

In this chapter some of the ways in which movement was used in the work with children are outlined together with my participation and observations of this work. Consideration is given to why and how movement and creativity may contribute to international development work with war-affected refugee children, and the place of DMT within this.

The field

Refugee or internally displaced people (IDPs) arrived in Serbia in several waves and from different parts of former Yugoslavia over the ten-year period of the war (1991 to 2001). Some of these people were housed in collective centres in Serbia created from converted schools, hospitals, factories, hotels, sports centres and barracks. A number of people remained in these centres for the duration of the war and continued to live in them after the war had ended.

The problems that refugee people face as a result of war can include the physical and emotional effects of experiencing or witnessing violence; and problems brought about through the migration and resettlement processes including language and access to basic resources such as housing, education, training, food, transport, sanitation, medical facilities and work opportunities. Development work can lead to further problems as donors take on a caretaking role leading to disempowerment and dependency. For many refugees the process of disempowerment begins immediately, 'when traditional familial or social support systems are lost as a result of migration' (Baron 2002). Refugee children may also experience loss of appropriate care from parents or caregivers because of the adults' responses to the war. In Serbia, children and families faced additional problems as a result of the economic sanctions imposed from 1992 to 1996, and the 78 days of NATO air strikes in 1999. Many informants stressed that all children in former Yugoslavia had been affected by the war. Graca Machel (1996) an expert appointed by the United Nations (UN) in June 1994 to make a study on the impact of armed conflict on children proposed:

> War violates every right of a child – the right to life, the right to be with family and community, the right to health, the right to the development of the personality and the right to be nurtured and protected.
>
> (Machel 1996: 11, Article 11.30)

War permanently changes the development of the child by fundamentally changing the world in which they live and their relationships within this world (Rieber 1998). One informant, however, stressed that life continues regardless of the conditions that surround it: 'I realized life needs no conditions, life is life all on its own . . . life creates conditions for itself' (extract from interview with a founding member of the organisation). The organisation I worked with recognised that refugee people have opinions and resources both within themselves and within the communities of which they are a part. They tried to harness and develop these resources through activities that used creative media including movement.

Methodology

The methodology used for the research was drawn from both dance ethnography (Buckland 1999) and DMT (Payne 1992, 1993a; Pearson 1996). This integration simultaneously facilitated and created challenges within the research. To my knowledge this is the first piece of academic research that has attempted to bring together dance ethnography and DMT from both practical and theoretical perspectives in the context of war-affected refugee children. I believe that this research is important in that it can begin to open doors to collaborations within and between these two fields and methodologies. It can also begin to open more doors to the acceptance of the value of the arts therapies within the context of international development work with war-affected refugee children.

Ethnography is a methodology derived from anthropological research and includes both the process of the research and the way it is described. The basis of ethnographic research is participant observation conducted through fieldwork and undertaken over a defined period of time, usually a minimum of one year. Through participant observation the researcher begins to understand the processes and meanings of the phenomenon being studied from the perspective of the participants. Ethnography has the potential to draw on various methods in response to participation, observation and negotiation in the field. Like DMT, dance ethnography works with *'multiple realities'* (Payne 1993b: 30).

In the field I used participant observation which included keeping daily field notes and journals, devising and organising formal interviews, documenting these using video and photography; and recording workshops using video and photography. I lived with a non-English speaking elderly Serbian woman, undertook intensive Serbian language training and had regular academic and clinical supervision by telephone and email for the duration of the fieldwork. In addition, a selection of informants in the field acted as informal translators and interpreters.

During the fieldwork I primarily participated in the work of a Serbian non-government organisation (NGO) called Zdravo da ste, which worked with refugee and internally displaced children and families living in collective centres and private accommodation. It was founded at the beginning of the war by a group of Serbian psychologists in response to individual concerns for the welfare of children. Teams composed of teachers and psychologists facilitated regular workshops with children at the offices of the organisation in different towns and cities in Serbia; at local cultural centres such as galleries, museums and parks; and at the collective centres. I participated in the work of one of these teams based in Belgrade. My work with this team involved participating, co-facilitating and occasionally leading regular workshops with pre-school and school-age children at the various venues. I also participated in weekly planning and evaluation meetings. In addition to this work, I facilitated several practical presentations and training on different aspects of DMT and drama and movement therapy for this and two other Serbian NGOs.

When I co-facilitated or led workshops for children I tried to integrate my understanding of the aims, objectives and approaches of the organisation with my knowledge and experience of DMT and community arts work, so that my work would complement and not contradict their work. The organisation was very clear that the work they did was not therapy, but was concerned with 'building relations' and finding 'possibilities for living' (extract from interview with a founding member of the organisation).

Through my participation I became an apprentice of their working methods with children. I was both an insider as a practitioner working in a field close to my own and an outsider as a researcher studying a specific situation.

I had initially entered the field with the intention of setting up individual and group DMT sessions with war-affected refugee children. I very quickly realised that this approach would not be possible because it would interfere with the work of Zdravo da ste. I therefore participated in their workshops as a volunteer. My knowledge and experience of DMT allowed me to interact with the children and facilitators within the workshop context and, when asked, to give feedback on the workshops and ideas for follow-up workshops. As the research progressed, I found tensions between my roles as a dance ethnographer and dance movement therapist. My increasingly involved participation as a volunteer appeared to be interfering with my research. In order to focus on the research, I tried to stop contributing to the evaluation and planning of the workshops, but this was not very well received by the people I was working with because of a fundamental notion and expectation of exchange. By withdrawing I was no longer sharing my understanding, skills and insights. My perceived experience of tension between dance ethnography and DMT, and between myself as a researcher and the people I was working with as a volunteer, persisted for the duration of the fieldwork.

Notions and applications of movement and creativity in the field

The movement work I observed in the workshops occurred in the context of a 'social frame', 'social happening' (extract from interview with a member of the children's team), or an 'event' (Torp 1989); where an event is set apart from daily life and occurs within a specific and limited time and place, and usually involves the coming together of a group of people for a specific activity (Bakka 1989). An event can also offer social interactions that are not necessarily allowable or possible in day-to-day social living (Dunin 1989).

The workshops occurred weekly, once or twice a month or at less frequent intervals. Before each workshop there was some kind of preparation time. These were often lively affairs where women from the Belgrade team gathered at the main office to make things for the workshops. Much time and care was put into this preparation and the activities were accompanied with discussions and evaluations of the work, strong black Turkish coffee and gossip. They were creative meetings where skills and ideas were shared and exchanged. I also wondered at their importance for the members of the organisation as a way to explore and express their own creativity and to help in their individual preparation and assimilation of the work.

The different workshops appeared to follow a similar pattern. They began with the journey to the workshop. On arrival space and time were given to arrive and explore the environment before the main workshop activity began. At the beginning of the main workshop activity the whole group were often brought together into a circle for introductions and preparatory work such as warming up the body, name games, greeting gestures, and introducing the main theme of the workshop. The large group was then divided into smaller groups often using games. The small groups then began preparing for, and becoming involved in, the main activity which they shared with the other groups on completion. The whole group was then brought together once more for a closing activity and clearing up. Frequently after a workshop had ended, food was shared between the participants and the workshop facilitators, either provided by the organisation or by the adult participants. I observed two kinds of workshops over the year: the first were self-contained workshops where the activity was completed within the one workshop; in the second the activities extended over several workshops. Sometimes the extended workshops were pre-planned, but sometimes they emerged as a response to the development of the activities in the workshops.

The organisation considered movement and dance to be one of a number of 'human potentials for expression', tools that could be 'discovered and actualised', and used alongside other media to find and develop the hidden potential inside each individual, and the 'voices of the future' (extract from interview with a founding member of the organisation), the potential for the future development of the society. They considered this human potential for expression to be 'indestructible' (extract from interview with a founding member of the organisation) and fundamental to human nature. Movement was often embedded within the activities of the workshops and used in the following ways:

- to create physical shapes, embody visual images, create and develop a story, prepare for or complete a workshop, explore and define an environment, remember previous experiences, acknowledge cultural festivals, facilitate exchanges between cultures, facilitate participation and activity, acknowledge the seasons, consolidate and share an individual or collective experience, acknowledge thresholds and boundaries, and learn written language
- as a medium for making choices, learning, documentation, communication, and as part of a journey
- to engage with sound, games, gesture, names, drawing, collage, and objects.

I was familiar with a multi-arts approach to using movement with other arts media from my own therapeutic work and training. What was different about this work was that members of the organisation did not consider their work to be therapy. The workshops did not target specific emotional or psychological problems present in the lives of the participants, or that emerged within the workshops, although this material was recognised and worked with by the psychologists and teachers on their regular visits to the collective centres and individual families outside the workshop context.

When they completed a workshop the organisation did not intentionally or ritually let go of imaginative and emotional spaces created through the work. In the work of the organisation, movement was considered as part of creativity, where creativity was not restricted to one art form, instead many 'aspects of creativity' (extract from interview with a member of the children's team) were used:

> I see creativity as life. It's not a means, it's not a tool, it's life and the people have such a capacity to create, an endless capacity to create. That's the life, to be creative. To create means to be alive. (Extract from interview with a founding member of the organisation, Belgrade)

The different creative media fed into one another within the activities, and the activities themselves developed in response to the children's participation in them. The description below, by a member of the children's team, is an example of how creative elements, including movement were applied within the context of a workshop at a collective centre:

> The thing that happened, happened through children playing. The workshop fell into following everything that was happening in the group of children. The workshop was at a collective centre, it was a mixed group of children from pre-school to first grade of secondary school. We started with a game but in some way we ended up with some important words. From the words that appeared we again tried to build up our new game. We divided into several groups. From the words the game was developed. The words were: stream, bird, kittens, and a dog. These words were written on pieces of paper, put into the basket and then everybody pulled a piece of paper with a word on it. My word was truth. Everybody made a movement, starting to relive these words. The children got into that fairly quickly. The story developed into a thing – there was a tree that grew in a field, it was a sunny day, birds were flying and you could hear the stream gargling, in that field the animals played, the kittens were playing hide-and-seek. Because my role was truth, I was all over the place following children and constantly asking the question 'Where is the truth?' Simultaneously [the children] said 'The truth is in our lives.' It was so strong that I am never going to forget about it. That was 'the thing' that happened in that workshop, it doesn't have an end. The important thing for me is that that potential will be preserved in children. The game and playing with children is not something simple, but is actually very

complex work and our joint work was brought into it. This was just one part of the workshop.

(Extract from an interview with a member of the children's team)

I was often given this example to show me the effectiveness of the work of the organisation in the context of their work with children. These primary school age children had ideas and concepts that appeared to be beyond their age, which contradicted traditional notions from psychology. Many of the psychologists within the organisation felt that their work was breaking new ground. The work had developed in response to the needs of the participants and the interactions within the workshop, the ways in which the work had developed did not necessarily fit into the traditional paradigms of psychology.

The above example not only illustrates how different creative media could interact and support one another within a workshop, but also shows how other activities developed through the activity itself and the children's inter-action with the process. Movement was used as part of play and games. It was also used to relive the words or *embody* the words and in this way created the basis for the formation and development of a narrative. Through these activities, children uttered what one informant described as fundamental truths, 'philosophy' (extract from interview with a founding member of the organisation). The above example also illustrates the importance of play and games within the work.

One result of experiencing war is that children stop playing (extracts from interviews; Lindon 2001: 17), two informants suggested that children and adults can become 'frozen' (extract from interviews with members of the organisation 2001–2) in response to their experience of war. Zdravo da ste tried to create possibilities for these children to find their resources for play again, through different activities and opportunities to meet and interact with other children and adults. Work with play was not restricted to work with the children but also extended to the adults.

Applications of movement in the workshops also included *etno*. 'Etno' or 'ethno' dance included regional structured choreographed movement forms from the region that had encompassed former Yugoslavia. Ethno was con-sidered to belong to everybody. One informant described ethno to be 'a kind of living . . . ethno is taking care about our lives' (extract from interview with a founding member of the organisation). Ethno was seen as a resource, part of a constantly changing living tradition passed within families, through the generations. Early in the development of their work, members of the organ-isation noticed that many people in the collective centres told stories about their lives before the war. Working with ethno created opportunities to tell the stories and to have them heard, allowing the stories to be placed in 'another social frame, not how it was, but how it is now' (extract from interview with a member of the children's team). Experiences from the past could be incorporated and used as resources in the present and for the future. In some of the workshops with adults I observed how movements from ethno dance usually accompanied by song would sometimes emerge out of the activities of the workshop. In the workshops with children I sometimes observed movement and song motifs from ethno dance that appeared to be incorporated in the children's games and play. These motifs included creating and passing under arches, and making circles and chains. One informant told me that dance could not be separated from other aspects of ethno because it was part of the 'whole social frame' (extract from interview with a member of the children's team), part of the way in which people organised and responded to their lives.

Creativity and movement were not only literally part of the work but were also metaphorically part of the language which the organisation used to describe their work: for example, 'we are building our relationships . . . some little steps through activities' (extract from interview with a member of the children's team); 'for the local people it was a journey of discovery' (extract from interview with a founding member of the organisation). Movement metaphors or metaphors from the creative process were used within the work to describe the process and the development of the work.

The experiences and effects of the workshops extended beyond the boundaries of the events themselves into the everyday and the future lives of the participants, as the example below describes:

> A few years ago we went to give the training to teachers. Among the teachers was one mother who used to be in a collective centre with her family in Belgrade. Her son is now in secondary school. They remembered the experience and workshops. We went to their small apartment and on his noticeboard there was the badge of [our organisation], he still keeps it, it's very important to him. I really think and believe that children have a chance. They can keep this in memory, they will keep this experience, but they can overcome this through development, through education, through meeting people. No one has the right to say 'It's ended', we have to do our best, that's to keep this process going on. (Extract from interview with a founding member of the organisation, Belgrade)

The activities of the workshops were part of a developmental process that facilitated the development of participants, including members of the organisation, and the development of the organisation itself; and by implication the wider society (Rieber 1998).

Conclusion

The problems that war-affected refugee children and families face are specific to their experience of conflict, migration and resettlement. This research suggests that work with the children is multidimensional both in terms of the disciplines and in terms of the creative media used. It cannot occur in isolation from other factors including access to choice and to basic resources and rights such as accommodation, health, transport, education, work opportunities, the families and communities in which the children belong and are surrounded by. Within the work of Zdravo da ste, creative movement was a central element but it was holistically connected to other elements. It was the whole event, as well as the elements that made up the event, that was important. The whole event was a process that had a beginning, middle and end, and was one stage within a larger life process.

Moving between different creative media within one activity created the possibility to move between different modes of understanding, expression and communication. Working between these different media gave the children a 'freedom' (extract from interview with a member of the children's team) to explore and the potential to find their 'treasures' (extract from interview with a member of the children's team) and 'hidden voices' (extract from interview with a founding member of the organisation).

I was asked by several different individuals and organisations from the field to give training in DMT. I did give a number of one- and two-day trainings as a way to give back to the people who had helped me in the research. These trainings were met with mixed responses. Some trainees felt that they had learnt a lot from the work and wanted me to do more long-term work in the future. Some people felt the work was no different from things they already knew from trainings in psychology and other forms of therapy such as transactional analysis. However, the overwhelming response was that further training was wanted, both to gain familiarity with skills and methods and to gain local and international professional qualifications and recognition. Providing opportunities for long-term and short-term professional training in DMT and other arts therapies in conflict or post-conflict areas is a potential area for development.

In terms of DMT practice with war-affected refugee children in the context of international development work, it would seem important to adopt a working practice that is flexible in its approach and in its use of the term 'therapy'. The working practice needs to be able to incorporate ideas and practices from other cultures which may seem to contradict basic tenets of DMT, such as ways of perceiving and understanding the client–therapist relationship. The notion of exchange is very important in this work, as is respect for the professional and personal experiences and approaches of the people from the home community. The approach also needs to adopt a multi-disciplinary and multi-arts approach in order to be able to work with as many people as possible and with the immediacy of the situation. Learning about, and working with, ethno or folk movement and arts forms both practically and theoretically can contribute to understanding of images, symbols and metaphors that emerge in the process of the work. Learning or speaking the spoken language or languages of the children, where possible, is also an important aspect of the work.

DMT is a unique form in that it actively attempts to use movement and dance to transform emotions and experiences. There are inherent skills which dance movement therapists have that can be passed on to other professionals in a context where little is known about this form. There are also many opportunities for the therapists to learn from members of the field and in this way to develop their own practice. Dance ethnography has an important role to play in DMT work with war-affected refugee children both in the United Kingdom and in the context of international development work. It can provide theories and methods that can contribute to understanding cultural difference, the importance and place of movement and creativity within a particular society, and understanding of cultural symbols that may emerge through the therapeutic process.

There are many themes that have emerged through the process of undertaking the research. The first concerns the definition and understanding of what a child is, what they are capable of, how their psychosocial processes develop and the effects of war on this development. The second theme concerns the negative and positive aspects of the notion of *refugee* and *refugeeness*, both as a label and as a way to construct a collective and individual identity as a survival tool and as part of the psychosocial process. The third theme concerns international development and the potential for change in working practices with, and perceptions of, war-affected refugee people. The fourth involves the notion of creativity and its fundamental place within developmental work. The fifth refers to the concept of play and its importance for both children and adults within the psychosocial process. Finally, the sixth theme concerns movement itself and its relationship to creativity, play, ethno and psychosocial development in the context of war-affected refugee children.

References

Bakka, E. (1989) Final comments, in: L. Torp (ed.) *The Dance Event: A Complex Cultural Phenomenon. Proceedings from the 15th Symposium of the ICTM Study Group on Ethnochoreology, Copenhagen 1988*. Copenhagen: ICTM Study Group on Ethnochoreology, p. 178.

Baron, N. (2002) Community-based psychological and mental health services for Southern Sudanese refugees in long-term exile in Uganda, in J. De Jong (ed.) (2002) *Trauma, War and Violence – Public Mental Health in Socio-Cultural Context*. London: Kluwer Academic/Plenum Press, pp. 157–203.

Buckland, T. J. (ed.) (1999) *Dance in the Field – Theory, Methods and Issues in Dance Ethnography*, Basingstoke: Macmillan.

Dunin, E. (1989) Dance events as a means to social interchange, in L. Torp (ed.) *The Dance Event: A Complex Cultural Phenomenon. Proceedings from the 15th Symposium of the ICTM Study Group on Ethnochoreology, Copenhagen 1988.* Copenhagen: ICTM Study Group on Ethnochoreology, pp. 30–34.

Lindon, J. (2001) *Understanding Children's Play*. Cheltenham: Nelson Thomas.

Machel, G. (1996) *Promotion and Protection of The Rights of Children – Impact of Armed Conflict on Children – Note by the Secretary General*. USA: United Nations Department for Policy Coordination and Sustainable Development (DPCSD) – A/51/306. Online. Available HTTP: <http://www.unicef.org/graca/> (accessed 6 June 2005).

Payne, H. (ed.) (1992) *Dance Movement Therapy: Theory and Practice*. London: Routledge.

—— (ed.) (1993a) *Handbook of Inquiry in the Arts Therapies – One River Many Currents*. London: Jessica Kingsley.

—— (1993b) From practitioner to researcher – research as a learning process, in H. Payne (ed.) *Handbook of Inquiry in the Arts Therapies – One River Many Currents*. London: Jessica Kingsley, pp. 16–37.

Pearson, J. (ed.) (1996) *Discovering the Self through Drama and Movement – The Sesame Approach*. London: Jessica Kingsley

Rieber, R. W. (ed.) (1998) *The Collected Works of L.S. Vygotsky. Vol. 5: Child Psychology*, trans. M. J. Hall. New York: Plenum Press.

Torp, L. (ed.) (1989) *The Dance Event: A Complex Cultural Phenomenon, Proceedings from the 15th Symposium of the ICTM Study Group on Ethnochoreology Copenhagen 1988*. Copenhagen: ICTM Study Group on Ethnochoreology.

Chapter 8

The body of culture

Transcultural competence in dance movement therapy

Sara Boas

Introduction

This chapter presents a framework for understanding the knowledge, skills and attitudes that support effective and ethical dance movement therapy (DMT) practice across cultural boundaries. I summarise and discuss a long-term qualitative inquiry conducted through cognitive-behavioural modelling, action research workshops and interviews with health, caring and managerial professionals from over 60 countries. Drawing on my application of the model in professional development programmes, my own clinical experience and interviews with other dance movement therapists, I discuss the implications of the ensuing Transcultural Competence model for DMT theory and practice. I provide a framework for practitioners to review their own practice and development needs, propose ways in which the DMT profession can be strengthened by giving greater attention to cultural issues in training and supervision, and make suggestions for future research.

How can we, while honouring our differences, acknowledge and use wisely our power to co-create the world in which we live? This core question informs my life work and was the stimulus for the Transcultural Competence research project, an exploration into the foundations of effective and ethical practice across cultural boundaries, which began in the mid-1980s and continues today. The purpose of this chapter is to present findings to date from this research, as they relate to DMT.

The name of the project points to some key assumptions. The term '*Trans*' means 'across', 'beyond' or 'surpassing'. This distinguishes my approach from 'cross', 'multi' or 'inter-cultural' studies, with their view of cultures as separate entities that come into contact while remaining distinct. I am interested in how we not only recognise and bridge our differences, but also **trans**cend them, finding unity in our common humanity and co-creating new cultural forms. The term '*Cultural*' keeps the focus on social dimensions of experience, activity and sense-making: the cultural bodies of individuals are born of, constitute and give rise to the larger body of culture. Finally, the term '*Competence*' draws our attention to active engagement; not only academic knowledge but pragmatic, professional know-how.

The research process

The core question above contains a paradox – diversity and unity. We can strive to embrace this tension, both honouring the depth of cultural differences and nurturing a society that fulfils universal human needs and potentials. However, this does not protect us from ethical dilemmas, when confronted with practices such as female genital mutilation that make sense within a certain cultural perspective but violate our humanistic values (Merry 2003). As therapeutic practitioners, we may be called upon to react to such practices. As DMT researchers, we need an approach that can encompass multiple perspectives (Payne 1993; Best 2000; McLeod 2001). Can the ethical practitioner-researcher respect the cultural value system which allows such practices, yet take a stand against them? My own commitment to embracing the unity-diversity paradox has led me to develop a research approach in which I explore a topic and gather data from diverse, seemingly incommensurable points of view. This approach, which I call multimodal inquiry, calls upon the many aspects of the researcher's intelligence described in Gardner's (1983) seminal work on multiple intelligences – linguistic, logical-mathematical, spatial, bodily-kinaesthetic, musical, interpersonal, intra-personal and naturalistic – and allows us to develop a multidimensional appreciation of the topic in question. The main steps of my multimodal inquiry into Transcultural Competence are set out below.

Informants

I identified eight individuals – four women and four men – who were viewed by peers and clients as outstanding in their ability to work effectively with people from diverse cultures. Selection was based on referral and interview; I did not use formal tools to measure or compare practitioner effectiveness. The eight informants were all therapeutic or personal development professionals practising in multicultural settings.

Cognitive-behavioural modelling

I conducted a series of interviews with each informant to model the cognitive and behavioural patterns associated with their practice in multicultural environments. This research method has been central to the field of neuro-linguistic programming (NLP), an offshoot of applied psychology with roots in structural linguistics, anthropology and humanistic psychology (Bandler and Grinder 1975a, 1975b, 1979). As Dilts and DeLozier note in their NLP encyclopaedia, 'the basic objectives of NLP are to model special or exceptional abilities and help make them transferable to others' (Dilts and DeLozier 2000: 790). NLP modelling is a specialised skill, which uses multiple 'perceptual positions' to gain a rich description of the ability in question; a perceptual position is a particular point of view within a system of interaction (Dilts and DeLozier 2000: 940).

As the researcher in the Transcultural Competence project I used four perceptual positions:

- *First position*: my identification with my own thoughts, feelings, priorities and beliefs.
- *Second position*: my empathic engagement with others' experiences (in this case, the informants).
- *Third position*: a more objective viewpoint, allowing observation and analysis of informants and critical evaluation of my own role in the system.
- *Fourth position*: my somatic sense of the 'relational field' of cultural encounters, not focused in others' experience but in the relations between them. This builds on Gendlin's notion of 'felt sensing' as the 'holistic, implicit bodily sense of a complex situation [containing] more than could be said or thought' (Gendlin 1996: 58). However, the focus here is on the therapist's own felt sensing, as advocated by Gilligan in his discussion of self-relations therapy (Gilligan 1997) and with the added refinement of identification with the relational field, rather than with either self or clients. This important data source is familiar to dance movement thera-pists, whose practice is likely to be continuously informed and guided by their bodily felt sensing of relational dynamics within the therapeutic setting (Sandel 1993; Loughran 2003).

I analysed my data to identify clusters, themes and patterns and to discern and make sense of the relationships between these. My approach corres-ponded to the early classical model of grounded theory as conceived by Glaser, with his focus on creative insight by an individual researcher, the emergence of theory through engagement with the material over an extended period of time and the development of initial hypotheses prior to conducting a systematic literature survey (Glaser and Strauss 1967). The result of this data analysis was the Transcultural Competence model.

Literature survey

The relevant theoretical and professional literature within several fields and disciplines, including the history of human consciousness, organisa-tional behaviour, anthropology and cross-cultural psychology, was reviewed. Insights from qualitative meta-analysis of this literature were incorporated in the model.

Participatory action research

Once this analysis had taken place and the initial framework was established, it was subjectively validated and refined in professional development workshops. Confidentiality agreements were established with each group.[1] Participants brought cases from their professional practice in therapeutic, educational and managerial roles. These cases formed the basis for facilitated individual and group inquiry and participants engaged with the model as part of their own professional development. The study was therefore susceptible to the usual complications of participatory research, in particular the 'Hawthorne effect', in which research participants steadily improve their performance as a result of the human attention and/or of the ongoing feedback (Mayo 1933; Adair 1984). Since the purpose of my project was and is instrumental, with the goal of improving effective and ethical professional practice across cultures, no attempt was made to mitigate this beneficial effect. To test the validity of the Transcultural Competence model as causal, or to test the efficacy of Transcultural Competence training, several consecutive control groups led by other researchers would need to be conducted, to ensure that the model, rather than my workshop leadership style, is the key variable (Mayo 1933; Adair 1984; Shayer 1992).

A handbook, presenting the framework, was given to each participant at the end of the workshop, after the experiential activities and dialogue (Boas 1989). This process continues and the model still undergoes minor additions and refinements.

Artistic inquiry

In addition to critical incident analysis and dialogue, the action research workshops included a wide range of activities, which we could call artistic inquiry (McNiff 1986, 1998; Hervey 2000). These activities included investigating Transcultural Competence through movement improvisation, drawing, music making and outdoor art.

Reflexive inquiry

Throughout the research process, I have sought to articulate how my own personal and professional cultural heritage shapes my thought and action, which in turn shapes my research process and its potential contribution to my professional field (McLeod 2001). This is particularly important in practitioner research, as the expert knowledge required to conduct specialised action research implies a vested professional interest in perpetuating one's own schema, and the authority of the practitioner role may motivate informants to confirm rather than refute prior findings. My reflexive process took the form of reflective and creative writing, movement improvisation, drawing and both academic and clinical supervision.

Key findings in relation to DMT

The data were striking in their diversity, as one would expect of multimodal inquiry. My research interest was not to reduce Transcultural Competence to one key variable, but to develop a detailed map of a multidimensional landscape. It is no surprise, then, that findings ranged from how practitioners interpret hand gestures to the role of unconditional love. These clustered into five kinds of competence, building up from specific cultural knowledge at the bottom, through intrapersonal and interpersonal skills, to generic, attitudinal competencies at the top. The findings can be summarised as a logical level diagram (Figure 8.1).

I shall use five mini-vignettes to present the five levels of the findings as they relate to DMT. The vignettes are illustrative and do not describe actual individuals. They are informed by cases presented by participants in professional

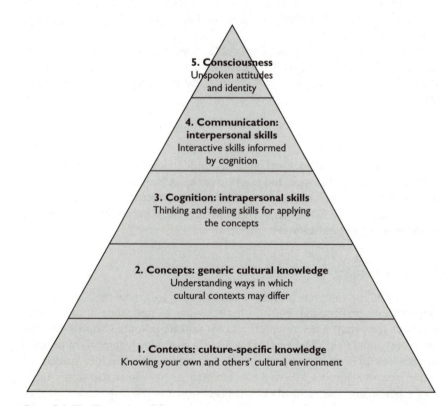

Figure 8.1 The Transcultural Competence model

development workshops and by my own interactions with clients and participants in workshops and clinical practice.

Transcultural contexts: knowing the cultural environment

> Zeka is new to DMT. Anna, his therapist, seeks to establish a connection with Zeka but finds it hard because he won't look her in the eye. He maintains eye contact for a fraction of a second before glancing down and to the left. This quick eye movement repeats itself throughout each session, especially when Anna addresses Zeka directly. She tries to 'hold' eye contact but he appears increasingly uncomfortable as she does so. It is clear to Anna that Zeka feels timid, even fearful; she wonders what past trauma is behind this. After several weeks, Anna is becoming disheartened. There is still no sustained eye contact and Anna fears that she is failing to establish a relationship of trust with Zeka.

The basis for working across cultures is knowledge of the context you are dealing with. A cultural context may be a nation, an ethnic, linguistic or religious group, an institutional setting, or an explicit collective identity such as deaf culture (Senghas and Monaghan 2002). Every aspect of a culture – from manners to monuments – is a clue to its deeper values. Because of this, a therapist never really knows her clients until she knows their context. Furthermore, whether we realise it or not, the context sets the unwritten rules of the game and defines the meaning of our behaviour – an idea elaborated by generations of cultural anthropologists and elegantly explored by Gregory Bateson in conversation with Carl Rogers (Kirschenbaum and Henderson 1990).

Anna is unaware that Zeka's eye movements are a conscious and conventional way to indicate respect for an elder. He feels safe and trusting in her presence and this is enhanced by the fact that Anna is older than him. She seems powerful and maternal as – in Zeka's world – a healer should be. When she tries to establish eye contact, he becomes confused. It is an unexpected and inexplicable rejection of his deferential manner. His discomfort grows as this potential mother-figure looks him straight in the eye, thereby implying intimacy of a more sexual nature.

Anna is unwittingly applying the assumptions and values of her own cultural context in the sessions with Zeka. She ignores the cultural heritage which forms the basis of Zeka's engagement in the therapeutic process and imposes her own rules: 'We are all equal ... we demonstrate equality by looking each other in the eye ... sustained eye contact expresses trust'. These unwritten rules are the product of her particular cultural heritage. Unexamined, their cultural source is denied and they live in Anna as natural truths. Her context defines the way she makes sense of Zeka's movements; his meanings have no place in her awareness.

The Transcultural Competence project brought me time and again to the same overwhelming conclusion: that we can only be effective, ethical practitioners in a multicultural society if we first and foremost become aware of our own cultural contexts. This done, the therapist is in a position to investigate the other cultural contexts, to find out what rules, assumptions, beliefs, values and history shape their clients' movement in the therapy space.

The second major finding of the project was the importance of fostering curiosity and exploring together the client's cultural context. We engage with a cultural context as a holistic lifeworld: the environment of cultural norms, rules and beliefs that structures experience and interaction, as described by the philosopher Jurgen Habermas (b. 1929) and developed by researchers in phenomenological sociology, psychology, anthropology and education (Schutz and Luckmann 1973; Habermas 1987; Good 1994; Sloan 1999; Sergiovanni 2004). By actively seeking to explore and discover other lifeworlds, it seems that we not only enrich our own, but also enhance the effectiveness of our therapeutic practice.

A third finding was that we are each the product of multiple contexts – what we could call the *multicultural self*. Practitioners who had examined the tensions, dynamics and mutual influences among their own inner cultural 'encounters', in the course of my professional development workshops, believed themselves to be better prepared for encounters with their clients' cultures than they had been previously. This is consistent with findings in self-relations theory (Muran 2001). If borne out, this observation could have significant implications for practitioner training and merits systematic inquiry.

So, context knowledge is the base, the foundation stone of Transcultural Competence. However, awareness of our own contexts will never be complete, let alone our understanding of the multiple, complex and constantly evolving cultural contexts we encounter in our work. Something more is needed to help us get to grips with this endless variety.

Transcultural concepts: understanding ways in which cultural contexts may differ

Priya has worked with her therapist, Louise, for several months and has identified a need to be more assertive in her relationship with her husband. A theme of protecting boundaries has emerged. Priya often arrives late and typically explains that she had to do something for another family member. When Louise asks Priya how she feels about this, she says that it's fine. Priya usually shakes her head while she says this and Louise notices that while the words say 'yes', the movement says 'no'. Louise is concerned that Priya's inability to acknowledge these violations of her boundaries may impede the progress of her therapy.

The next level of the findings takes us from the infinite complexity of 'different cultures' to the relative simplicity of 'how cultures differ'. This is a more abstract and conceptual kind of cultural knowledge, based on generalisations about significant dimensions of culture. For example, some cultures favour a blunt communication style whilst others are more indirect; some cultures believe in fate, others in free will; some emphasise competition, others co-operation. As well as such folk concepts, there is an extensive research literature providing a proliferation of cultural dimensions models. The four dimensions referred to below are drawn from the widely used model developed by Geert Hofstede (1991).

Priya, like millions of others with South Asian heritage, indicates 'yes' with a side-to-side movement of the head. Louise lacks this basic context knowledge and misreads Priya's gesture. On top of this, Louise is unaware of key concepts that could have been helpful. One such concept is the *collectivist-individualist* dimension, which distinguishes cultures in which the group or community is perceived as the basic unit of society from those in which the individual is supreme. In Priya's lifeworld the basic unit of society is not the individual but a collective. Priya has stated that she wants to be more assertive with her husband and Louise supports this goal, but it means different things to therapist and client. Louise, the therapist, imagines Priya standing up for her own individual needs. Priya wants to better balance her husband's demands with those of her children for the sake of family balance and harmony.

Furthermore, Louise's high uncertainty avoidance contrasts with Priya's low uncertainty avoidance. The uncertainty avoidance dimension distinguishes cultures in which ambiguity and change are tolerated from those in which people attempt to control the future by making and implementing detailed plans. Louise values flexibility and responsiveness within the session, but her punctuality is a core value and an important way of providing the therapeutic holding environment. Priya, with low uncertainty avoidance, expects to go with the flow of life. For her, the theme of boundaries concerns subtle aspects of sexuality and spirituality – as realms of collective experience. Priya's discomfort from the last-minute family arrangements which lead her to arrive late for sessions arises only from the fact that her therapist insists on discussing them!

We can identify a third dimension here. Initially labelled *masculinity–femininity* by Hofstede, this dimension distinguishes between cultures in which people generally relate to one another in either a competitive or a co-operative manner. It is often renamed *tough–tender* to avoid reducing it to gender roles. Louise's 'tough' culture leads her to view the world in competitive terms – Priya's interests compete with her children's needs and her husband's demands. Priya's more 'tender' culture means that her goals are shaped by ideals of co-operation, sharing resources and nurturing each person.

Thinking back to Anna and Zeka, we see Hofstede's fourth dimension at play. The *power distance* dimension distinguishes between cultures' expectations of the existence and expression of hierarchy. Anna comes from a low power distance culture and likes to be 'on a level' and 'seeing eye to eye', both literally and metaphorically. Zeka's culture is high power distance: he feels reassured by the elder's power and expresses this by his respectful distance.

The Transcultural Competence findings indicate that conceptual knowledge of the dimensions of culture (whether folk concepts or from the research literature) support effective and ethical professional practice. As well as raising awareness, such concepts provide a common language for talking about our differences; they can help us to notice hidden differences and compare our values and assumptions. For the therapist who is finding it hard to connect with a client, conceptual knowledge may be a first step towards the development of vital empathy (Rogers 1975).

However, the findings also indicate that consistent application of one conceptual model may undermine effective practice. Practitioners with a strong allegiance to one specific cultural dimensions model (either a folk concept such as 'primitive-modern' or a research-based model in which they had been trained) were apparently less responsive to clients' varying needs than others with a more fluid intellectual approach. At the other end of the spectrum is the complete lack of a conceptual 'lens' to alert practitioners to cultural differences. So, conceptual knowledge of cultural dimensions is the second level of Transcultural Competence. We need to do our homework, but without losing our lively curiosity.

These first two levels of the model – summarised as contexts and concepts – are the knowledge base of the effective and ethical practitioner. But DMT is a field of practice: knowledge is not enough.

Transcultural cognition: thinking and feeling skills for applying the concepts

Bettina leads an open DMT group in a drop-in centre for refugees. She brings great commitment to her work and the group has some long-term users. Abed attends his first session and seems keen to enter the process. Bettina seeks to create a safe space for Abed, mirroring movements and matching his rhythm whilst being careful not to impose contact. At the end of the session Abed leaves abruptly and does not return for further sessions. Some time later Bettina hears that Abed has told the centre's receptionist that he will not return because 'Bettina was so unfriendly'.

Knowledge of different cultures and awareness of how cultures differ are the basis of Transcultural Competence, yet these have little value until they are applied. The next level of findings identifies key thinking and feeling skills. Exercised before, during and after client sessions, these cognition skills help us to imagine and feel our way into another lifeworld. Here, cognition refers to a range of skills including the ability to become aware of your own prejudices and assumptions, to actively assess your own thinking process, to shift between different perceptual positions and to reconcile opposing values. The findings in this under-researched area have been particularly rich. For the purposes of this chapter, I shall present just one of the cognition skills, which is especially relevant to DMT.

First, however, we can think back to the concepts and see how Bettina's tough culture is reflected in her direct, straightforward, fact-based communication style. Abed's relatively tender culture leads him to expect more feeling-based communication, explicit verbal encouragement, and smiles. Bettina has not developed the cognition skill which would equip her to identify this need.

A key finding in the Transcultural Competence project was the crucial role of *perceptual position flexibility*: the ability to move freely between several different points of view. I referred earlier to the four perceptual positions used in NLP (Dilts and DeLozier 2000). This fourfold classification – identification with self, other, observer or relationship – proved inadequate to map my findings. I therefore defined two further perceptual positions. 'Zero position' is an individual perspective, but not grounded in personality or ego. 'Infinity position' refers to an inclusive, transcendent identification with the whole human family, all living beings, or the cosmos (we might explore the correspondence between zero position and the idea of individual soul, infinity position and universal spirit). All six perceptual positions are critical to Transcultural Competence; many research participants found their professional practice to be compromised by their preference for certain perceptual positions and neglect of others.

Bettina's preferred positions are: first, third, zero and infinity. Her highly developed first position is reflected in her passion for her work. She is a committed member of the multidisciplinary team and often takes a stand on ethical issues if she feels that her core values may be violated. She is able to move into third position to critically reflect on her own practice and consider ethical principles. Through many years of spiritual practice she feels familiar with the freedom of zero position and the bliss of infinity. However, Bettina does not easily enter second position – the place of empathy. Second position involves feeling what the other feels; seeing the world through the other's eyes. Bettina goes through the motions of attunement, but does not easily access the empathic experience. This, combined with her passionate commitment (first position) to her value of 'giving space' and her clear thinking (third position) on ethical issues, leads her to keep a physical distance from Abed which he experiences as cold and unwelcoming. Had Bettina been able to step out of her own lifeworld and into Abed's, if only for a moment, she would have noticed his different experience of space and been aware of his disappointment and confusion.

Perceptual position flexibility is but one of the cognition skills with a central role in effective and ethical practice; such skills are the basis for developing a multidimensional, multicultural view. However, it is only a view, not yet a full-bodied engagement. The cognition skills are intrapersonal; therapeutic practice is by its very nature interpersonal.

Transcultural communication: interactive skills informed by cognition

> Maria is starting a new group in a mental health residential unit. The group members are from diverse cultural backgrounds and Maria is keen to address this openly. She wants everyone to feel included and to participate in forming the culture of the group. Maria regularly makes this explicit and invites people to speak out if anything is unacceptable from their cultural perspective. No one raises concerns and Maria takes this as a sign that no cultural difficulties have arisen. Occasionally Maria asks how people feel with the process; the answer is the same every time 'Fine!'

The fourth level of findings describes a set of vital communication skills, including meeting the other person on their ground, speaking their language – both verbal and non-verbal – and defining shared values (which may be few and far between). Almost all the dance movement therapists I have met are highly skilled in the main body of the communications skills identified by the project: the movement awareness, observation, attunement, adjustment and synchronisation that enable client and therapist to develop their unique movement dialogue, led chiefly by the client and without the need for words. However, the findings also highlight the need for more explicit verbal communication where possible: articulating unspoken assumptions and checking understanding of a radically different point of view.

In our vignette, Maria is well intentioned. She builds on her context knowledge, conceptual awareness and cognition skill to identify and address a real issue for the group. However, she does so in a way that is bound to fail. Maria is asking group members to do something they cannot do without violating their values. Several are from collectivist cultural backgrounds: to stop the group process and speak out as a lone voice would be both inconsiderate and humiliating. Some are from contexts with high power distance: to question the group process would challenge the therapist's authority. A few have high uncertainty avoidance: they feel confused by the open-ended suggestion. One or two are from tough cultures: they want to get on with the action and are not yet comfortable being asked to articulate their feelings.

After several weeks, Maria realises the hopelessness of her request. She adapts her communication by providing a structured exercise, with a 'talking stick' which is passed around to each group member, asking them to describe (rather than judge) the process they have just engaged in. By removing the request for critique and providing this clear task with everyone involved, Maria begins to realise that seldom does 'Fine!' mean 'fine'.

Contexts, concepts, cognition, communication: in the first year of the project, the Transcultural Competence model stopped there. Then I met, interviewed and observed an outstanding individual. He had extraordinary knowledge of the many cultural contexts he encountered in his work. His mastery of cultural concepts was dazzling. The agility of his cognition was astounding. His communication skills were highly developed and unusually wide-ranging. But I felt that something was missing. Further inquiry led me to conclude that his understanding, adaptability and responsiveness were in the service of a clear unspoken message: 'My culture is right, your culture is wrong; you will learn to do things my way.' The outcome was a fifth level in the model, which is the very essence of Transcultural Competence.

Transcultural consciousness: unspoken attitudes and identity

> Frank has recently moved to take up a DMT post in a community centre. He has decided to become better informed about his client population by reading about their culture, religion and history. After some weeks in his new role, Frank is troubled by sleep difficulties and feelings of nausea and disorientation. These symptoms decrease at the weekends and return during the working week. Frank is concerned; this has not happened before and bringing it to supervision seems to make no difference.

Transcultural consciousness is the fifth level of the model and in recent years has become my main focus within the project. The attitudes and identity referred to here as consciousness arise from the four other levels. However, consciousness determines how the other levels of competence are used. You can be effective by virtue of your knowledge and skill in the first four levels of the model. The fifth level makes you ethical.

Transcultural consciousness refers to a cluster of higher order capabilities. Key elements include uniting the zero and infinity perceptual positions to cultivate a fluid and inclusive sense of identity in which notions of 'us and them' dissolve: developing epistemological flexibility so that radically different worldviews can be experienced with ease; and raising and reiterating questions about global ethics. Linking these competencies is an attitude towards humanity which can best be called universal love – or kenosis – the power of which seems to be recognised in all the world's cultures (Garrard Post et al. 2002). This is in turn underpinned by transcendent states that can be strengthened at a neurological level through certain kinds of spiritual practice (Varela et al. 1991; Austin 1999). We see that Transcultural consciousness, although harder to capture in words than the previous four levels, can also be actively developed.

What has all this to do with Frank's misery? This brings us full circle to the multicultural self. Just as context knowledge needs to be applied to self, so does this *inclusive consciousness*. Frank sees himself as an open, accepting and caring person. As a gay man living far from the country of his birth, he has critically examined notions of culture and identity. He practises meditation and actively nurtures the knowledge, skills and attitudes that correspond to the five levels of the Transcultural Competence model.

After months of confusion and moments of despair, Frank decides that he needs to enter a deeper exploration of the issues. Through facilitated movement improvisation, letting his body do the thinking, Frank finds himself pacing the studio with the strutting gait and rasping voice of a persecutor. This leads him to ask questions. He discovers that in his grandparents' generation, his ancestors were involved in an ethnic conflict which is part of the history of the community with which he now works. These power struggles live on in Frank's body memory; reawakened, they demand to be addressed. Frank summons the courage to explore beyond the boundaries of his familiar sense of self and takes more time for quiet meditation. In doing so he acknowledges and extends loving kindness to the different parts of his own heritage – persecutor and victim alike. Only then do his psychosomatic symptoms pass. Writing of our Cultural Embodiment work, Sandra Reeve and I surmised:

> The body reveals its knowledge to the mind. Movement releases transgenerational, cellular memory and it becomes clear that we don't know how much we know, about ourselves, our ancestors, our stories and our histories.
>
> (Boas and Reeve 2003: 21)

In the same report we highlighted the importance of 'identifying difference and power relations within ourselves, as a means of ultimately honouring our own different cultures as equal to one another' (Boas and Reeve 2003: 21).

This attentive, loving listening to all our ancestral voices, this inner democracy, may be the basis for effective, ethical DMT practice, as it is the basis for a democratic, multicultural society. Just as the therapeutic group may be viewed as a social microcosm, we can find within our own selves a microcosm of our group practice. And here we see the magnitude of the challenge. For which of us extends loving kindness to all parts of self? Who does not deny the existence of our own censored voices? Do we not project the darkness elsewhere, onto our own foreign bodies, our inner outsider, our hidden 'other'?

No body

The title of this chapter belies my view of the cultural dimension of humanity. For – as others have clearly shown – there is no 'body' of culture (le Goff

1989; Davis 1997; Latour 2004; Shilling 2004). There are only cultural bodies – people moving – and even these are always in formation and transformation, products and creators of a larger – a larger what? If not a body, what metaphor will serve? Here is the crux. The very idea of culture limits and divides us. Yet only the dominant can indulge in cultural ignorance. To avoid becoming naive mini-tyrants and colonisers, we must acknowledge culture. And we must transcend it. How do we hold both: body and no body; culture and no culture? The answer may be in the space we make for these seeming contradictions, within the present moment that is both coming into being and passing away. Paradoxically perhaps, our practice may be all the more ethical when we relax the boundaries of the self and give our full attention to the here and now of the myriad diversity between us and within us. This glorious, crashing, stellar multiplicity of incommensurable experiences, beliefs, memories and dreams; the infinite variety of lifeworlds we strive to know and only ever glimpse in passing.

Implications for DMT

For the individual dance movement therapist, I have outlined elsewhere some suggestions for nurturing one's own Transcultural Competence (Boas 2004); nor is this the place to discuss how the model translates into specific methods and techniques. Here, I shall comment on some broader implications as I see them.

Training

There is scope for DMT training and professional development to include more systematic and comprehensive education in the knowledge, skills and attitudes of Transcultural Competence. Training institutions could provide reading lists for developing the relevant knowledge base, drawing on research literature in anthropology, education, transcultural nursing, counselling and psychiatry, organisational behaviour and cultural studies (D'Ardenne and Mahtani 1989; Hofstede 1991; Orbe 1997; Moodley 1999; Warnier 2001; Miyaji 2002; Rousseau 2002; Arpin 2003; Coker 2003; De La Mata and Cubero 2003; Gard 2003; Gebru and Willman 2003; Butz and Besio 2004; Glittenberg 2004). In addition, the core cognition and communication skills can be actively developed in clinical skills training. Finally, experiential workshops can enable deep, personal exploration of transcultural consciousness – a necessary preparation for professional practice across cultures.

Supervision

Providers of supervision can use the five levels of the model to extend the range of responses to case material. For instance, the therapist in supervision might be encouraged to identify their own cultural contexts, develop their context knowledge, study and apply cultural concepts, tell the story of a session from the six perceptual positions, role play client interactions, or expand their consciousness. A multimodal approach to supervision can support this, incorporating movement, dialogue, drawing, mask work, stillness, silence, and so on.

Professional identity

The professionalisation of DMT is accompanied by much debate and soul-searching about our collective identity. We would do well to raise our cultural self-awareness as a community of practice. Broadly speaking, DMT professional culture is low power distance, low uncertainty avoidance, individualist and tender. How does our professional culture shape the movement culture of our DMT groups? To what extent do we require our clients to adapt to our unwritten rules? If we claim to be reflective, critical practitioners, we need to address these questions in our daily practice. Dare we acknowledge our cultural prejudices and limitations as a profession? I speculate that we need to do so. In particular, we can become much more effective in working with other communities of practice – the medical psychiatrists, for example, with their relatively high power distance, high uncertainty avoidance, tough professional culture. The degree to which DMT has a clear voice and strong presence within multidisciplinary teams is partly a function of our level of transcultural competence.

Suggestions for further research

Whilst many dance movement therapists around the world work in multicultural settings with skill and sensitivity, the published DMT literature pays scant attention to culture. DMT has ethnographic roots through Franziska Boas – pioneer of dance as therapy, anthropologist and daughter of the great anthropologist and anti-racist Franz Boas. Both explored the relationships between culture, healing and dance (Boas 1888; Boas 1944). However, DMT has known only a brief flowering of publications on culture (e.g. Hanna 1990; Antinori and Moore 1997; Dosamantes-Beaudry 1997; Coseo 1997; Callaghan 1998; Dokter 1998; Subramanyam 1998; Dosamantes-Beaudry 1999). In these writings, culture tends to be reified in national or racial terms and presented as a basis for personal identity, determined by ancestry or childhood environment, which may be lost or fragmented and which the therapist aims to understand in order to overcome prejudice, raise self-awareness, or adapt her communication style to match that of the client. Even current research addresses context knowledge rather than a broader transcultural framework (e.g. Sakiyama and Koch 2003). With this narrow research base, almost any inquiry into the role of culture in DMT will strengthen our stance. My recommendations for future research are as follows.

First, we need to conduct ethnographic research into *the culture of DMT* as a community of practice, with particular attention to its relations with other professional communities and with client populations. This should include a consideration of power relations and their impact on DMT practice.

Second, we would do well to understand the *group as a social microcosm* in which therapist and client work together to dance a world into being. This builds on an understanding of cultural agency: whilst we are shaped and constrained by the socio-cultural circumstances of our birth and development, we are also active agents of culture, continually co-creating those same circumstances of our coming-into-being (Bourdieu 1977; Giddens 1991; Clark-Rapley 1999; Nellhaus 2004).

Third, we should examine *leadership in DMT group therapy*. This theme was researched in the 1980s, with a restricted definition of leadership (Johnson *et al.* 1983; Koch 1984). New research could develop an understanding of shared leadership that encompasses both the therapist's role and group members' ongoing co-creation of the group's movement, dynamics and culture.

Fourth, we can conduct *evaluations of professional DMT practice across cultures*. This could combine self-assessment, observation and interview to triangulate user, practitioner and third-party perspectives, so as to validate findings from the Transcultural Competence project. In particular, the idea that there is an optimal level of conceptual certainty – as discussed above – merits further research.

Fifth, we can develop *movement-based cultural dimensions concepts*. This could integrate anthropological studies of the body with existing movement analysis tools and so refine the interpretation of movement in DMT. Since the ground-breaking work of anthropologists such as Gregory Bateson, Margaret Mead and Edward T. Hall, in the first half of the twentieth century, proxemic studies have highlighted differences in how people of varying cultures experience and manage movement and interpersonal space (Bateson 1980; Hall 1981). One could build on this rich literature by conducting a meta-analysis of ethnographic studies of movement in specific cultural contexts, together with the more universalistic movement analysis and cultural dimensions literatures. This would be a basis for identifying patterns and distinctions in cultural movement and exploring their possible significance in relation to notions of power, purpose and other social constructs. The resulting movement-based cultural dimensions model could be used in theoretical and practical training of therapists working in multicultural settings. In developing such a model, we need to protect the tension between universalistic and particularistic perspectives, as exemplified in Richard Schechner's careful discussion of the future of ritual (Schechner 1993).

Finally, we can contribute to a *multidimensional understanding of the human body* by carrying out DMT practitioner research together with a much needed survey of relevant primary research in anthropology, cross-cultural psychology and neuroscience. The human body – culturally created and creative – moves at the heart of DMT and deserves to be better understood.

Note

1   A group discussion was facilitated at the start of each workshop, defining what confidentiality would mean in practice. The principles generated and agreed by the group were reiterated and confirmed by the participants. Please note that all individuals and cases in this chapter are fictional and illustrative.

References

Adair, G. (1984) The Hawthorne effect: a reconsideration of the methodological artifact, *Journal of Applied Psychology* 69, 2, 334–345.

Antinori, D. and Moore, P. (1997) The controlled approach exercise in cultural diversity training with clinicians, *The Arts in Psychotherapy* 24, 2, 173–182.

Arpin, J. (2003) Masters of their conditions: at the crossroads of health, culture and performance, *Transcultural Psychiatry* 40, 3, 299–328.

Austin, J. H. (1999) *Zen and the Brain: Toward an Understanding of Meditation and Consciousness*. Cambridge, MA: MIT Press.

Bandler, R. and Grinder J. (1975a) *The Structure of Magic – I: A Book About Language and Therapy*. Palo Alto, CA: Science and Behavior Books.

—— (1975b) *Patterns of the Hypnotic Techniques of Milton H. Erickson, M.D.*, Vol. 1. Cupertino, CA: Meta Publications.

—— (1979) *Frogs into Princes*. Moab, UT: Real People Press.

Bateson, G. (1980) *Naven*. London: Wildwood House.

Best, P. A. (2000) Theoretical diversity and clinical collaboration: reflections by a dance/movement therapist, *The Arts in Psychotherapy* 27, 3, 197–211.

Boas, F. (1888) On certain songs and dances of the Kwakiutl of British Columbia, *Journal of American Folklore* 1, 49–64.

Boas, F. (1944) *The Function of Dance in Human Society*. New York: Boas School.

Boas, S. (1989) *Transcultural Competence*, self-published handbook. Online. Available HTTP: <http://www.boastl.com> (updated 2001; accessed 12 May 2004).

—— (2004) Developing transcultural competence, *e-motion: Quarterly Newsletter of the Association for Dance Movement Therapy*, 14, 5.

Boas, S. and Reeve, S. (2003) Cultural embodiment: reflections on an ADMT conference workshop, *e-motion: Quarterly of the Association for Dance Movement Therapy (ADMT) UK*, 14, 4.

Bourdieu, P. (1977) *Outline of a Theory of Practice*. Cambridge: Cambridge University Press.

Butz, D. and Besio, K. (2004) The value of autoethnography for field research in transcultural settings, *Professional Geographer* 56, 3, 350–360.

Callaghan, K. (1998) In limbo: movement psychotherapy with refugees and asylum seekers, in D. Dokter (ed.) *Arts Therapists, Refugees and Migrants: Reaching Across Borders*. London: Jessica Kingsley.

Clark-Rapley, E. (1999) Dancing bodies: moving beyond Marxian views of human activity relations and consciousness, *Journal for the Theory of Social Behaviour* 29, 2, 89–108.

Coker, E.M. (2003) Narrative strategies in medical discourse constructing the psychiatric 'case' in a non-western setting, *Social Science and Medicine* 57, 5, 905–916.

Coseo, A. (1997) Developing cultural awareness for creative arts therapies, *The Arts in Psychotherapy* 24, 2, 145–157.

D'Ardenne, P. and Mahtani, A. (1989) *Transcultural Counselling in Action*. London: Sage.

Davis, A. D. (1997) Identity notes Part II: redeeming the body politic, *Harvard Latino* 2, 267.

De La Mata, M. L. and Cubero, M. (2003) Cultural psychology approaches to the study of the relationship between mind and culture, *Infancia y Aprendizaje* 26, 2, 181–199.

Dilts, R. and DeLozier, J. (2000) *Encyclopedia of Systemic NLP and NLP New Coding*. Online. Available HTTP: <http://nlpuniversitypress.com/html2/PaPo30.html> (accessed 12 May 2004).

Dokter, D. (1998) Being a migrant, working with migrants: issues of identity and embodiment, in D. Dokter (ed.) *Arts Therapists, Refugees and Migrants: Reaching Across Borders*. London: Jessica Kingsley.

Dosamantes-Beaudry, I. (1997) Embodying a cultural identity, *The Arts in Psychotherapy* 24, 2, 129–135.

—— (1999) Divergent cultural self construals: implications for the practice of dance/movement therapy, *The Arts in Psychotherapy* 26, 4, 225–231.

Gard, M. (2003) Being someone else: using dance in anti-oppressive teaching, *Educational Review* 55, 2, 211–223.

Gardner, H. (1983) *Frames of Mind: The Theory of Multiple Intelligences*. New York: Basic Books.

Garrard Post, S., Underwood, L. G., Schloss, J. and Hurlbut, W. B. (2002) *Altruism and Altruistic Love: Science, Philosophy and Religion in Dialogue*. Oxford: Oxford University Press.

Gebru, H. and Willman, A. (2003) A research-based didactic model for education to promote culturally competent nursing care in Sweden, *Journal of Transcultural Nursing* 14, 1, 55–61.

Gendlin, E. T. (1996) *Focusing-Oriented Psychotherapy: A Manual of the Experiential Method*. New York: Guilford Press.

Giddens, A. (1991) *Modernity and Self-Identity: Self and Society in the Late Modern age*. Cambridge: Polity Press.

Gilligan, S. G. (1997) *The Courage to Love: Principles and Practices of Self-Relations Psychotherapy*. New York: Norton.

Glaser, B. and Strauss, A. (1967) *The Discovery of Grounded Theory*. Chicago: Aldine.

Glittenberg, J. (2004) A Transdisciplinary, transcultural model for health care, *Journal of Transcultural Nursing* 15, 1, 6–10.

Good, B. J. (1994) *Medicine, Rationality, and Experience: An Anthropological Perspective*. Cambridge: Cambridge University Press.

Habermas, J. (1987) *The Theory of Communicative Action, Vol. 2: Lifeworld and System: A Critique of Functionalist Reason*. Boston: Beacon Press.

Hall, E. T. (1981) *The Silent Language*. New York: Anchor Books, Doubleday.

Hanna, J. L. (1990) Anthropological perspectives for dance/movement therapy, *American Journal of Dance Therapy* 12, 2, 115–126.

Hervey, L. W. (2000) *Artistic Inquiry in Dance Movement Therapy: Creative Research Alternatives*. Illinois: Charles Thomas.

Hofstede, G. (1991) *Cultures and Organisations: Software of the Mind*. New York: McGraw-Hill.

Johnson, D. R., Sandel, S. L. and Eichel, V. (1983) Structural aspects of group leadership styles, *American Journal of Dance Therapy* 6, 17–30.

Kirschenbaum, H. and Henderson, V. L. (eds) (1990) *Carl Rogers: Dialogues*. London: Constable.

Koch, N. S. (1984) Content analysis of leadership variables in dance therapy, *American Journal of Dance Therapy* 7, 58–75.

Latour, B. (2004) How to talk about the body? The normative dimension of science studies, *Body and Society* 10, 2, 205–229.

Le Goff, J. (1989) Head or heart? The political use of body metaphors in the Middle Ages, in M. Feher, R. Nadddaff and N. Tazi (eds) *Fragments for a History of the Human Body*. New York: Zone Press.

Loughran, E. (2003) The therapists' use of body as a medium for transference and countertransference communication, *Dissertation Abstracts International, Section B, Sciences and Engineering*, 63, 10-B, 4911.

McLeod, J. (2001) *Qualitative Research in Counselling and Psychotherapy*. Newbury Park, CA: Sage.

McNiff, S. (1986) Freedom of research and artistic inquiry, *The Arts in Psychotherapy* 13, 4, 285–292.

—— (1998) *Art-Based Research*. London: Jessica Kingsley.

Mayo, E. (1933) *The Human Problems of an Industrial Civilization*. New York: Macmillan.

Merry, S. E. (2003) Human-rights law and the demonization of culture. *Anthropology News* February 2003. Available HTTP: <http://home.comcast.net/~drduvall/HumanRights.htm> (accessed 12 May 2004).

Miyaji, N. T. (2002) Shifting identities and transcultural psychiatry, *Transcultural Psychiatry* 39, 2, 173–195.

Moodley, R. (1999) Challenges and transformations: counselling in a multicultural context, *International Journal for the Advancement of Counselling* 21, 2, 139–152.

Muran, C. J. (ed.) (2001) *Self-Relations in the Psychotherapy Process*. Washington, DC: American Psychological Association.

Nellhaus, T. (2004) From embodiment to agency cognitive science, critical realism, and communication frameworks, *Journal of Critical Realism* 3, 1, 103–132.

Orbe, M. P. (1997) *Constructing Co-Cultural Theory: An Explication of Culture, Power, and Communication*. London: Sage.

Payne, H. (ed.) (1993) *Handbook of Inquiry in the Arts Therapies: One River, Many Currents*. London: Jessica Kingsley.

Rogers, C. (1975) Empathic: an unappreciated way of being, *The Counselling Psychologist* 5, 2, 2–10.

Rousseau, C. (2002) Uncertainty and transcultural clinical practice, *Evolution Psychiatrique* 67, 4, 764–774.

Sakiyama, Y. and Koch, N. S. (2003) Touch in dance therapy in Japan, *American Journal of Dance Therapy* 25, 2, 79–95.

Sandel, S. (1993) The process of empathic reflection in dance therapy, in S. Sandel, S. Chaiklin and A. Lohn (eds) *Foundations of Dance/Movement Therapy: The Life and Work of Marian Chace*. Columbia, MA: Marian Chace Memorial Fund of the American Dance Therapy Association.

Schechner, R. (1993) *The Future of Ritual: Writings on Culture and Performance*. New York: Routledge.

Schutz, A. and Luckmann, T (1973) *The Structures of the Life-World*. Illinois: Northwestern University Press.

Senghas, R.J. and Monaghan, L. (2002) Signs of their times: deaf communities and the culture of language, *Annual Review of Anthropology* 31, 69–97.

Sergiovanni, T. J. (2004) *The Lifeworld of Leadership: Creating Culture, Community, and Personal Meaning in Our Schools*. San Francisco: Jossey-Bass.

Shayer, M. (1992) Problems and issues in intervention studies, in A. Demetriou, M. Shayer and A. Efklides (eds) *Neo-Piagetian Theories of Cognitive Development: Implications and Applications for Education*. London: Routledge.

Shilling, C. (2004) *The Body in Culture, Technology and Society*. London: Sage.

Sloan, T.S. (1999) The colonization of the lifeworld and the destruction of meaning, *Radical Psychology* 1, 2. Online. Available HTTP: <http://www.radpsynet.org/journal/vol1-2/Sloan.html> (accessed 12 May 2004).

Subramanyam, A. (1998) Dance movement therapy with South Asian women in Britain, in D. Dokter (ed.) *Arts Therapists, Refugees and Migrants: Reaching Across Borders*. London: Jessica Kingsley.

Varela, F., Thompson, E. and Rosch, E. (1991) *The Embodied Mind: Cognitive Science and Human Experience*. Cambridge, MA: MIT Press.

Warnier, J-P. (2001) A Praxeological Approach to Subjectivation in a Material World, *Journal of Material Culture,* 6, 1, 5–24.

Chapter 9

Another royal road

Freudian thought applied to authentic movement

Kedzie Penfield

The interpretation of dreams is the royal road to a knowledge of the unconscious activities of the mind.

(Freud 1909/1991: 769)

Introduction

Freud recognised words (which he termed parapraxies or Freudian slips) and dreams as direct expressions of the unconscious. He also saw his work as a process of making the unconscious more conscious through the relationship between the therapist and the client (Freud 1924). There are two points I would like to make with this in mind:

- Movement, like a dream, is another 'royal road' which offers access to the unconscious.
- Words and movement are two different languages[1] through which my clients and I explore their inner worlds. Freud and his followers offer concepts, which help to do this work and it is a few of these concepts I would like to apply to clinical examples given in this chapter.

The selection of concepts discussed here is based on those I have found useful in clinical practice. Much has been written about all of them (the unconscious, free association, transference/countertransference, projection) so the main thrust of this chapter is to exemplify them through clinical material. However, I will discuss my understanding of these and related concepts.

Movement psychotherapy

Psychotherapy is a widely used term meaning different things to different practitioners. For me it is a psychodynamically based theory used in work between a client and a therapist. Like many of my colleagues, I have adopted the term 'movement psychotherapy' to name the work that we do with our clients: usually a mixture of dance and movement-based therapy using various psychological frameworks such as Jungian, Freudian, Adlerian, person-centred or core process (Payne 1992). As I trained as a psychoanalytical psychotherapist in a training programme that bases its work on Freud and object relations theories, I am heavily influenced by that particular approach.[2]

The movement[3] psychotherapy in which I am involved takes place in private practice with individuals who are, for the most part, functioning normally in their professional and personal lives. The work is about helping the client to develop a better relationship between her internal and external world, although the presenting problems are usually to do with stress in relationships or work. For instance, an individual comes complaining about her[4] husband but soon finds herself talking (or moving) about her relationships to her brothers or her father – perhaps mixing up their names (a Freudian slip) or becoming angry with me when I appear to be similar to one of these relatives (transference).

Soon these experiences in our sessions begin to open questions, insights, dreams and movement reminiscent of childhood times and she becomes aware of her fear, hatred, anger, love for these men and the patterns they and she share. The stories from a dynamic unconscious begin to be discovered, giving her more choice to consider what she wants to do or change in her deciding behaviour. Her conscious actions become more informed by her unconscious processes rather than made on impulse, reaction or patterns that simply repeat themselves over and over again.

The unconscious

Freud began the development of a theory that established the importance of the unconscious in the human mind and a technique to consider it:

> The aim of our efforts may be expressed in various formulas – making conscious the unconscious, removing the repressions, filling in the gaps in memory: they all amount to the same thing.
>
> (Freud 1924: 442)

One of the ways that the unconscious is expressed, besides through dreams, is the parapraxis ('slip') both verbal and non-verbal which he called 'inadvertent actions' (Freud 1901). He describes several non-verbal 'slips' that have meaning such as when a colleague, Stekel, described how he inadvertently untied the bow holding an attractive woman's dress together:

> I was not aware of any dishonourable intentions, yet I had performed this unskilful movement with a conjuror's sleight of hand.
>
> (Freud 1901: 167)

Stekel's thought reveals his desire for the woman which, until that moment, was unconscious and only became clear through a movement whose meaning could not be avoided.

I suggest that spontaneous movement or spontaneous speaking can both be direct expressions of the unconscious. The movement in authentic movement (or the words free associating to a dream, an experience, or another mental event) could be seen as a fluid, continuous 'slip' of the unconscious into consciousness. Payne (2003, 2006) notes this phenomenon in authentic movement describing it as: 'a completely self-directed approach in which participants may discover a movement pathway that offers a bridge between the conscious and the unconscious' (Payne 2003: 33).

Two forms for two languages

Unconscious material can be expressed through many languages that form a 'bridge' between unconscious and conscious experience – visual art, movement, music and literature – but this chapter is devoted to words and movement. I am using the word 'Form' to mean the structure of physical arrangement and procedures in a session. For example, in psychoanalytic work a chaise longue or bed is used on which the client semi-reclines or lies, and speaks, facing away from the therapist, for 50 minutes. All discussion takes place in this Form; except for handing over invoices or receipts or other such business, no transactions take place face to face except in the first and last sessions. There are exceptions to this, such as when someone does not wish to use the couch, but here I am describing the usual way it is used in psychoanalytical psychotherapy.

The Form used for authentic movement is an open space in which the client moves with her eyes closed for an agreed period of time. When the time is past (anywhere from seconds to hours) the observer (called a 'witness' in authentic movement) indicates the end of the move by saying it is past or ringing a bell. Following this, the mover may take a time of transition (thinking, writing, drawing) before coming to join the witness and speak of her experience. The observer usually remains silent until the mover asks for witnessing and this is given with great attention to what the mover has said; what she has chosen to speak about and the words she has used. All of this parallels the psychoanalytical psychotherapist who also listens more than speaks and tries to use words that the client has used when she does speak. Similarly, in both these Forms time is used as an external boundary. For example, no matter what movement is taking place or what is being spoken about, within the limitation of courtesy the therapist indicates that the time is past. In both Forms there is often a blanket available, on the couch or at the side of the space.

It seems to me there is a contiguous relationship between these two Forms. If we put them on a continuum with what I shall call couch work on one end

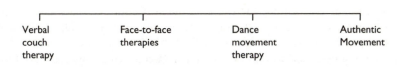

Verbal	Face-to-face	Dance	Authentic
couch	therapies	movement	Movement
therapy		therapy	

Figure 9.1 Verbal to Movement Form continuum

of the continuum and authentic movement on the other, we could place face-to-face verbal therapies next to the couch work end; then put dance movement therapy next before placing authentic movement at the other end of the continuum (see Figure 9.1).

Many verbal therapies that use the face-to-face Form use concepts such as transference, countertransference and projection which Freud discovered in the couch work Form. Many dance movement therapists use improvisational structures which are similar to authentic movement in guiding the client to move in a spontaneous, unedited manner, and these result in spontaneous movement expressive of inner states (Penfield 1992). In this chapter, I am concentrating theoretically on the two Forms at each end of the continuum. In practice most dance movement therapists, including myself, will use a mixture of Forms so I will also include them in the clinical material below. For instance, music may help to crystallise the expression of the improvised movement while authentic movement usually takes place in silence or with sounds made by the mover. Words may clarify or interpret a movement idea or the therapist may offer a movement to embody an emotion or mood emerging through the verbal or non-verbal events taking place between therapist and client (Penfield 1992). In contrast, in authentic movement the witness does not move in this interactive manner with the mover.

Just as the client on the couch does not see the analyst behind them, the mover in authentic movement has her eyes closed so does not see the witness.[5] I believe the two languages are equally powerful: the expressive paths between the conscious and unconscious worlds no longer need to vie for a more important place in the order of things. Authentic movement provides a space in which the grammar of the individual's movement language can develop; just as lying on a couch in psychoanalytic psychotherapy provides a space for the grammar of the individual's dreams to develop. Perhaps it does not matter which language is used, but there are several aspects to consider:

• Both therapist and client will have preferences for one or other language, a greater or lesser sense of safety in one or other, and this needs to be respected.
• Individuals who are trained in these areas (for example, dance or literature) often use their technical skills to defend themselves against the very material they are trying to access. For instance, this could be the case with the dancer who executes aesthetically pleasing shapes or gives

a sense of performing for the external world rather than listening to spontaneous movement impulses from her internal world; or the academic who constantly refers to theoretical explanations rather than allowing her mind to roam freely in a non-censoring way. They are both struggling with their previous learning and may have to learn to let go of these technical skills in order to engage fully in the evolution of a new relationship with themselves and their history.

• The transition from one language to the other can be problematic. For example, if someone is speaking it can be difficult to interrupt and suggest moving and vice versa (see the clinical example below for one way to overcome this difficulty).

The question is when to intervene with a suggestion or direction. Going back to our continuum the two extremes invite the client to participate in solo expression during a session with little or no comment, direction or suggestion from the therapist. This will vary widely of course and depend on the style of the individuals and their working relationship, but both forms have specific guidelines which restrict the action and words of the therapist more than the two modes of work in the centre of the continuum.

Each language is, of course, very different in approach, each has its own training and discipline, either of which take years to understand. Training enables me as the clinician to reflect on a session after it has occurred. For instance, I use Laban Movement Analysis in movement psychotherapy as a skill base to observe the movement that I see, just as I use writing as a skill base to record and consider the words I have heard. The Laban framework is also a useful one (Schmais and White 1989) to learn in order to analyse and understand one's own movement character, just as one is required to engage in personal therapy to understand one's psychological/emotional self.

The danger with the subject of this chapter is that it avoids the power and character of movement in and of itself. I do not mean that movement and words are the same or interchangeable. Words may give a kind of insight, movement may shift a dynamic memory that we could not put into words. Parallel to dreams, that other 'royal road', movement, has its own logic, grammar, narrative and characteristics unique to each individual. All of these can be vehicles to explore the inner world through a free associative process. I hope the character of movement in its own right is evident in the clinical vignettes presented in this chapter.[6]

Free association

Freud proposed that the client on the couch engages in a kind of stream of consciousness monologue in which 'free association' could play a large part and give information about the internal story of the individual:

He adopted the unheard-of plan of simply asking the person whose mind he was investigating to say whatever came into his head.

(Strachey 1962: 18)

Gomez (1997) describes this Form as:

The patient, lying on a couch with minimum distraction, the analyst out of view, simply gives words to her awareness. The analyst listens with non-prescriptive, non-judging 'free floating attention' for the blocks, themes, modes and trends in the patient's words, manner and silences.

(Gomez 1997: 26)

There seems to me to be a parallel process in movement. Escobar (2003) has put this succinctly:

Movement association is like a stream of consciousness in movement: I invite my clients to let whatever comes have its space and time – it may develop it may not. Your body will take a movement and flow with it – let that happen.

(Escobar 2003: 1)

This is similar to the process of unedited speaking described above. It is also equally difficult. The lack of eye contact in both Forms usually frees the two individuals from the ordinary constraints of interaction, such as looking for a certain response or trying to guess from a facial expression what the other may be thinking. However, most of us as clients find this open, uncensored expression of our inner selves difficult to begin with. It takes time to build the skill and trust which enables such concentration and open bridging between the inner and outer worlds. Whitehouse (1978), known as the originator of authentic movement, commented in an interview with Sherman:

The reality of the inner life is where I work and it comes out in movement. I am looking at the physical movement as a revelation, as a show of the inner thing.

(Whitehouse 1978: 30)

The witness, or therapist, observes the movement just as the psychoanalytical psychotherapist listens, in a very particular way. Whitehouse goes on:

Therefore I am not saying 'The shoulders are up, the mouth is this way.' I take that in but it's minor. What I am looking at is the psychic attitude displayed by the physical movement.

(Whitehouse 1978: 31)

Gomez (1997) describes the therapist using her attention to become aware of 'modes and trends'. Similarly Janet Adler comments during her film, *Still Looking*:

> Patterns emerge: Bonnie finds herself upside down over and over again. When Susan feels emotional she often brings her hands to her neck. Kate's pattern: she moves most truthfully when her head is covered.
>
> (Adler and Aginsky 1988: 15 minutes in)

As a psychoanalytical psychotherapist, I may look for themes and patterns in the verbal stories, memories and dreams told to me by the client on the couch. There is a process of 'getting to know' the internal voice of the client through this unstructured, free association, whether through words or movement.

The use of the word 'authentic' in the name of this Form is interesting and perhaps misleading. It could mean the more direct the expression between the unconscious and the movement appears to be, the more 'authentic' the movement, or 'truthful' to use Adler's word in her film (1988). Just as one may hear a difference between edited and unedited, free associative processes in the spoken material, there may be an observable difference between the movements that are more spontaneous and those which are narrative or mimetic. However, most colleagues with whom I have spoken do not appear to have a clear definition of which movement is 'authentic', free associative or directly from the unconscious, just as most psychoanalytic psychotherapists will not have concrete criteria for identifying what is spoken directly from the unconscious.

Authentic movement invites an individual (or a group) to close their eyes and follow whatever movement impulse comes into their bodies. Janet Adler describes this as follows:

> In the dark and silence, journeys begin with feelings, images sounds memories thoughts and sensations. Gates to the unconscious open as movers descend.
>
> (Adler and Aginsky 1988: five minutes in)

In the film we then see her clients engage in extraordinarily expressive movements (though we do not know their meaning), which seem totally spontaneous and unchoreographed. Similarly, I may not know the meaning of a dream, a memory or a body gesture of my client until I know more about her story and our relationship. The context of the relationship between myself, the client and her past is crucial to understanding these expressive events. Thus my experience as a therapist in a psychoanalytic role or in an authentic movement witnessing role is exactly the same. When I am witnessing a body moving the Form is different from that of sitting behind my couch listening to a client speaking, but the experience within me feels the same. For instance the following clinical example took place in movement but, as I will show, could have taken place verbally.

Anne

Anne came to work with me as an art therapy student who needed to engage with personal therapy in her training. She was 25 years old and a talented artist who felt she wanted to work with other people therapeutically. She was attractive, well educated, and seemed to have few problems; she claimed she was only doing this therapy for her training. We met twice a week and, after about six months, she realised that she was in the work for herself as well as for her training. This session occurred about nine months after we had begun.

On arrival, Anne said that she had been at a party the night before and asked if she could begin the session with a move. We agreed on ten minutes and as soon as the bell rang she closed her eyes and began swaying from side to side. After a few minutes she lost her balance a little and swung into a turn; she began gesturing and turning in what looked almost like a dance with her arms opening invitingly to the space around her. She became more and more dance-like in her motions and finished with a flourish as the time came to an end. I felt I had watched a lovely (in my judgement) performance.

Afterward, she spoke to me of her enjoyment of moving and what a good time she had at the beginning of the party the night before. She asked me to verbally witness her dancing mode of movement and I said I felt I was in the presence of a performance that I enjoyed. She thought for a moment then asked to move again – this time for 15 minutes.

She began with a similar swaying but this time it developed into turning her head as if looking for someone. This pulled her body into turns going first one way then the other until she added her arms which opened her upper body widely to one side, then pulled it together into a closed ('shielded' was the word that came into my mind) shape on the other. This increased until it included a level change going to the floor where she sat rocking in a sort of neutral verticality until a few moments before the end of the movement time when she reached out her hand as if meeting someone. After the bell rang to end the movement, it took her a few moments to open her eyes and return to the side of the space.

As she spoke it was clear that something emotional had happened. She began to cry when remembering her open/close movement as 'putting on a show' on the one hand and 'hiding' on the other. She described her sense of shyness in being seen to move in such a simple, quiet movement as rocking. She commented that the end of the movement felt very different for her. She had arrived at a quiet place inside herself from which she wanted to meet the person she saw the night before, without performing or trying to prove anything. She did not ask for any witnessing from me, rather she tried to say how new it felt to simply move, knowing I was there, and not 'show' me something.

I did not say very much as it seemed to me that something had shifted both in her relationship to herself and to me. She had changed from seeing me as the judging (albeit benign) parent to a supportive witness. I felt this resulted in her accepting more of herself as a vulnerable individual rather than as a competent, beautiful performer.

My interpretation that her movement was a performance could also be seen as a countertransference reaction on my part. I identified (Klein 1945, discussed in Hinshelwood 1989: 179–204) with her need for an audience and this experience, verbalised to her, brought a realisation to her of how she used performance to relate to other people – a behaviour which she wished to change. The transference from her inner world of a performer/audience relationship into our session or, in using another concept, the projection of her parental figures onto me which I then experienced (countertransference) as an appreciative audience, enabled us to understand her performing self as a defence against a more vulnerable aspect of herself. This is, of course, a positive transference experience which is usually easier to handle than a negative or destructive transference for both therapist and client.

However the concept and the way it works to move the process along is the same no matter what the material or Form used. Etchegoyan (1991) states it clearly:

> The moment the transference is resolved, the patient is able to face his problems differently from before.
>
> (Etchegoyen 1991: 266)

He describes the therapist's responses, often called reciprocal or countertransference, as phenomena resulting from the analytic setting:

> The setting is instituted precisely so that these phenomena can come into being: for the patient to develop his transference and for the analyst to accompany him in the sense of a musical counterpoint, resonating to what comes initially from the patient.
>
> (Etchegoyan 1991: 268)

Perhaps this took place between Anne and myself in this piece of work. It could have taken place verbally as well in the following (hypothetical) manner: Anne is on the couch recounting the fact that she went to a party the night before this session. Partly due to a dream she has in the early morning, she begins to free associate to that event and remembers other parties she attended as a child. This leads on to memories of being dressed up by a servant and asked to perform at the party, reciting poems and stories she has learned. I think about her transference and wonder if I am the parent or servant in her mind at this moment. My feeling in the moment (my counter-transference) is one of admiration for this charming and interesting person. This brings me to ask her if she feels she must perform for me to keep my interest. The question strikes a chord with Anne who then muses about her experience of parties as a metaphor for many of her relationships and she eventually comes back to a specific person she met at the party the night before. She begins to think (and feel) differently about herself in that situation with that person and in relation to the other people she met there.

I cannot claim the transference was 'resolved' in the way Etchegoyan (1991) may mean, but the concepts of transference, countertransference and projection helped me track a process of discovery for Anne which could have taken place in either Form. The concept of projection overlaps with transference and can also be applied to either Form.

> *Projection* Lit. throwing in front of oneself. Hence its use . . . to mean 'viewing a mental image as objective reality.'
>
> (Rycroft 1995: 139)

In describing a 'witness circle' (when one or more movers have several individuals witnessing their movement) Adler writes:

> The mover can project her experiences of parents, siblings, or other pri-mary figures in her life onto two or three witnesses. She can embody her projections safely in such a format, allowing the presence of more than one witness to affect her work.
>
> (Adler 2002: 96).

It seems to me the client described above did exactly that; she projected her need for an audience onto me which she was then able to think about both verbally and physically.

One difference between the guidelines in authentic movement and those in psychoanalytic work is the use of interpretation. In couch work it is considered as part of the technique but it is not usually used in authentic movement. This difference is exemplified in the example above: within the authentic movement Form I would not have asked if she felt she had to perform for me after the move. I would simply report my experience, as witness, of her performance as I did. Perhaps this is a question of technical procedure. I suspect it is never possible to engage with another individual's expression without interpretation, projection or judgement. Using the con-cepts of transference and projection the therapist/witness can use her internal reactions to inform herself about the client's internal process.

The debate about when and how to offer something from oneself as a therapist verbally continues in both fields of work. The psychoanalytical psychotherapist is classically silent, only offering comments which may help the thought process of the client or raise her awareness of some particular issue. The witness is also silent and usually remains still and outside the moving area of the mover-client. However, there are exceptions to these guidelines and the choices made probably have to do with the style and temperament of the two individuals involved in the process. For instance, my statement that I had experienced a beautiful performance was an opinion of my own which, one could argue, I should have contained and not shared with the client. Since the question did seem to help the client carry her work forward, however, it was an appropriate intervention.

To return to the realm of movement in relation to the process, the following vignette is explored the other way around; the actual event occurred in the verbal couch Form but could equally have happened through movement.

Ben

Ben was a psychoanalytical psychotherapy client who came three times a week, used the couch, and engaged in therapy for four years. He came because he was living with his mother to whom he was devoted and, though he was in his mid-thirties, felt he could not leave. His mother was, and always had been, physically frail, and his father, idealised by the family, died when he was ten years old. As an only child he had assumed the mantle of the 'man of the house' and had always lived in the family home with the exception of some years spent in a childless marriage when he was in his mid-twenties. The atmosphere in his family seemed to emphasise that everything was all right. Despite the tragedy of the father's death he and his mother could struggle on because they had each other. The result was a sense of being stuck. On the one hand he wanted to leave his mother and her home, as he had tried to do with his first marriage, and make another life for himself; on the other he felt he had to stay with her as she was estranged from her family and had no one else to care for her. His sense of guilt for his father's death as a result of cancer plus an extremely complex interdependency between them had kept him there. Financially it had also been advantageous for him to live rent-free in this home; although a skilled computer programmer he had never had a lot of money and was careful with what he did earn.

In a session early on in the analysis, before the transference in my awareness had developed clear positive or negative characteristics, he lay on the couch and spoke of his problems with his mother. In trying to describe the uncomfortable feeling he had he used his hands in a way which symbolised the situation. His left hand attempted to cradle the right hand which kept taking a claw-like shape as if attacking the cradling hand. I felt I was witnessing someone struggling with extremes in his life, such as cruelty–kindness, love–hate. He kept speaking while doing the hand gestures and eventually verbalised a quality of cruelty between his mother and himself he had not thought about before. I do not know if he was aware of how explicitly (to my eyes, anyway) his non-verbal actions expressed the experience he put into words. In terms of the transference, I felt I was a trusted friend or a polite therapist who was beginning the process of getting to know the stories of this particular individual. I could not tell from any countertransference feeling, for instance, if he was indirectly saying he experienced me as either cradling or attacking him, or both.

Looking at this event from the Form of dance movement therapy, a more interventionist approach than authentic movement, the scenario might play itself out as follows. I invite the patient to continue with this 'hand dance' and the claw shape draws into the shape of a fist in order to 'cuddle into' the left cradling hand. The movement repeats itself with the hand turning from claw to fist shape and back again while rotating in relation to the left hand, the claw motion scraping and scratching the palm of the other hand. I encourage him to stand up and make the movement larger; using his whole body to 'play' the part of first one hand, then the other. He identifies the claw hand as his mother, the cradling hand as himself and begins to allow emotions of rage to emerge with the movements of the 'claw' person, and despair with the movements of the 'cradling' person, as he makes more postural versions of each. Eventually he finds himself doing the same movement for both, a kind of twist with both arms being brought together to hit the torso. He repeats this many times, working up to a frenzy of energy until he sits down exhausted.

In fact, none of this full body movement happened but in either Form the destructive atmosphere underlying Ben's living situation seemed to have been clearly formulated. He began a journey of separation from his mother which took four years, with many dreams and painful insights. Although he had not moved out of her house when he chose to finish his therapy with me, he had managed to change to a more lucrative job, build an extension to the house and live more independently of his mother. The process may or may not have taken less time if it included movement but I do wonder if it may have enriched the process of his therapy.

Taking this same material into the self-directed authentic movement Form, the whole sequence might have emerged in a similar way during perhaps a ten-minute movement experience. I would not have invited Ben to continue with the hand gesture (I would not choose the movement to be followed), nor would I have encouraged him to amplify it. Instead, we would have agreed the movement time and space and he would have closed his eyes and followed his own movement impulses. The movement sequence might have stayed gestural yet resulted in the same journey described, or it might have taken a totally different course. All of this is speculation but I believe that his process of discovery of unconscious material could have taken place through either Form.

In the context of assessment, movement can occasionally be helpful in clarifying the issues to be addressed, particularly if the client wishes to use a mixture of authentic movement and verbal psychotherapy. The following example shows the informative power of movement, in this case cautioning me against taking on a new client.

Amanda

Amanda was a successful actress who had to spend much of her time on the road either touring or going abroad to film on location. She had heard of my dance movement therapy work through a friend and was interested in the idea of dance being used in personal work. She telephoned to make an appointment but the only time she had available was on a weekend so we agreed on a day and time a few weeks away. I explained that I usually had at least two assessment sessions with someone before making a final decision about whether or not we would work together.

She arrived promptly and entered my studio. She was a tall, graceful woman whose presence seemed to fill the space. I realised with surprise that I had seen her in a lead role in a play recently (her private name was different from her stage name) but decided not to admit that in an effort to keep the analytic space free, so to speak, for a new relationship to develop. She had engaged in a series of relationships with both men and women and my impression was that she wanted time to consider difficulties she was experiencing in her present relationship.

She talked about her parents and siblings, an individual story but not a unique one, so I will move on to the process rather than the content of our work. She spoke for about half the session at which point I suggested she might want to move. She looked surprised but admitted she probably should. I said it was only a suggestion but she had come specifically with movement on her mind. She agreed but said she felt scared and did not know what to do. I decided not to pursue this verbally but suggested we stand up and go into the space together. I thought if I initiated the transition from sitting/talking to moving perhaps it would be easier for her to do so. She followed me, taking off her shoes and walking into the space which we moved through for perhaps half a minute. I talked her through a kind of centring warm-up: sensing the space, the floor underneath her feet, her breathing. She seemed to relax and after a minute or so stood still, then closed her eyes as if listening. Although she did not have training in authentic movement she had attended workshops in several non-verbal therapies. As is normally the case, I was using an adaptation of authentic movement whereby I encouraged her spontaneous gesture of the body which might express a story, emotion or state of inner being.

She looked quite firm in her stance so I stopped talking and stepped back to witness what movement might emerge. She began swinging her arms gently around herself then pressing her hands down and stepping carefully but firmly around the space. I had the impression of a huge person carving through the space, claiming every part of it as if there was no spot for anyone or anything else. Although she did not hit any wall or furniture I had the impression I was in the presence of a bully not allowing anything or anyone into her territory. After a few minutes she came to a quiet standing and opened her eyes. As often happens with this kind of moving with eyes closed, it took a moment or two for her to focus and return to her seat.

She then spoke about the relationship between her parents and her search for her own place in the family. I was interested in her story and looked forward to the possibility of working with her. In discussing this she commented firmly that she could only attend sessions about once a month due to her touring and rehearsal schedules. Our time was up soon after so we agreed to meet again in a month's time.

Soon after she left I realised I felt disturbed by something and uncomfortable about agreeing to the possibility of working with her. One aspect of this was that I had seen her in a dramatic play. My mind had fantasies and impressions of her in the role she had been performing which may have contaminated the objective stance I wanted to have in order to work with her. I remembered the movement work she had just done with me and my impression that there did not seem to be any space available for anyone else in the room when she moved. Thinking about the countertransference image of bullying that I had experienced during her movement work, it seemed to me that she was bullying both herself and me into providing an inadequate time to deal with important personal issues relating to her parents and early experience in her family of origin. After discussing both the content and the process of the session with my supervisor I felt I would not be able to do the work in the infrequent times allocated.

I do not know enough about her story to do anything but speculate about this. Perhaps she identified with her father who may have bullied the family through his absence. Maybe she was bullying herself to set up an impossible therapy timeframe rather than allowing herself time and space where more frequent sessions could provide the containment she needed. Given that the idea of bullying came from my mind, not hers, was it possible for me to see her as herself rather than, in part, the character I had seen her play? Was the performer/audience roles we had first occupied with each other (albeit unbeknown to her since she was unaware I had seen her performance at the theatre) taking up so much space in my mind that I could not make space for her individual, private self? If we had been able to meet regularly twice or three times a week, maybe we could have worked through these questions.

This, as I have said, is speculative, but I was clear that I did not feel able to provide the space she needed within the time she could allocate to the work. On the one hand I felt frustrated that a concrete detail such as her profession had prevented me from engaging in what promised to be very rewarding work. On the other hand I wondered if her choice to work with me as someone who required frequent and regular meetings was not only repeating a pattern of asking the impossible of herself but also ensuring that she would not have to get into difficult parts of her inner world.

In the event, she came for our second assessment session. We had a complex discussion but in the end we agreed it was unrealistic to work together, given the other demands on her time. Her movement statement had expressed a situation that I did not hear in her verbal story. It gave me the opportunity to think through the implications of the proposed time structure and my own experience of her in relation to the work in a clearer way than I would have done working solely with her words.

Conclusion

I have always been fascinated by the 'how' rather than the 'what' of these kinds of psychotherapeutic processes. The 'what' may be governed by the chemical changes in the brain, shifts in energy fields around the bodies involved or other processes we are still discovering. For example, neuroscience can now document changes in neuronal pathways in relation to therapeutic encounters. Conzolino (2002) writes clearly about 'neural network integration' and mental health; looking at dissociation in relation to traumatic experiences. He comments:

> Dissociation reflects a pathological expression of the plasticity that organizes and integrates neural networks.
>
> (Conzolino 2002: 24)

And:

> All forms of therapy are successful to the degree to which they have found a way to tap into processes that build and modify neural structures within the brain.
>
> (Conzolino 2002: 45)

However, I am only qualified to look at the 'how' of this work which I see as the evolution of the relationship between the members of the 'therapeutic alliance' (Etchegoyen 1991) to each other and to themselves. Given that this journey is about exploring the internal world of the client, I propose that 'another royal road' (in addition to verbal psychotherapy, among others) to that internal world is movement originating in the body. Concepts developed by Freud and his followers such as transference, countertransference and projection give us ways to understand the process going on between therapist, client and this unconscious material and can be applied to whichever Form is being used. These ideas, even if they are not 'true' in the concrete way of the neurones in our brains, act as conceptual tools that enable us as therapists to do our work.

I would encourage movement therapists interested in psychodynamic thinking to continue using theories growing from Freud and other thinkers. Although they do lose the power of movement, the two aspects go well together because movement, like dreams, give us another royal road to a knowledge of the unconscious activities of the mind (Freud 1900). Perhaps the psycho-neurological research presently being undertaken needs to include an awareness of dance movement therapy research and practice. Therapists using authentic movement similarly need to be aware of recent research in the neurosciences. In any case, I do not believe that one person, Form or framework holds all the concepts we need in order to do this kind of work. I welcome further research, thought and discussion between practitioners of many different trainings and approaches.

Notes

1 Dance movement therapists often call movement the 'modality' in which they work. 'Domain' is another word I use to indicate this other non-verbal 'language' of our bodies' movement.
2 There is a difference between a psychoanalyst and a psychoanalytical psychotherapist. Since I trained as the latter (a slightly different intensity of programme – four, not five times a week analysis; two, not three training patients; a differently qualified training analyst, etc.) I will refer to that title in this chapter.
3 I am differentiating between working with the body as a static structure and working with the body as a moving, expressive entity. In this chapter I am focusing on the body's actions – gestures, postures, qualitative movement changes of any kind.
4 For simplicity I will refer to clients as 'she' throughout unless I am clearly referring to a man.
5 In my own analysis I occasionally got up from the couch and moved; the movement material was taken into interpretive work just as my words or dreams.
6 I have changed details and combined several people's stories in order to protect the identity of those involved. In some instances, writing in the present tense, I have invented possible clinical material based on my experience in the two languages, as illustrations. I have visited all four areas on the continuum described in order to continue exploring how one framework and domain can aid another in terms of practical clinical choices.

References

Adler, J. (2002) *Offering from the Conscious Body: The Discipline of Authentic Movement*. Vermont: Inner Traditions.

Adler, J. and Aginsky, Y. (1988) *Still Looking*. A 28-minute film available on video. Berkeley, CA: Center for Media and Independent Learning.

Conzolino, L.J. (2002) Rebuilding the brain: neuroscience and psychotherapy, in D.J. Siegel (ed.) *The Norton Series on Interpersonal Neurobiology*. New York: Norton.

Etchegoyen, R.H. (1991) *The Fundamentals of Psychoanalytic Technique*. London: Karnac.

Escobar, T. (2003) Movement free association. E-mail (13 November 2003).

Freud, S. (1900/1991) *The Interpretation of Dreams*. Harmondsworth: Penguin.
—— (1901/2002) *The Psychopathology of Everyday Life*. Harmondsworth: Penguin.
—— (1924/1960) *A General Introduction to Psychoanalysis*. New York: Washington Square Press.
Gomez, L. (1997) *An Introduction to Object Relations*. London: Free Association Books.
Hinshelwood, R.D. (1989) *A Dictionary of Kleinian Thought*. London: Free Association Books.
Payne, H.L. (ed.) (1992) *Dance Movement Therapy: Theory and Practice*. London: Routledge. Introduction pp. 1–17.
—— (2003) Authentic movement, groups and psychotherapy, *Self and Society* 31, 2, 32–36.
—— (2006) Wellbeing and embodiment: authentic movement in bodymindspirit development, in J. Corrigall, H.L. Payne and H. Wilkinson (eds) *About a Body: Working with the Embodied Mind in Psychotherapy*. London: Routledge.
Penfield, K. (1992) Individual movement psychotherapy: dance movement therapy in private practice, in H. Payne (ed.) *Dance Movement Therapy: Theory and Practice*. London: Routledge.
Rycroft, C. (1995) *Dictionary of Psychoanalysis*. London: Nelson.
Schmais, C. and White, E. (1989) Movement analysis: a must for dance therapists, in American Dance Therapy Association *A Collection of Early Writing: Toward a Body of Knowledge*, Vol. 1. Columbia: ADTA Publications.
Strachey, J. (1962) Sigmund Freud: a sketch of his life and ideas, S. Freud in *Two Short Accounts of Psycho-Analysis*. London: Pelican.
Whitehouse, M. (1978) Conversation with Mary Whitehouse. Reprinted in P. Pallaro (ed.) (1999) *Authentic Movement: Essays by Mary Stark Whitehouse, Janet Adler and Joan Chodorow*. London: Jessica Kingsley. (Also in *American Journal of Dance Therapy* 2, 2, 1978).

Chapter 10

Birth moves

Dance movement therapy and holistic birth preparation

Monika Steiner Celebi

Introduction

Holistic birth preparation (HBP) draws on the tradition of dance movement therapy (DMT), psychoanalysis and yoga. This pilot study gathered feedback from women, who attended holistic birth preparation classes. Women found classes effective in helping them to respond to their bodies' needs and in using breathing and relaxation strategies during the birth. They also valued the emotional support they gained from meeting other pregnant women. The analysis of semi-structured interviews indicated that women needed space in a small, unhurried group environment where they could prepare physically and emotionally for the birth of their babies, as well as share experiences and gather information. Bodily experiences were considered an important and effective preparation in terms of raising a woman's determination and confidence in her ability to give birth rather than being the passive recipient of information handed to her. Dance movement therapists are in a unique position to contribute towards antenatal education in helping childbirth educators think about the most effective format in which to pass on information and help prepare women for birth.

The current debate about the different paradigms of birth encompasses diverse positions from the technocratic to the bio-psychosocial and the holistic (Raphael-Leff 1992). Their implications for birth practice and birth preparation are profound. Holistic birth preparation falls into the latter group. It is part of a tradition that advocates a low tech/high touch model (Walsh and Newburn 2002). HBP views the pregnant woman as a whole person who is going through tremendous life changes (Raphael-Leff 2001).

Rationale for the research

Childbearing practices reveal a society's basic values and beliefs, as well as attitudes towards bodies, babies and women. Birth raises strong, primitive anxieties about life and death in all of us (Raphael-Leff 2001). However, midwifery lecturer Anderson (2000) states we need to accept that birth is a hormone-driven process, and interference increases anxiety and sabotages the release of oxytoicin (Anderson 2000). Teixera *et al.* (1999) have demonstrated that the psychological state of the mother affects birth outcome. Fear and anxiety during labour will heighten a woman's response to pain (Simkin 1986), which then interferes with labour leading to the use of medical procedures. Kitzinger (2000) says that Western society has lost the structures and the knowledge for ritual, which can help reduce or contain anxiety (Kitzinger 2000).

It has been found that most women use a combination of medical and non-medical forms of pain relief (Spiby *et al.* 2003). Simkin and O'Hara (2002) found non-pharmacological methods for pain management, particularly the use of breathing during labour (Green 1993), reduced the use of medication and the subsequent total dose required (Simkin and O'Hara 2002). Evidence of alarmingly high medical interventions rates in the United Kingdom (Department of Health 2004) makes the search for effective alternative coping strategies more urgent.

The National Institute for Clinical Excellence Guidelines (NICE 2003) states that pregnant women should be offered antenatal classes. They stress that it is possible to build a woman's confidence in her ability to give birth. Spiby *et al.* (2003) conclude that antenatal classes offer women information and ways of coping with pain and emotional distress. However, women attending antenatal classes have not always found it a satisfying experience (Hillan 1992). Spiby's (2003) research calls for birth preparation to be effective and for research to identify the circumstances which influence the use or discontinuation of coping strategies. However, this study does not tell us exactly the manner in which midwives introduced coping strategies, nor how information about their potential benefits was imparted.

Holistic birth preparation

HBP draws from eastern and western approaches to physical, mental and spiritual well-being. Three pillars support it: dance movement therapy, findings from psychoanalysis and yoga.

Dance movement therapy

In this approach DMT is used to understand and work with body energy, which can be blocked, free flowing, or overactive (similar to the chakras in yoga philosophy). A variety of techniques is utilised such as movement sequences, relaxation, music and visualisation, which has been shown to increase well-being and reduce anxiety (Ritter and Graff Low 1996; Weber 1996; Lord 2002). Grounding as well as experiencing and owning the body (Alperson 1974) are DMT concepts, which are highly relevant to working with pregnant women. Kinaesthetic empathy – the ability to be in tune with each other non-verbally – is seen in DMT as the most important tool for establishing trusting and safe, holding relationships (Sandel 1993). DMT, as adapted for use in HBP, therefore fosters body awareness, adjustments to changes in the body and the mind, as well as having the potential to reduce anxiety and encourage trusting relationships.

Psychoanalysis

The psychoanalyst Raphael-Leff (2001) urges inquiry into the conscious and unconscious fantasies and fears surrounding birth. In this approach a woman's feelings about her ability to contain and nourish the unborn baby, to give birth, and to parent, will be important aspects of the emotional work she needs to undertake during pregnancy. She has to prepare to birth her baby, as well as to give birth to herself as a mother (Stern *et al.* 1998). A pregnant woman may feel extremely open to both her inner physical and her emotional world (Raphael-Leff 2001). This can raise anxiety, which can be understood as a signal of internal or external danger threatening the equilibrium and the sense of safety in a person (Fromm-Reichman 1955). Women need a safe space to discover, recognise and articulate their feelings at this important time in their lives. Antenatal classes, which take into account these conscious and unconscious processes, and allow their expression in an accepting, safe, non-judgemental ambience, are more likely to help women contain their anxiety and look beyond the 'wall' of labour (Wiener 2002).

Yoga

Yoga is a philosophy and a practical method (Mehta and Arjunwadkar 2004) that aims to calm the fluctuations of the mind. The term yoga is Sanskrit and means 'to yoke', that is to link mind and body, the individual and the world around (Steiner-Celebi 2003). Yoga teaches mastery of postures called asanas. These are modified for safe use in HBP with special emphasis on body awareness, grounding, extending the spine and opening the chest. This could be compared to Siegel's concept of mastery of technique as a prerequisite for further emotional work (Siegel 1995). For a pregnant woman to be anxious is normal (Raphael-Leff 2001), but yoga helps to recognise and contain this anxiety by teaching breath awareness, breath control (pranayama), relaxation, visualisation and meditation. These techniques help to create space in the body and in the mind. Breathing awareness allows women to observe feelings such as anxiety without having to act on them. This is called emotional intelligence (Goleman 1996). Another aspect of yoga used in HBP is its spiritual dimension. For some people birth is akin to a spiritual journey (Davies 2002). Yoga using breath awareness promotes a calm mindset and encourages a positive attitude towards contractions, which can be seen as challenges on that journey to parenthood. The assumption is that giving meaning to the pain of contractions will strengthen a woman's ability to deal with fear and the pain of labour (Frankl 2000) and also encourage a degree of detachment. The latter is different from the Western therapeutic approach of immersing oneself in one's feelings. Mastery of yoga is based on regular and repeated practice (Mehta 2002).

Components of holistic birth preparation classes

HBP aims to help women contain their anxiety. It wants to equip them with confidence and a belief in their innate abilities to cope with the challenges of labour, birth and early parenting. It does this by creating a space where women can explore and own the physical, emotional, cognitive and spiritual aspects of pregnancy and birth. HBP is not promoted as a panacea, since there is always a possibility of physical problems.

The women who come to HBP classes are either self-referred or sent by midwives, health visitors and general practitioners. They commit to attend for a minimum of one month and a maximum of six months. On average they attend for about three months. The maximum number of participants in any one of the HBP groups is 12, the average is 10 women. Spaces become available when women reach full term. Then new group members join the group. This set-up is comparable to a slow-open DMT group. It creates a different dynamic from a closed group where everyone starts and ends at the same time, or an open group where women would participate on a drop-in basis. It means that at the start of each HBP class it is important to make time for introductions, stage of pregnancy and any other events or questions women want to share, and so create a space which feels safe like a benign 'holding' environment (Winnicott 1982; Raphael-Leff 2001).

The initial part of the session takes about half an hour. This is followed by about 40 minutes of yoga-based poses. Their aim is to help women to stretch and strengthen their bodies, to help them adjust to their constantly shifting centre of gravity and to become aware and improve their posture, extend the spine and open the chest to make breathing more efficient; also to synchronise their movements with their breathing. The women learn pelvic floor exercises, positions for labour and breathing whilst sitting still and meditating. The women are encouraged to listen to their bodies, to acknowledge any aches and to adjust to them. This can be seen as a first stage labour rehearsal. They also work in pairs, giving and receiving physical support and touch. The body and its constant changes provide the basis for both information gathering and for the expression of emotions. When the women focus on their bodies, their feelings about the pregnancy and birth often emerge. This process helps women to recognise how their anxiety expresses itself in their bodies. They can experiment with movements and explore how breathing can help them contain their fears. Recognising tension in the body is the first step towards identifying anxiety in the mind (Alperson 1974). Women are encouraged by the facilitator to express their worries, dreams, hopes and fears about childbirth and about parenting.

The facilitation of the group is akin to that of a DMT group. The facilitator may move with and alongside the women, or remain still and give verbal suggestions. There is always the opportunity for women to opt out if something does not feel right. As a matter of fact not following a suggestion is often praised, since women then learn to follow their inner impulses rather than an external authority. To listen to their bodies is therefore used as a way of empowering women, so that they learn to trust themselves and know that they are the experts in their birthing process. Touch (always with permission) is used to adjust women's posture and help them become aware of areas of holding and tension. The mood and energy level of the class are reflected in the facilitator's words or movements.

Each class then has 20 minutes relaxation and another half an hour to talk about any issues which might arise. The women appear to show great interest in each other's experiences and supportive relationships between them are formed. They talk about their relationships with their midwives, partners, their mothers and their in-laws. Sometimes they talk about stopping work, which may be a real shock to their self-image demanding great adjustments. Sharing these changes that are happening in their lives provides a common experience which enables women to create strong bonds in a relatively short time. They often forge friendships with classmates, which give support during pregnancy and those precarious first weeks and months of parenting, sometimes even continuing into later years.

Because of the non-directive nature of the discussions the women feel free to pool their knowledge together with input from the facilitator. In this way they learn about the role of hormones in pregnancy and labour, the reasons for pelvic floor exercises, the lie of the baby and its implications for birth, possible medical interventions, birth provisions in the community, options for pain relief and so forth. The women feel free to ask questions; they are empowered to own the level and direction of the conversation. After the birth of their babies, mothers come and join the class discussion in the last half hour of the session. They show their babies to the group, share their birth stories and their experiences of parenting a newborn baby.

HBP classes provide women with an outlook towards birth that aims to be realistic yet positive, with a belief in their ability and power to give birth as countless women have done before them. The women practise visualisation of their babies, and themselves as part of the human chain, which strengthens their trust in their bodies and their capacity to endure labour. In meditation no specific religion is promoted, just the breath/spirit as an object for meditation and as a manifestation of the life force that sustains every living moment of existence. The breath is also linked to movement, including movement rituals which, as they become familiar, may help to contain anxiety and kindle women's hope in their strength and their ability to cope.

Research of birth preparation classes

Introduction

In recent years there has been growing interest in women's experiences of birth, as well as the effectiveness of antenatal classes (Spiby *et al.* 2003). Interviews conducted by the author between November 2003 and February 2004 with midwifery managers in four counties in the Southwest of England confirmed the numerous accounts from pregnant women, namely that there is no uniformity between classes. The skills and interests of the person leading the class appear to determine the manner of the provision. Women partaking in publicly provided antenatal classes report conflicting experiences. For instance, one woman recalls her experience of an antenatal class: 'The lady, who taught us relaxation was so anxious, her voice shook as she read the instructions out loud.' This contrasts with another woman's comment that the teacher was reassuring and calmed her fears with her positive attitude. In the UK the health professionals employed by the hospital or local health service mostly teach antenatal classes (Spiby 2003). Some classes are taught privately, such as those facilitated by active birth teachers, yoga teachers or movement therapists. Antenatal classes are also offered by trained educators of the National Childbirth Trust (Robertson 1999).

Rationale for research

NICE guidelines call for evidence for the best method to deliver antenatal education. They state that women need to be invited to contribute to any future designs for antenatal education in order to convey issues they feel are important to learn about and to feel empowered by their pregnancy and birth experience (2003). The current research can be seen as part of this trend.

Aims

The primary aim of this study was to explore which components of holistic birth preparation women found beneficial; second, to explore women's thoughts and experiences of antenatal classes in general; third, to establish which aspects the women found to be important. It was hoped that by hearing the women's voices a contribution would be made to the discussion on the training of birth educators, enabling an improvement in the approaches, quality and relevance of the antenatal classes offered by the public sector.

Methodology

A qualitative approach was chosen in order to understand the complex world of the lived experience from the point of view of those who live it (Jones 1985). This approach promotes studies that are 'led' by the subjects' experiences; therefore the research questions need to have an open focus. More than one collection tool was used because there are different ways of making sense of the world (Institute of Health Sciences 2004). Consequently questionnaires with open-ended questions, semi-structured interviews and one repertory-grid-based, in-depth interview were undertaken. Ethical considerations were important since birth is a highly emotive time, and sensitive and personal information was revealed. Women were informed of the aims of the study and confidentiality was assured. They gave their approval for the use of the information they disclosed. The research was considered a pilot, exploratory in nature, aimed at laying the foundations for a more extensive further study.

Recruitment

Women were self-selected. In total 20 women's responses were collected and analysed. All had participated in HBP classes conducted by the researcher. Their ages ranged from 24 to 42 years and all were educated and from a middle-class background. In the first stage, questionnaires were sent out to women who had given birth within the last year. They were first and second time mothers. Women in the second stage of the research were currently still partaking in HBP classes and pregnant with their second child. A convenient time for the interviews at their homes was arranged.

Data collection

At the first stage 45 questionnaires were sent out to women who had participated in HBP classes within the past year. They were asked to evaluate the usefulness of HBP classes with the aim of improving the class delivery. Women were requested to comment on three main elements:

- the aspects of classes they found useful for the birth
- elements they would have liked more of
- any other comments.

Of the questionnaires 16 were returned (35 per cent) and analysed to find recurring themes. A thematic analysis is summarised in Table 10.1.

An evaluation of stage one findings informed and clarified the main components of HBP as set out in the text above. However, to learn more about women's needs and requirements of antenatal classes, more research was

Table 10.1 An evaluation of holistic birth preparation classes

Components of HBP classes, women found useful	Percentage	An example of women's comments
Stretching and releasing aches	80	'The classes helped with backache during pregnancy and prepare for the birth.'
Learning to focus on breathing	73	'I was able to use the breath to cope during labour.'
Learning to relax	73	'I managed to stay calm and relaxed, when all was chaos.'
Talking to other mums	60	'The relaxed atmosphere helped to make friends; it was reassuring to hear others' stories and concerns.'
Finding out what positions are comfortable	50	'I used positions to deal with contractions.'

required. Consequently, as a second stage of the (still ongoing) research four interviews were undertaken. Three of these were semi-structured and conducted with women who had all been to HBP classes for a minimum of five and a maximum of seven weekly sessions. Women's ages ranged from 34 to 36 years and they were 32 to 37 weeks pregnant. They were asked about their experiences of antenatal classes:

- the aspects they liked, disliked (and why), what they enjoyed (or not), what they thought were the most important/least important elements
- whether they had formed impressions of antenatal classes from conversations with friends and if so to comment upon these.
- the forms of pain relief they had learned of and thought they could use.

Interviews lasted approximately one hour each. The researcher took notes, which were then fed back to the women to achieve respondent validation. The women drew on their own and their friends' experiences of five kinds of antenatal classes (those provided for free by the National Health Service, and private classes such as provided by the National Childbirth Trust, active birth classes, antenatal yoga classes and holistic birth preparation classes). The data were analysed according to elements, groups and categories. Themes that emerged are summarised in Tables 10.2 and 10.3.

The fourth interview was conducted in depth using the repertory grid method, based on personal construct theory (Kelly 1963). This is an interviewing technique used to arrive at straightforward descriptions of how a person views the world, or some smaller part of it, in his or her own terms. It is particularly effective in guarding against researcher bias (Jankowitcz 2004). A construct is the basic unit of description and analysis. To construe means

Table 10.2 Themes emerging from antenatal classes: those components which women valued

Component	Reasons women gave
Getting information and exploring options on labour and birth	• To get confidence, not to be terrified, because information frightens and empowers • To adopt a positive approach to birth; to find out about conventional and alternative pain relief, about possible side effects, self-help strategies, tips i.e. perineal massage • To find out about home birth, about 'Doulas' and independent midwives • To learn how to avoid induction, unnecessary intervention and complications • To gain knowledge on how to speed up/slow down the birth
Sharing experiences with other pregnant women	• To find out that everyone goes through similar fears, worries, anxieties, similar stages • To make friends • To hear good and bad birth stories because it helps to know that each birth is different • To be able to ask questions because you can question people, not books
Preparing for birth – focusing on the body	• To do pregnancy-appropriate exercises like stretching • To become aware of tension in the body • To learn strategies and techniques to relax and to breathe • To try out many different positions for the first and second stage of labour • To learn about being upright • To open possibilities of new ways of coping, like chanting for instance
Preparing for birth – mentally 'making time'	• To focus on being pregnant, to think about baby, to identify feelings • To clear the mind and make space • To create a positive attitude towards pain • To become assertive (not to lie flat), to feel empowered • To recognise fear of birth, fear of intervention, to know that not all is rosy, sometimes things can go wrong, therefore to discuss cot death, postnatal depression and that it is normal to worry about a new baby • To express concerns such as possible links between birth experience and postnatal depression

Special issues for second timers	• To use the class to go over earlier birth experiences because now there is: less/more fear of birth • To make time to think about what will happen after the birth, like new more complicated relationships with sibling and family dynamics, since there are more people to worry about • To explore feelings such as guilt that this time there will not be any exclusive time with baby like first time, and sadness that there may not be another child

Table 10.3 Themes emerging from antenatal classes: those Components which concerned women

Component	Reasons women gave
Timing of class	Appropriate for due dates, and therefore not too close to the birth in case baby comes early
Make up of class	If members are too diverse not all needs can be met
Addressing partners' needs	Partners have less time, but communication with them is important and could be facilitated in small groups

to make sense of something, to find meaning. A construct always represents a contrast, and this needs to be spelled out before the meaning of the whole construct is clear.

The repertory grid interview presented here is an illustration. The aim was to elicit constructs about women's attitudes to birth preparation and the benefits desired from antenatal classes. The respondent (Jane) was 24 weeks' pregnant. In the initial conversation with the researcher she identified 12 elements that she associated with a variety of antenatal classes she had experienced, such as active birth, antenatal yoga, HBP and classes at the local health centre (see Figure 10.1 for these elements). Using triadic comparisons, Jane and the researcher discovered ten constructs, which help them to understand how Jane thought about the topic of birth preparation and its effectiveness for coping with birth (see Figure 10.1 for these constructs). Jane then rated each construct against each of the 12 antenatal class elements. Her ratings tell us what she thinks about the different elements (see Figure 10.1 for these ratings). Figure 10.2 depicts a cluster analysis of Jane's interview.

Jane (Interview 1), Domain: antenatal classes
Context: effectiveness of birth preparation, 12 elements, 10 constructs

Construct	Practising positions	Discussing dad's role	Watching a video	Being told hospital and NHS policies	Listening to lectures	Talking in small single-sex groups	Meeting professionals	Meeting mums	Asking questions at leisure	Thinking about options	Practising making sounds	Practising assertiveness
knowing my body's needs – being told my body's needs	3	5	3	5	2	5	3	3	5	2	1	2
being present – planning ahead	3	5	5	3	1	3	1	3	3	5	1	1
getting support – being on your own	1	2	1	3	1	2	2	2	1	3	2	4
being determined – being susceptible to persuasion	1	4	1	4	2	3	2	2	1	1	2	1
feeling positive – feeling negative	2	2	2	2	2	3	2	2	1	2	1	1
emotional – cerebral	1	5	3	4	2	3	2	4	4	5	1	3
feeling part of – feeling removed	1	5	4	4	2	2	2	2	1	2	1	1
standing/moving – lying down	1	2	5	3	5	3	3	2	2	1	2	2
don't care what others think about me – being quiet	2	3	4	4	2	2	2	2	1	1	1	1
experiencing – information gathering	2	3	4	3	5	2	5	1	4	3	1	3

Figure 10.1 Repertory grid interview

100 90 80 70 60

being present – planning ahead
knowing my body's needs – being told my body's needs
experiencing – information gathering
emotional – cerebral
don't care what others think about me – being quiet
feeling part of – feeling removed
being determined – being susceptible to persuasion
feeling positive – feeling negative
standing/moving – lying down
getting support – being on your own

100 90 80 70 60

Practising making sounds
Meeting mums
Talking in small single-sex groups
Practising positions
Discussing dad's role
Thinking about options
Practising assertiveness
Asking questions at leisure
Meeting professionals
Listening to lectures
Watching a video
Being told hospital and NHS policies

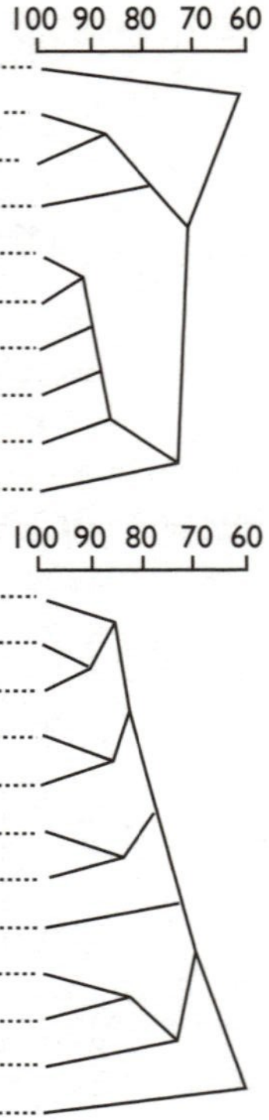

Figure 10.2 Cluster analysis of Jane's grid

Discussion

The main components of HBP that women found beneficial related to two time spans, before and during the birth. Before the birth women said the classes helped them to adjust to their changing body and prepare mentally and physically for the birth. They said they benefited from exploring positions, breathing, relaxation and the emerging supportive relationships with other pregnant women. During the birth women found coping strategies they had learned such as breathing, relaxing and changing to comfortable positions useful.

These results confirm findings by Spiby *et al.* (2003). One woman, who had an emergency Caesarean section, commented: 'I managed to use my breathing at times of high stress and anxiety.' Other comments included: 'I would have preferred a fixed routine', which may refer to her anxiety and the importance of repetition. Another wrote: 'I wanted to practise more breathing.' These statements are similar to the comments made by other women in a research conducted by Spiby *et al.* (1999), where a desire to spend more time practising coping techniques was expressed. Implications for antenatal teachers may be that coping strategies need to be taught and practised repeatedly over a period of time to be effective in times of need. These findings and feedback from the first stage of this study influenced the delivery of HBP classes subsequently, with more emphasis on breathing, explorations of positions, relaxation and time for the development of supportive relationships.

When asked about which components of antenatal classes women considered important, it transpired that they fell into five main categories:

1   Getting information on and hearing about options such as hospital procedures and self-help alternatives, as well as homebirth, the importance of a doula, and so forth.
2   Sharing experiences, good and bad, with other women. The format of classes, which enabled women to feel free to ask questions, appeared to increase their confidence. Perhaps it contributed to them creating new and supportive relationships.
3   Preparing for the birth physically. They said that they wanted to pay attention to the physical experience of being pregnant, recognising tension in the body and practising strategies to relax, as well as explore different positions for labour and for birth.
4   Preparing for the birth mentally and having time to think and feel. They wanted to explore their attitudes to pain. Whilst they endeavoured to endorse an assertive and positive attitude towards birth, they also expressed a need to express their fears and worries.
5   Attending refresher classes for second time mums, where they could go over prior birth experiences and express their special concerns regarding changing family dynamics.

Concerns women expressed were:

1   The timing of classes, especially if they were too close to the due date, in case baby arrives early.
2   The make-up of classes, particularly if the people in the class were from too diverse backgrounds. They were worried that some people's needs would not be met.
3   The involvement of their spouses with the birth process, specifically worries about how this might be achieved.

Jane's repertory grid in-depth interview showed two distinct clusters of constructs. One was to do with her knowledge of her body and her experiences, as opposed to being told about her body's needs, gathering information and being cerebral. This may express the contrast between internal ownership of knowing about her body and her feelings in contrast to external ownership, that is, other people's views imposed upon her. Jane rated herself as owning more of her experiences in small, single-gender groups, and less so when watching a video, meeting professionals or listening to lectures.

The other cluster appeared to be about the dichotomy of being upright, standing and moving, feeling positive, determined and not caring about what others thought about her compared to being quiet, susceptible to persuasion, feeling negative, lying down and (interestingly) feeling removed. This indicated a greater likelihood of Jane owning her experience when she felt assertive and active. From a mental health point of view 'feeling part' of an experience may indicate a greater likelihood of psychically integrating the birth rather than feeling 'removed', which may indicate the need to defend herself emotionally and to distance herself from the birth and maybe the baby (Raphael-Leff 2001). Jane's grid also showed a link between actively practising positions, assertiveness, making sounds, thinking about options, to being determined and feeling positive. This indicates for me the benefits of exploring and practising positions, making sounds and reflecting on possibilities in antenatal classes to increase a woman's self-confidence and her ownership of the birth process. On reading these research findings a year after the collection of the data, Jane commented:

> My birth experience seems both a long and also only a short time ago. I remember vividly how I could use the knowledge I had gained from the antenatal classes. It gave me the confidence to cope at times of panic, to calm my breathing, move into more comfortable positions and visualise the baby coming further down the birth canal. Being active helped me to stay in control and cope without resorting to drugs. Reading the research findings made me realise that I get so much more out of being active, than being a passive recipient, and also it brought home to me how much more I can be in tune with my body than I give myself credit for.

These comments may point out that holistic birth preparation helped Jane to become more aware of, and in tune with, her body, which helped her to feel in control and empowered by her birth experience.

Two further constructs, which were more separate from the two main clusters, were identified: being present compared with planning ahead, and getting support compared with being alone. This indicates to me that they are important considerations in their own right and should be explored further.

The dendrogram of elements showed the closeness between such elements as single-gender groups, meeting mums and making sounds, which may indicate the importance of single-gender groups enabling women to feel free to express themselves. There was an affinity between practising positions and discussing the father's role, which may point towards the benefits of hands-on sessions with the fathers. Thinking about options for labour and birth and practising assertiveness could indicate the importance of connecting thinking with practical exercises, such as role play, movement or visualisation in classes.

Meeting professionals, listening to lectures and watching a video were all grouped together and appeared to place Jane in a more passive position. Asking questions at her leisure and being told about hospital and NHS policies seemed to be elements that stood quite separate from other elements. They are both about information gathering, yet they do not seem be linked closely at all in Jane's grid. Further study may want to look into reasons for this, and find out if this gap is also applicable to other women. Jane's experience of feeling supported was least when she was listening to a lecture, but more likely to happen when she was in contact with other women. She felt least determined when watching a video. Being a passive recipient of information did not appear to boost Jane's confidence, rather she felt encouraged when she was doing things and being active.

Critique

These findings will be affected by the sample, which was made up of a self-selected group of educated women, who were articulate and had the capacity and desire to prepare emotionally, physically and intellectually for the arrival of another child. Women said they wanted to be in a setting that was relaxed, informal and friendly and which allowed for (a) the exploration of options for childbirth and of their feelings; (b) gave them time and space to adjust to their changing physical and emotional realities.

The repertory grid interview painted one woman's mental landscape in depth. It gave insights into how she thought about and experienced different forms of birth preparation. These interviews were pilot studies. Further research with a larger cross-section of the population is desirable to place the present findings into a wider context. However, Leamon (2004) puts the case that individual voices should be heard to raise new ideas.

The researcher/interviewer was also the person conducting the antenatal classes that the women were attending. However, the questions were posed in such a way as to encourage women to draw from a whole range of experiences, their past and present, their own and their friends'. The already existing relationship with the researcher may also have enabled women to feel comfortable enough to reflect and share their private thoughts.

Conclusions

The women who attended HBP classes highlighted the benefits of body awareness, breath awareness, relaxation and contact with other pregnant women. They pointed out the importance of regular practice of coping strategies. Interviews further raised the value of gathering information, preparing physically and mentally for the birth, sharing of experiences with other pregnant women as well as going over prior birth experiences and their changing family dynamics.

Body-based experiences, such as exploring posture and labour positions, making sounds, breathing and relaxation, were considered by the women to be an important and effective preparation in terms of raising a woman's determination and confidence in her ability to give birth rather than being the passive recipient of information. However, this study was conducted on a limited sample of women from a narrow socio-economic background and more extensive research is needed.

If, however, giving birth requires embodied knowledge rather similar to breastfeeding (Hodnott 1999) it will be difficult to learn it intellectually. We should ask, perhaps, what circumstances would foster this kind of embodied learning. Antenatal educators may wish to consider their teaching format and their mode of teaching when preparing women for birth and early parenthood. Pregnant women could be encouraged to move their bodies and reflect on their feelings in small, single-gender groups. The practice of coping strategies, coupled with giving voice to feelings and thoughts, may raise women's confidence in their ability to be involved, assertive and active during birth.

The construct 'knowing about my body' as opposed to 'being told about my body' is of particular interest to dance movement therapists who are professionals in a unique position to contribute towards antenatal education. They can draw on their understanding of the connection between mind and body and on the importance of creating a holding group environment. If pregnant women feel safe they will be able to explore their changing bodies and voice their feelings about the literal and the symbolic baby within, as well as discuss the reality of the upcoming birth and parenthood.

Pregnancy and birth are important stepping-stones in the maturation process of becoming a mother. It is often highly charged, yet also a time that increases a woman's receptivity for change and for learning new ways of being and of coping. By understanding the holistic nature of birth preparation, dance movement therapists can move between different disciplines and contribute to HBP, thus creating an interface between therapy, prevention and education and therefore supporting women to take control of the birth process.

References

Alperson, E. D. (1974) Carrying experiencing forward through authentic body movement, *Psychotherapy: Theory, Research and Practice* 22, 211–214.

Anderson, T. (2000) Have we lost the plot?, *NCT New Generation*, September, 16–17.

Davies, L. (2002) Antenatal classes and spirituality: an oxymoron or opportunity for transcendancy, *Practising Midwife* 5, 11, 16–18.

DoH (2004) *Maternity Statistics for England for 2002–03*. Online. Available. HTTP: <http://www.dh.gov.uk/PublicationsAndStatistics/Statistics/StatisticalWorkAreas/StatisticalHealthCare/StatisticalHealthCareArticle/fs/en?CONTENT_ID=4086521&chk=wV7ZSA> (accessed 19 May 2005).

Frankl, V. (2000) *Man's Search for Meaning*. London: Beacon Press.

Fromm-Reichman F. (1955) Clinical significance of intuitive processes of the psychoanalyst, *Journal of American Psychological Society* 3, 82–88.

Goleman, D. (1996) *Emotional Intelligence*. London: Bloomsbury.

Green, J. M. (1993) Expectations and experiences of pain in labor: findings from a large prospective study, *Birth* 20, 2, 65–72.

Hillan, E. (1992) Issues in the delivery of midwifery care, *Journal of Advanced Nursing* 17, 2, 274–278.

Hodnott, P. (1999) Qualitative study of decisions about infant feeding among women in East End of London, *British Medical Journal* 318, 7175, 30–34.

Institute of Health Sciences (2004) Critical appraisal skills programme: making sense of evidence, in Institute of Health Sciences *Critical Appraisal Skills Programme Workshop Pack*. Oxford: Institute of Health Sciences.

Jankowitcz, D. (2004) *The Easy Guide to Repertory Grids*. Chichester: Wiley.

Jones, R. (1985) *Depth Interviewing. Applied Qualitative Research*. Aldershot: Gower.

Kelly, G. A. (1963) *A Theory of Personality: The Psychology of Personal Constructs*. New York: Norton.

Kitzinger, J. V. (2000) *Rediscovering Birth*. London: Little, Brown.

Leamon, J. (2004) Sharing stories: what can we learn from such practice?, *Midwifery Digest* 14, 1, 13–16.

Lord, D. L. (2002) Exploring the role of somatic education in experiential well-being, *Dissertation Abstracts International Section A: Humanities and Social Sciences* 63, 4-A, 1269.

Mehta, M. (2002) *Health through Yoga*. London: Thorsons.

Mehta, M. and Arjunwadkar, K. (2004) *Yoga Explained*. London: Kyle Cathie.

National Institute for Clinical Excellence (NICE) (2003) *Guidelines on antenatal care: routine care for the healthy pregnant woman*. Online. Available HTTP: <http://www.nice.org.uk/pdf/CG6_ANC_NICEguideline.pdf> (accessed 19 May 2005).

Raphael-Leff, J. (1992) *Psychological Processes of Childbearing*. London: Chapman & Hall.

—— (2001) *Pregnancy: The Inside Story*. London: Karnac.

Ritter, M. and Graff Low, K. (1996) The effects of dance movement therapy: a meta-analysis, *The Arts in Psychotherapy* 23, 3, 249–260.

Robertson, A. (1999) *Empowering Women*. Camperdown: ACE Graphics.

Sandel, C. S. (1993) The process of empathic reflection in dance therapy, in S. Sandel, S. Chaiklin and A. Lohn, (eds) *Foundations of Dance/Movement Therapy: The Life and Work of Marion Chace*. Columbia, MA: Marion Chace Memorial Fund of the American Dance Therapy Association.

Siegel, E. (1995) Psychoanalytic dance therapy: the bridge between psyche and soma, *American Journal of Dance Therapy* 17, 2, 115–128.

Simkin, P. (1986) Stress, pain and catecholamines in labour, *Birth* 13, 234–240.

Simkin, P. and O'Hara, M. (2002) Nonpharmacologic relief of pain during labour: systematic reviews of five methods, *American Journal of Obstetrics and Gynecology* 186, 5, 131–159.

Spiby, H., Henderson, B. and Slade, P. (1999) Strategies for coping with labour: does antenatal education translate into practice?, *Journal of Advanced Nursing* 29, 2, 388–394.

Spiby, H., Slade, P. and Escott, C. (2003) Selected coping strategies in labour: an investigation of women's experiences, *Birth* 30, 3, 189–194.

Steiner Celebi, M. (2003) Preparing for birth – a holistic approach, *Spectrum, Journal of the British Wheel of Yoga* 3.

Stern, D., Bruschweiler-Stern, N. and Freedland, A. (1998) *The Birth of a Mother*. London: Bloomsbury.

Teixera, J., Fisk, N. and Glover, V. (1999) Association between maternal anxiety in pregnancy and increased uterine artery resistance index: cohort, *British Medical Journal* 318, 153–157.

Walsh, D. and Milburn, M. (2002) Towards a social model of childbirth: Part 2, *British Journal of Midwifery* 10, 9, 540–544.

Weber, S. (1996) The effects of relaxation exercises on anxiety levels in psychiatric inpatient, *Journal of Holistic Nursing* 14, 3, 196–205.

Wiener, A. J. (2002) The brick wall of labour, *Practising Midwife* 5, 2, 38–39.

Winnicott, D.W. (1982) *Playing and Reality*. Harmondsworth: Penguin.

Chapter 11

Embodiment in dance movement therapy training and practice

Bonnie Meekums

Introduction

Dance movement therapy (DMT) by definition involves the body in both practice and training. DMT supervision also frequently makes active use of the body's wisdom in order to aid reflexive practice (Penfield 1994; Scarth 1995; Best 1999, 2003; Payne 2001a; Meekums 2002). Verbal approaches to psychotherapy may be viewed as embodied practice (Shaw 2003), though the extent to which embodied learning is a conscious element within training programmes may vary. The research on which we rely for evidence-based practice is, however, still largely a linguistic, cognitive pursuit in which the promptings of the body are ignored both in the research process and in reporting. The challenge for dance movement therapists is how to forge links between what we can know about embodiment from multidisciplinary theoretical perspectives and what we know through our embodied practice, in order to develop innovative and integrated approaches to learning, research and practice (including supervision).

This chapter will address embodiment in DMT, first by considering the concept in relation to the dominant discourse in which 'mind' and verbal articulation are privileged over body and the non-verbal. The metaphor of 'position' is used to highlight the inherent power dynamics within this discourse. This cultural context sets the scene within which DMT training strives for authority whilst foregrounding somatic intelligence and embodied learning, including the role of the emotions in knowledge production.

Having considered these key concepts, the contribution of this chapter is to offer a model by which the phase-specific and embodied therapist–client relationship within DMT can be understood. The model is drawn from creativity theory and builds on some of my previous writing concerning research and therapy processes. A case illustration is given of this model at work with a client diagnosed as suffering from anorexia nervosa.

Embodiment and the dominant discourse

The concept of embodiment can be treated in two distinct ways. The first is in the sociological sense, of our bodies as areas of discourse. The term discourse used here does not denote a discussion, but a set of beliefs and structures that determine the meanings we attribute to our experiences. The discourses available to us at any one time influence the range of our responses. They are enshrined in institutions and language, and are intrinsically linked to power and authority (Ryan 2001). They are embodied and internalised. Thus, our experiences of our embodied selves are shaped by these discourses, expressed in the stories we tell ourselves about our lives and the world. The dominant Cartesian discourse privileges mind over body. The wisdom of the body is thus denigrated with respect to intellect, and embodiment becomes problematic. The challenges posed by Foucauldian (Foucault 1980) and feminist analysis to the dominant discourse are potentially liberating, as we discover that the gendered body can be subjected to 'inscriptions' or meanings derived from the exercise of power. These meanings affect our subjective experience, but are open to deconstruction.

A key body metaphor used by post-structuralists in deconstructing power relations is that of 'position' (Ryan 2001). Different positions carry different kinds and degrees of power. We construct narratives about our experience, influenced by discourse, in which we position ourselves and are positioned by others. From this vantage point we perceive the world (Ryan 2001). However, we can potentially reposition ourselves, and we also position others.

A key question therefore for dance movement therapists might be concerned with how we position ourselves or are positioned by the institutions within which we practise, teach and research. Is our teaching, research and practice afforded an equivalent position to that of our colleagues in other disciplines? Do we risk becoming obsessed with words and measurement, ignoring embodied wisdom? We also need to consider how we position our clients and our students, and how our clients and students in turn position themselves and us. What power differentials are there? How much does our own internalised sense of devaluation as embodied selves within the dominant discourse affect the way we teach our students and mentor our novice practitioners?

Despite the usefulness of post-structural analysis, Prain and Hickey (1998: 20) claim that 'the Cartesian mind/body split has merely been supplanted with the inscriber/body substitute, and hence the body's agency in developing a sense of embodiment is once more denied, suppressed, or relegated to a peripheral role'. Essentially, the body becomes an object of theory and analysis rather than a lived subjectivity. It therefore becomes necessary to consider embodiment in terms of the body as agent and in action (Prain and Hickey 1998; Beckett and Hager 2002; Sparkes and Smith 2002).

Embodiment in dance movement therapy training

The theory and practice of DMT is essentially inconsistent with Cartesian propositions of a mind/body split in which mind is privileged over body. It also potentially subverts assumptions that the body is merely a passive recipient of gendered inscription. The active body is implicated pedagogically in DMT training. DMT respects the lived body as an active source of knowledge production. As Payne (2004: 11) comments: 'It is about "knowing" (feeling) from the inside'. Embodied learning within DMT training is especially evident in the training group (TG). An example of experiential learning via the group and dance movement processes, the TG makes use of the body's wisdom as its vehicle, thus drawing implicitly on traditions from within dance, psychotherapy, education and body–mind practices derived from eastern traditions.

But the body is not unproblematic within DMT praxis. DMT training derives from dance as an art form. The arts, within the Cartesian discourse, are seen as less important and useful than, for example, hard science. Within the arts, dance is primarily associated with women or gay men, whose position may be viewed by society as inferior (hence the jibes commonly suffered by young men when they take up dance as a field of study). Dance training develops strength and stamina (qualities genderised as masculine), yet female dancers in some settings still (and despite the development of postmodern dance forms including contact improvisation) appear to develop bodies and movements that deny this.

Added to this, the discipline of dance may require a denial of certain information deriving from bodily experience. It is impossible to continue dancing on *pointes* with bleeding toes, unless the dancer dissociates to a degree and ignores the promptings of her body. I have personally witnessed young male dancers from one professional company using anaesthetic spray on painful muscles following a particularly athletic performance. Dance can be used as an escape from the troubles of the world, precisely because of this asceticism and the trance-like qualities it brings. Many dancers know how to 'dance it out' when feeling low. The use of mirrors, still prevalent in all major dance studios, also privileges external/visual references over internal kinaesthetic information. The combination of denial of bodily experience and the tendency to develop a thin, underdeveloped body despite its strength and stamina may be two of the factors that contribute to a high risk of eating disorders amongst female dance students (Joseph *et al.* 1982; Buckroyd 1994). DMT demands opposing coping strategies to those described above. In DMT, we expect our students to enter fully into their bodies, to pay attention to nonverbal and somatic information, to use dance as symbolism rather than as escape (though this may have some benefits), deepening their understanding of the human condition. This may pose a problem for some students if previously they have cultivated a denial of bodily cues in order to survive.

Learning styles are gendered[1] (Barrett and Lally 1999). It is probably no accident that there are far more women than men in the DMT profession. The core practice skills of embodied dance movement, emotional sensitivity and relatedness are typically symbolised as feminine within most Western cultures. However, DMT training in Britain is at the level of postgraduate study. This requires critical and analytical skill that may present a challenge to anyone whose self-concept is unbalanced and restricted by socially constructed, gendered expectations of women. Greben (2002: 15) has observed that dancers 'commonly see themselves as much less talented and able to learn in areas other than dancing than they in fact are'. Tutors faced with such distressed learning (Curzon-Hobson 2002) must be mindful of their delicate role in encouraging and modelling simultaneously: 'feminine' qualities like embodied empathy as displayed in rhythmic entrainment of movement and sound between two individuals (Trevarthen 2001); and a genuine passion for academic pursuits and specifically for research.

Embodiment and somatic intelligence

Gardner (1993) identified seven forms of intelligence: logical-mathematical, spatial, musical, linguistic, intrapersonal, interpersonal and bodily-kinaesthetic. His theory revolutionised the concept of intelligence, previously held to be either linguistic or mathematical. However, his view of bodily intelligence maintained the dominance of mind over body, as he viewed it as the ability of the individual to use mental processes in order to co-ordinate body movement. This definition was undoubtedly influenced by biological references to the kinaesthetic apparatus, and is thus limited. It fails to consider how the body might influence the mind, or how somatic information might be derived from other body systems. I therefore prefer to use the term 'somatic intelligence' to describe this complex relationship.

It has been argued that learners can benefit from developing 'emotional intelligence' (Beard and Wilson 2002): 'the ability to use your understanding of emotions, in yourself and others, to deal effectively with people and problems in a way that reduces anger and hostility, develops collaborative effort, enhances life balance and produces creative energy' (Bagshaw 2000, cited in Beard and Wilson 2002: 120). Some dance movement therapists might take issue with this definition of emotional intelligence. For example, it may be necessary to express anger first and learn to tolerate difference, rather than simply aim to reduce uncomfortable emotions. Perhaps more useful is the allied concept of 'emotional literacy' (Park 1996; Sharp 2001). This is described within the context of school education as developing in pupils 'a capacity to know what it is they feel, to express those feelings in an appropriate fashion and to empathise with the feelings of others' (Park 1996: 57). This definition too remains inadequate. Given the fact of position, who determines what is an 'appropriate fashion' in which to express emotion?

I would argue that emotional literacy is dependent on somatic intelligence due to the fact that we recognise our emotions through their specific associated body processes. Somatic intelligence, I would suggest, can be viewed as the wisdom derived from attending to the body, and all emotional literacy depends on this faculty. Thus, both in DMT praxis and in emotional literacy, somatic intelligence is key.

There is ample anecdotal evidence of somatic intelligence within DMT praxis. Several forms of psychotherapy make use of somatic intelligence (Gendlin 1981; Shaw 2003; Totton 2003), though Shaw argues that this has been largely absent from discourse. Somatic intelligence is also evident in many body–mind practices based on Eastern philosophies. Here, body, mind and spirit are one (von Durckheim 1977).

Powerful evidence for the role of embodied emotions in learning, decision making and reasoning can be found in the work of the neuroscientist Damasio (1999), who developed his 'somatic marker' theory after examining people who had damage to certain regions of the brain. The ability to learn from emotionally charged experience was compromised in those persons with damage to the prefrontal region and right parietal region of the brain. Their powers of logic remained intact, as did their other emotional capabilities, but they often displayed an inability to decide rationally and advantageously in situations of risk or conflict.

The embodied relationship in dance movement therapy practice

As a result of my doctoral research, I developed a creative, spiralic model of the recovery process with respect to child sexual abuse trauma, and identified the importance of the therapeutic relationship and group relationships as vector catalysts[2] to the recovery process (Meekums 1998, 1999, 2000). I then developed my ideas further in relation to DMT praxis (Meekums 2002). A similar model had previously been used to describe the research process (Meekums 1993). The developments from the doctoral research presented here incorporate two new phase-specific aspects of the therapeutic relationship not previously described, namely *Probing, questioning and challenging* and *Releasing*. It is important to state that I do not see this model as 'true' in the sense of being exclusive to other explanations. Rather, I view any theoretical model as a 'convenient fiction' (Herman 1992: 155) that is useful so long as it makes sense to somebody and has practical application. It is one of many narratives concerning the DMT process and is summarised in Figure 11.1.

I refer to my model as the WISE/EMPoweR model. The four key stages in the client's development are described as

- Warm-up (W)
- Immersion (I)

- Seeing things differently (S)
- Evaluation (E).

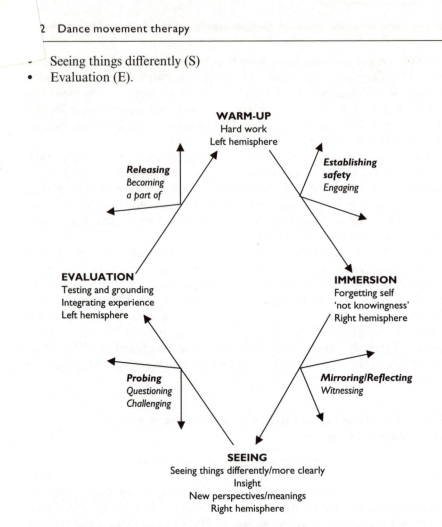

Figure 11.1 The WISE/EMPoweR model of therapeutic change

These processes are supported through task-specific *vector catalysts* (Meekums 1998, 1999, 2000, 2002) within the relationship. The vector catalysts are:

- Establishing the conditions of safety (E)
- Mirroring, reflecting and witnessing (M)
- Probing, questioning and challenging (P)
- Releasing (R).

Clients entering DMT are in a stage of preparation, analogous to the *Warm-up* of a DMT session (Meekums 2002). There may be anxiety or expectation and the journey before them may feel daunting. The client must first feel emotionally and physically safe (Meekums 1998, 1999, 2000, 2002). I have argued elsewhere (Meekums 2000) that the core conditions proposed by Rogers (1957) can be seen as constituting the optimal conditions for *Establishing the conditions of safety* within the therapeutic relationship. The DMT practitioner conveys unconditional positive regard, empathy and genuineness both verbally and non-verbally. This aspect of the relationship is thus embodied.

Research by Payne (1996) demonstrated the need for safety in a DMT personal development group within training. The theme of safety recurred in interviews with DMT participants, its establishment allowing greater self-disclosure in both movement and words. My own research (Meekums 1998, 1999, 2000) revealed similar findings with members of an arts therapy group for survivors of child sexual abuse. Taken together and in the light of other literature examined above, these two pieces of research suggest that the importance of clients feeling safe may be common to more than one setting in which personal development is expected, including that of the student engaged in experiential learning.

The establishment of conditions of safety within the therapeutic relationship allows for clients to *Immerse* themselves in a state of 'not-knowing', which is essentially a trust and willingness to open up and see experience afresh and is a 'right brain' state. Payne's (1996) research has shown this in the DMT personal development group within training, as well as in authentic movement (AM) (Payne 2001a). My research (Meekums 1998) similarly identified its importance in multimodal arts therapies groups for women survivors of child sexual abuse, and I have since demonstrated its importance within DMT clinical practice (Meekums 2002).

A client who witnesses another in movement will experience an embodied empathic response (Payne 1996; Meekums 2002). Neurophysiologic research concerning the existence of so-called 'mirror neurones' indicates that these neurones allow us to learn by imitation and also fire as a kind of 'body memory' when the observer sees someone else performing an action that is already within the individual's repertoire (Rizzolatti *et al.* 1996; Williams *et al.* 2001). In the TG or DMT group, this empathic response may be formalised as in the role of client or therapist, or of witness in AM. On other occasions, the firing of mirror neurones may lead to physically mirroring the quality of movement (Meekums 2002). These possibilities, facilitated by right brain function, may or may not be accompanied by verbal reflection.

As a result of this *Mirroring, reflecting and witnessing* by self, therapist and other clients in a group setting, insights emerge related to the movement metaphors (Meekums 2002) with which the client has engaged via her somatic intelligence. These insights represent a subtle change in perspective which I refer to as *Seeing things differently*. These new meanings open up the possibility of creating different scenarios for the future. I have referred to this stage as grounding of insights in everyday life (Meekums 2002), or *Evaluation*. I would argue that, while the *Evaluation* process often happens quite organically, the therapist and other clients in a group setting can assist the process through gently *Probing, questioning* and *challenging*. This demands a slightly more distanced embodiment, and more left brain function. Eventually, the relationship must end, which requires an attitude of *Releasing* on the part of both therapist and client. The emotions accompanying such release will resonate in an embodied experience.

The cycle referred to in Figure 11.1 can be viewed both in microcosm, as in one DMT session, and in macrocosm, across the whole therapy. In either case, the form may be viewed as a spiral, in which topics and themes are revisited many times. The path taken around this spiral is not necessarily even or sequential. Each client carves out their own path in relation to the therapist, fellow clients in the case of group therapy, and their own internalised narratives.

Embodiment in dance movement therapy within an eating disorders context: a case study

The following case material is taken from a series of group DMT sessions that took place in a private eating disorders unit (EDU).[3] I have chosen to focus on one case study, that of a young woman called Jayne.[4]

Jayne had been diagnosed as suffering from anorexia nervosa. At the time I met her for assessment purposes, she had already been resident for a few months. Like all of the women in the unit (there were no male patients at all), her weight was closely monitored by nursing staff. Her mealtimes were closely observed and her diet controlled.

We met in the more comfortable of two lounges, used at other times by residents. This was also to become the group room. Jayne, at 21 years of age, was not one of the youngest in the unit, which took women from the age of 16 years, neither was she one of the oldest (my oldest client was in her fifties). She normally lived with her parents, but I quickly discovered that her role in the family carried pivotal responsibility. She described her family as 'living on an edge', caused apparently by her father's unemployment and subsequent money worries. I recall in that very first meeting experiencing an embodied maternal countertransference.[5] It was almost as if at times I wanted to take her into my womb to keep her safe and nourish her. I noticed my body's message, but its significance only became clear to me much later.

Jayne had danced from a young age, but always felt guilty about the financial cost to her parents. Hence, when she was of an age to do so, she began paying for lessons herself. Jayne had got a job when her father left his, so that she could pay for her own dance classes and continue her A level[6] studies. At around the same time, she was dating a young man. In biology classes at school, several of the class were weighed in order to demonstrate the concept of body mass index. Jayne discovered that she was the heaviest in the class, and promptly began dieting. Thus began her obsession with food reduction, and eventually she was hospitalised. This led to the loss of her job and a failure to complete her A level studies. The end result was that Jayne felt even more responsible for her family's financial situation.

Jayne was typical of many of the young women I encountered in the EDU. Anorexia is strongly associated in the literature with high-achieving young women (Lawrence 1984), but often has the effect of interrupting studies and careers. Anorexia is also a risk in young dancers (Joseph *et al.* 1982; Buckroyd 1994) like Jayne. However, there was another important aspect to Jayne's story. Her determination to lose weight was associated with a strong belief that she was not good enough as a person. I had a sense of a young woman who had always disciplined herself (first in the dance training, and now by denying herself food) and who somehow felt responsible for the whole family. I noticed that she apologised almost every time she opened her mouth to speak, and she frequently asked for my approval. She also displayed agitated movements in her hands. It later transpired that Jayne constantly worried that she had upset someone. I wondered if she had ever felt able to be playful, or indeed if she had ever felt truly accepted and loved.

Buckroyd (1994), writing about the context of therapy for women with eating disorders (EDs) in a dance school, suggests that ED is essentially a psychosomatic illness, in which the body symbolises what the individual is unable to articulate verbally. She suggests that non-verbal approaches to therapy may therefore have particular value for this group of individuals, as they 'might provide a bridge from the somatic to the verbal' (p. 109). Buckroyd and her colleagues used art and movement but not DMT. However, they did acknowledge the importance of bodily awareness in the therapy: 'An eating disordered person is frequently very confused about the physical signals that she gets from her body, so body awareness is one for the corner-stones of the experiential work' (p. 113). The activity of art making she claims 'reflects the somatic activity of an eating disorder' (p. 114). Essentially, it seems that Buckroyd is acknowledging the importance of developing somatic intelligence in the eating disordered individual.

Following assessment, I invited Jayne to one of the inpatient DMT groups to be run in the lounge in which we had met. I decided to use a very simple structure for these groups, beginning with a short check-in, a warm-up of the body, then moving into free improvisation with a prop (for example, stretch cloth) and finishing with a verbal debriefing and short movement ritual. One of the young psychiatrists co-worked with me. My primary goal was initially to *Establish the conditions of safety*. This, I hoped, would provide a group experience in which the women could slowly begin to 'come out of their shells' within a supportive and safe atmosphere. I also wanted to introduce the idea of choice, as many of their lives had been marked by over-control either externally and/or internally. The EDU necessarily reflected this atmosphere of control, in an attempt to keep these young women alive. My other goal therefore was to avoid any tendency to set up my DMT sessions as 'good' compared to the 'bad' EDU. I did this by reinforcing the fact that the controls exerted on them by the EDU were benevolent, and encouraging the young women to take responsibility for the fact that it was their own decision to withdraw food that had led to these controls being introduced.

In our first group DMT session (in the stage of *Warm-up*), I noticed that Jayne locked her knees, as if she could not trust herself to stay upright otherwise. When *Immersing* herself in throwing a ball, she threw underarm because she thought she would be unable to find sufficient strength to throw overarm. I *Mirrored* my observation to her, both verbally and kinaesthetically, encouraging her to expand her repertoire. She was surprised to find that she could in fact be quite powerful when throwing overarm (*Seeing things differently*). She also remarked during verbal processing that she had particularly valued being given a choice within the session, for example, about what music we might use, what prop she wished to work with, and even whether or not to move (*Evaluation*). Nevertheless, Jayne continued for many weeks being preoccupied with thoughts that she had upset someone. This made it impossible at times for her to focus on the here and now experience of the group, or to take in feedback from others.

In session two, I became aware of how some of these patterns had developed, and made sense of my own early embodied countertransference. Jayne was *Immersed* in wrapping her fingers in the circle of elastic with which the group sometimes moved together. She was able to link this action to her wish to hide her feelings (a new insight, and therefore an example of *Seeing things differently* or more clearly). She then used a stretch cloth to wrap her body in, and began rocking. This she associated with her need to merge with, and be symbolically 'fed' by, her mother. She revealed that she avoided asking for a hug from her mother, as she feared a repeat of the rejection she had come to know in similar situations. In the following session, she returned to the stretch cloths, and actively chose one to represent her mother. She initially sat far away from this cloth symbolising, I felt, her usual avoidance of rejection. But as our movement improvisation progressed, she explored her need, identified in the previous session, to be enveloped and rocked by this cloth/ mother. When I asked her how it felt to be in that state (*Probing/questioning*), she remarked that she knew now that she had done nothing wrong, and that everything would be OK (*Evaluation*). There was no longer anything to apologise for. I did my best to encourage Jayne to internalise and own this state (and separate the feelings of self-acceptance from the reality of a rejecting mother) by recreating her body memory without the cloth, first with eyes closed and then with them open as she engaged with the group. However, this was early in Jayne's therapy and the following week she was as preoccupied as ever with her concern that she had upset someone. I was not perturbed by this, as I have previously (2002) conceptualised this kind of apparent retrogression within therapy as merely visiting a familiar vista, but from an elevated vantage point on the spiral (see Figure 11.2). The instillation of hope (on this occasion held by me) has been described by Yalom (1995) as a key therapeutic factor within group psychotherapy.

Jayne's awareness of the link between her relationship with her mother and her own obsessive thoughts of having upset someone may have contributed to a period of apparent depression just before Christmas. In session five she reported that her eyes and limbs were heavy. I noticed her playing with her rings. She sat on the edge of her chair, and when asked what she needed she replied, 'I don't need anything.' I chose not to challenge this statement, as I felt that if I further alluded to her 'insides' at this early stage in her therapy, this could be experienced by her as persecutory.

Jayne had enormous difficulty making even the simplest of choices. She initially said that she was looking forward to going home for Christmas, but later retracted this statement as she simultaneously created the image of a large lollipop out of the balloon and a cloth. I wondered privately whether this lollipop might symbolise her ambivalence about food. I was struck by its similarity to a large, perhaps overpowering (or withholding) breast. Despite Jayne's potential ambivalence, when she returned in the New Year I noticed she was saying please and thank you less frequently than before Christmas. Her movements were distinctly calmer, with only a little nervous gesture in her right hand. I had rearranged the group membership over Christmas. The group now comprised younger women whose movement expression was timid and showed limited expansion or affect, leaving Jayne in the position of 'old hand'. She made the decision to speak first in the check-in, and initiated movements in a group improvisation using whole body action rather than her previously split-off gestures, and an all-round use of space that I had not seen her use before.

This new leadership role within the group continued. In session seven, we *Immersed* ourselves in a movement improvisation around the theme of 'little' and 'big', as this had emerged from the women's verbalisations during the

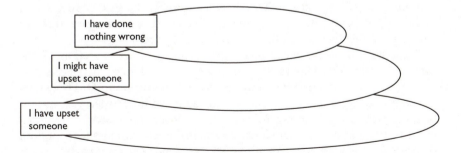

Figure 11.2 The spiral process in psychological therapies

check-in (a form of verbal *Warm-up*). Jayne adopted a foetal position, wrapped in cloth, which I witnessed. She reflected that she felt safe and secure, but noticed that she needed to have her head outside of the cloth, to avoid feeling claustrophobic (*Seeing things differently or more clearly*). During our verbal *Evaluation* Jayne disclosed that she had been reminding her mother that she was now '21, not three'. I began to wonder if she was ready to become bigger, more adult and more assertive.

Jayne's movements continued to be much freer, and I even saw her using humour in one of the group sessions. Soon after this, however, I had to tell the group that I would be leaving in two months' time. Jayne said she was upset and declared that this was her favourite group. The need to protect herself within this affective state was visible in her body as she adopted a quasi-foetal sitting position. But her stated upset was tempered by the knowledge that her parents had said they would allow her to return home (there had been some reluctance to do so previously). In the next session Jayne wondered aloud if the stretch cloth could take her weight. Although there were not enough people in the room to lift her, we all lifted the cloth around her body as she lay in it, and 'rocked' her (*Immersion*). We were reminding her, I realised later, of her earlier symbolised experience of being rocked. She said that she felt safe, secure, and a sense of belonging. This embodied insight was in contrast to her earlier sense of privation, and thus is an example of *Seeing things differently*. Later, she processed (*Evaluation*) that moving together in the DMT group meant both belonging, and having the right to be different, to choose.

Sadly, the following week I heard that Jayne had forced the secure window in her room and contemplated throwing herself out. This occurred following a conversation with her father, in which he revealed that he did not want her to go home after all. She did manage to attend the group, with some support, but her movements were very inner directed, reflecting an unwillingness to engage with others. This time, the stretch cloth reminded her of making beds during her former work in an elderly people's home (EPH), of her positive relationship with the residents, and of her sadness when they died. I wondered if she was also thinking of the impending ending of her relationship with me and with the group. This, like her work in the EPH, had been an experience of belonging and acceptance. She ended by remarking that she wished she could hug her mother without fear of rejection.

The following week, Jayne had been detained under a section of the Mental Health Act. This resulted in a loss of freedom as her meals and movements were once more strictly controlled. In our group DMT session, she began crying, and said that here she felt accepted for who she was, not for how she looked. But her anger at her loss of freedom seemed to be turned inwards. Her movements were inner directed (though with moments of both strength and tenderness). We discussed her tendency to turn her anger inwards by overworking and self-starving. Jayne was stimulated by one piece of music to disclose that her parents were in continuous conflict. She also revealed that she only felt she deserved positive attention if she 'bought' it with gifts.

There was an unfortunate mix-up shortly after this, when Jayne had to see her individual therapist. This was the only one of 14 group DMT sessions that Jayne missed. The group was slowly being dismantled, as group members were redirected to other activities pending my departure, or were too ill to attend. Jayne was the only group member present for the last two sessions. Whilst sad at the loss of the group, Jayne remained committed. The themes emerging from Jayne's improvisations were to do with 'dancing to her own tune', symbolising her separation/individuation (Mahler 1979) and a *Releasing* attitude. Jayne played with the ball and beanbag, and shared memories of playing on her own on holiday, away from others. She told me of her decision to live, and to look forward to travelling, thus making it obvious that far from echoing unhappy times this new separation would be positive (*Seeing things differently*). I was aware that Jayne knew that my departure had been precipitated by my own decision to travel and that her statement could signify an unconscious wish to merge with me. Her movements were stronger in these sessions, and her voice more emphatic. She made good eye contact and looked 'at home' in her body. Once again, she spoke of moving together as meaning she was accepted and not 'the horrible person I thought I was'.

In her final session, Jayne told me of her fears about finishing because this had been the only place she had been able to express certain feelings. However, I was able to remind her that she had a productive relationship with her individual therapist. She had by now achieved her target weight and was able to feel good in her body. In particular, she was able to appreciate feeling more energised. She chose a green cloth that was reminiscent of work we had done together regarding her mother. She *Immersed* herself in rocking to the music, which sang of family conflict, and she remembered arguments between her mother and father, echoed now in her own relationship with her brother (*Evaluation*). This led into free movement, in which she asked if she could follow my movements for a while, demonstrating perhaps her dependency needs and her fear of separation. However, this led into some leaderless movement, and we found an ending together, without speaking. At the end of our last session together, Jayne spontaneously gave me a hug and we parted (*Releasing*).

Jayne was one of the residents who completed a proforma evaluating her experience in the group. She said that she felt proud that her confidence had grown to the extent that she could now 'suggest ideas and movements that the group can do'. She also remarked: 'I found it difficult at first to say how I was feeling but now I feel comfortable sharing my problems without feeling guilty about wasting someone's time.' The most important thing she had done, she said, was the piece of work based on relationships with mothers, because she had discovered 'other people had similar issues and it was good to be able to talk about it'. Jayne's statement illustrates Yalom's (1995) concept of universality (the sense that one is not alone) as a therapeutic factor in group psychotherapy.

She was able to identify some key learning that had taken place through her involvement with the DMT group, suggesting that DMT may offer a form of experiential learning: 'I have learnt that everyone is entitled to their own opinion and it is OK to say how you feel . . . Life is important and definitely worth living. Talking about your problems makes dealing with them a lot easier.' Given that anorexia nervosa is a life-threatening illness that has been likened to a hunger strike (Orbach 1993), Jayne's commitment to live is significant. It is interesting that she identified talking as a healing factor, because she also recalled in her feedback that she was unable to speak in the group at first. Her comments both here and in the *Evaluation* at the end of each session suggest that her ability to speak about her feelings was only made possible by moving together, and the feeling of acceptance this brought her.

Embodiment in therapy for clients with ED is especially significant, given that the ED itself can be viewed as a form of somatised symbolism. The embodied relationship between Jayne and myself and between her and the other group members appears to have facilitated a new embodied relationship with herself. In particular, the experience of moving together and of discussing important and universal themes arising out of the movement gave her an experience of belonging that fundamentally contradicted her conditions of worth (Mearns and Thorne 1988) and thus enabled her to move on.

Moving together in this case meant having the opportunity to move in time with others (thus facilitating a sense of belonging), but also being allowed and even encouraged to experience what it felt like to move in ways that expressed individuality without fear of rejection by the group. For example, we often moved together with a stretch cloth, all positioned around one large piece of material. The group would be asked to choose the music, from a range that included various ethnic styles, rock, pop, ballads, and so on. The instruction was simply to see what emerged as we began to move, and for group members to share any images or associations that occurred to them. Sometimes, one or more of the group members would move quite minimally, while others would move enthusiastically. All of these modes of expression were contained by the group, and no one was judged or cajoled into pretending to feel anything other than what they were feeling at the time. This was extremely important, as many of the women in the group had previously coped by appearing to be happy when they actually felt sad. Later, when we discussed the movement, I would sometimes name how it felt to me, in my own body, when I witnessed their embodied expression. It was also at this time of evaluation that group members began to speak more meaningfully about the images they had been working with as they moved.

Conclusion

This chapter proposes a model for understanding the therapeutic process within DMT. Building on my previous writing and research, I have introduced the importance of the developing relationship between client and therapist. I have attempted to develop these ideas within a framework of embodiment, linked to the central idea of somatic intelligence as a cornerstone of DMT.

The presentation of ideas is necessarily simplified, in order to begin to draw the boundaries of processes that are essentially human and therefore complex. Above all, despite the discrete roles and processes I have assigned to client and therapist, DMT is a co-creational act that changes all of us. We all are potential witnesses for each other.

Notes

1   This term does not imply that learning styles are innately male or female, but that they are symbolised as either masculine or feminine. Boys and girls are encouraged by society to acquire the characteristics assigned to their gender roles. Such roles are, it is argued, limiting for both sexes.
2   I use this term because the relationship has directionality. It can of course assist the therapeutic process when optimal, but when deficient in certain qualities it not only has the effect of slowing the therapeutic process, but of reversing it.
3   My thanks to the staff and residents at eating disorders unit at which this research took place.
4   The client name is a pseudonym and some details are deliberately disguised. The client has signed a consent form for details of our work together to be used in this way.
5   Lewis (1984) refers to this phenomenon as 'somatic countertransference'.
6   A level is the term used for Advanced level studies, taken in England and Wales normally between the ages of 16 and 18 and resulting in A level examinations at 18.

References

Barrett, E. and Lally, V. (1999) Gender differences in an on-line learning environment, *Journal of Computer Assisted Learning* 15, 48–60.

Beard, C. and Wilson, J.P. (2002) *The Power of Experiential Learning: A Handbook for Trainers and Educators*. London: Kogan Page.

Beckett, D. and Hager, P. (2002) *Life, Work and Learning: Practice in Postmodernity*. London: Routledge.

Best, P. (1999) Improvised narratives: dancing between client and therapist, *E-Motion ADMT Quarterly* 11, 4, 17–26.

—— (2003) Interactional shaping within therapeutic encounters: three-dimensional dialogues, *USA Body Psychotherapy Journal* 2, 1, 26–44.

Buckroyd, J. (1994) Eating disorders as psychosomatic illness: the implications for treatment, *Psychodynamic Counselling* 1, 1, 106–118.

Curzon-Hobson, A. (2002) A pedagogy of trust in higher learning, *Teaching in Higher Education* 7, 3, 265–276.

Damasio, A. (1999) *The Feeling of What Happens*. London: Heinemann.

Foucault, M. (1980) *Power/Knowledge: Selected Interviews and Other Writings 1972–1977*, ed. C. Gordon, trans. C. Gordon, L. Marshall, J. Mepham, K. Soper. Brighton: Harvester Press.

Gardner, H. (1993) *Frames of Mind: The Theory of Multiple Intelligences*, 2nd edn. London: Fontana.

Gendlin, E. (1981) *Focusing*. London: Bantam.

Greben, S.E. (2002) Career transitions in professional dancers, *Journal of Dance Medicine and Science* 6, 1, 14–19.

Herman, J.L. (1992) *Trauma and Recovery*. New York: Basic Books.

Joseph, A., Wood, I. and Goldberg, S. (1982) Determining populations at risk for developing anorexia nervosa based on selection of college major, *Psychiatry Research* 7, 53–58.

Lawrence, M. (1984) Education and identity: thoughts on the social origins of anorexia, *Women's Studies International Forum* 7, 4, 201–209.

Mahler, M. (1979) *The Selected Papers of Margaret Mahler*, Vol. 2. New York: Jason Aronson.

Mearns, D. and Thorne, B. (1988) *Person-Centred Counselling in Action*. London: Sage.

Meekums, B. (1993) Research as an act of creation, in H. Payne (ed.) *Handbook of Inquiry in the Arts Therapies: One River, Many Currents*. London: Jessica Kingsley.

—— (1998) Recovery from child sexual abuse trauma within an arts therapies programme for women, unpublished PhD thesis, University of Manchester, Faculty of Education.

—— (1999) A creative model for recovery from child sexual abuse trauma, *The Arts in Psychotherapy* 26, 4, 247–259.

—— (2000) *Creative Group Therapy for Women Survivors of Child Sexual Abuse: Speaking the Unspeakable*. London: Jessica Kingsley.

—— (2002) *Dance Movement Therapy: A Creative Psychotherapeutic Approach*. London: Sage.

Orbach, S. (1993) *Hunger Strike: The Anorectic's Struggle as a Metaphor for Our Age*. Harmondsworth: Penguin.

Park, J. (1996) Emotional literacy: the most essential skill, *Educational Therapy and Therapeutic Teaching* 5, 57–60.

Payne, H. (1996) Student experiences of a dance movement therapy group in Higher Education, unpublished PhD thesis, University of London.

—— (2001a) Authentic movement and supervision, *E-Motion ADMT Quarterly* 8, 4, 4–7.

—— (2001b) Student experiences in a personal development group: the question of safety, *European Journal of Psychotherapy, Counselling and Health* 4, 2, 267–292.

—— (2004) Becoming a client, becoming a practitioner: student narratives of a dance movement therapy group, *British Journal of Guidance and Counselling* 32, 4, 511–532.

Penfield, K. (1994) Nurturing the working therapist, *Association for Dance Movement Therapy Newsletter* 6, 4, 4–5.

Prain, V. and Hickey, C. (1998) Embodied learning in English and physical education: some cross-disciplinary insights, *Curriculum Perspectives* 18, 3, 15–22.

Rizzolatti, G., Fadiga, L., Gallese, V. and Fogassi, L. (1996) Premotor cortex and the recognition of motor actions, *Cognitive Brain Research* 3, 131–141.

Rogers, C. (1957) The necessary and sufficient conditions of therapeutic personality change, *Journal of Consulting Psychology* 21, 2, 95–103.

Ryan, A. (2001) *Feminist Ways of Knowing: Towards Theorising the Person for Radical Adult Education*. Leicester: National Institute of Adult and Continuing Education.

Scarth, S. (1995) Supervision on the move, *E-Motion ADMT Quarterly*, 7, 2, 12.

Sharp, P. (2001) *Nurturing Emotional Literacy: A Practical Guide for Teachers, Parents and those in the Caring Professions*. London: David Fulton.

Shaw, R. (2003) *The Embodied Psychotherapist: The Therapist's Body Story*. London: Brunner-Routledge.

Sparkes, A. and Smith, B. (2002) Sport, spinal cord injury, embodied masculinities, and the dilemmas of narrative identity, *Men and Masculinities* 4, 3, 258–285.

Totton, N. (2003) *Body Psychotherapy: An Introduction*. Maidenhead: Open University Press.

Trevarthen, C. (2001) Setting the scene: a window into childhood. Keynote speech at the 7th Professional Conference of the United Kingdom Council for Psychotherapy: Revolutionary Connections: Psychotherapy and Neuroscience, Warwick University, 7 September.

von Durckheim, K.G. (1977) *Hara: The Vital Centre of Man*. London: Mandala.

Williams, J.H.G., Whiten, A., Suddendorf, T. and Perrett, D. (2001) Imitation, mirror neurones and autism, *Neuroscience and Behavioural Reviews* 25, 287–295.

Yalom, I.D (1995) *The Theory and Practice of Group Psychotherapy*, 4th edn. New York: Basic Books.

Chapter 12

The lived experience of students in a dance movement therapy group

Loss, physical contact and the dance movement therapy approach[1]

Helen Payne

Introduction

This chapter documents some of the uppermost themes to emerge from an analysis of the data from a larger qualitative and collaborative research study (Payne 1996a) which asked how dance movement therapy (DMT) trainees experienced the DMT personal development group on their training and whether this linked to practice. The rationale for this was not to offer a method of providing a DMT group in higher education but to elucidate meanings derived from the students' experience, which may assist in providing some links to practice.

There has been a growing interest in the nature and purpose of personal development (PD) groups in the training of therapists for some time although little research to date. An overview of relevant research studies concerning PD groups in the training of psychotherapists, counsellors and arts therapists may be found in Payne (1999). The study aimed to explore the DMT students' perceptions of a two-year, weekly, closed DMT personal development group over six terms (60 weeks), before, during and following their postgraduate training in DMT. The third year follow-up focused further on their thoughts of how the group experience related to their eventual practice.

The context for the study was researched by an international survey (Payne 2002b) comparing arts and psychotherapies programmes with PD/experiential/training group component. Themes described here are concerned with the importance of loss for the group; physical contact and experiences of the approach to DMT provided (the facilitation and method of the DMT group itself). Other themes arising from the in-depth, systematic, three-year research study can be found in Payne (2001, 2004).

Trainees' experiences of personal development groups

Studies that document the therapist's perception of group process in clinical settings in both arts therapies and psychotherapy are profuse (for example, in DMT: Desamantes 1990; Schmais 1981, 1985, 1998 and Siegal 1995). However, few inquire into the student experience of the PD group. Izzard and Wheeler (1995) study a self-awareness group in counsellor training and call for a creative approach to researching PD groups. Most relevant though is an investigation into an authentic movement group experience as it impacted upon qualified psychotherapists' (n = 20) private practice. Outcomes included self/other differentiation development, which was seen to reduce the tendency to over-identify with client material (Lucchi 1998). The study reported here had a focus on the quasi-group therapy aspect of training as described by Truax and Carkuff (1967). It is similar to that of Newman and Collie (1984), which explored the PD group as a drama therapy group in higher education. It shares the fact that the PD group as experiential learning is a non-assessed part of the training, as in Aveline's (1986) study evaluating perceptions of a 12-week 'training group'. Small and Manthei (1988) conducted a study investigating psychotherapy trainee perceptions in post-session evaluations with the facilitator from a 24-week, non-assessed experiential group. However, neither of these related studies linked learning experiences/outcomes to practice.

Research into the individual client's experience of therapy has been a growth area for some time (McLeod 1990; Caskey *et al.* 1984; Lietaer and Neirinck 1988; Martin and Stelmaczonek 1988; Hill 1989; Rennie 1990; Watson and Rennie 1994; Grafanaki and McLeod 1995; Hill at al 1993; Seligman 1995; Bischoff and McBride 1996; Howe 1996; Paulson *et al.* 1999; Etherington 2000; Paulson *et al.* 2001; Ryden and Lowenthal 2001. Clients themselves have reported their individual experiences of personal therapy such as Dinnage (1989), Lott (1999) and Sands (2000). Findings from these studies differ significantly from therapists' perceptions of the therapeutic process (such as Orlinsky and Howard 1986; Elliott and James 1989; Bachelor 1991; Heppner *et al.* 1992; Gershefski *et al.* 1996) and can equally contribute to theory and practice in the psychological therapies. Perhaps through research into student experiences there can be more understanding of the lived experience of the trainee, which can contribute to the development of theory, training and practice.

Few studies, however, ask for perceptions of clinical DMT group therapy experience (Payne 1992) and none to date invite students' views of experiential personal development groups in the psychological therapies. One study in counselling considers the value of personal therapy to therapist practice from the therapist's viewpoint Macran *et al.* (1999). Wilkins (1999, 2000), also in higher education using an arts therapies approach exploring the group process in a collaborative style, studied undergraduate human communication students' perceptions of a person-centred approach to psychodrama in an experiential learning group. Unlike this study the facilitator was also the researcher and responsible for student assessment.

The context

The research involved one cohort on a postgraduate diploma in DMT training, held in an institute of Higher Education (HE) on one day per week for two years amidst other similar programmes in drama and art therapies. Clinical lectures were shared by programmes together with intensive weeks. Ongoing clinical placements, supervision and skills workshops were undertaken weekly. Assessment was by several clinical and seminar papers, an autobiography in dance and other formative work. DMT practice in settings such as hospitals, special schools and day centres was assessed by case studies and manager, supervisor and tutor appraisal in situ. The DMT group was held at the same time, same venue each week with the same facilitator (not the author). She was an experienced DMT practitioner practising in the NHS and accredited in psychoanalytical and humanistic approaches to psychotherapy. Supervision was provided for the DMT group by another therapist employed by the institution. The DMT group involved both movement and stillness, verbal reflection and vocalisation. Students were provided with information on the nature of the group, its aim and learning outcomes. It was confidential, closed and all journal entries were private to the student. It was assessed solely on a minimum attendance of 80 per cent. The researcher was also the programme tutor for 18 months of the project.

Methodology

The author's experiences of facilitating DMT groups in clinical settings, personal development groups for DMT and drama therapists in training and research in client perceptions were the seeds for the growth of the research idea. Despite evaluations of the personal development/experiential group components of programmes in the institution, there was no evidence of their contribution towards student learning or practice. Therefore the research sought to gather student reflections on the DMT group experience, inviting them to contribute to the sense making of these, and make links to DMT practice during and following training.

It was important to use a methodology consistent with the values inherent in the programme, the DMT approach and the researcher's practice. The approach selected belongs to the philosophy found in the humanistic (Reason and Rowan 1981) or 'new paradigm' view towards research. These premises include research 'with' rather then 'on' people, deep respect for the participant, the idea of human agency, the importance of feeling, dialogical/co-constructive approaches to sense-making and honouring the complexity of human existence where a subjective, dense, 'thick description', holistic web of knowing is sought rather than an objective 'truth' (Geertz 1973).

The researcher monitored her own bias (Heron 1981; Reason 1988) such as desire for evidence to demonstrate the effectiveness of the group for practice and 'bracketed' these off to avoid preconceptions for the purpose of the project. The self-reflexivity (Schon 1988; Steier 1991) by the researcher as part of the field being studied is crucial to validity since it demonstrates how the story is created by the researcher(s). The study complied with Stiles (1983) who recommended, for quality control, that all informants be invited to agree the findings. Participants were asked for comments on transcriptions and analysis where possible. Wyatt (2002: 179) states that 'another way of achieving credibility ... is by consulting research participants themselves and asking them to read and comment on the outcomes of data analysis'.

The frequent debriefings with participants allowed for further thoughts to be given on the design and any pitfalls arising from the research process. Both the researcher and facilitator were interviewed once the group had terminated as part of the reflexivity process and the researcher kept a reflective journal to raise awareness of power dynamics and highlight any preconceptions. The study aimed to empower participants and provide a supportive, challenging research group (Reason 1994). Normally in collaborative/participatory inquiry (Heron 1971; Torbert 1981; Reason 1988; Olesen *et al.* 1994; Erikson and Stull 1998) phenomena outside the research group are studied. However, the two phenomena – the DMT group and the students' experience of clinical practice in relation to it – were within the research study group. Spaniol (1998) followed a similar collaborative approach in an art therapy inquiry. In this world of inquiry the reader is invited to enter the picture painted by the representation described and share in the dialogue between the data and researcher. Berrol (2000) in DMT research in the USA advises a case for phenomenological, post-positivist approaches to DMT inquiry (Lincoln and Guba 1985; Moustakas 1994), as has McNiff (1998), in advocating art-based research. Edwards (1999), Forinash (1995) and Junge and Linesch (1993a, 1993b) recommend qualitative social sciences methods in US music and art therapies respectively and Payne (1996b) proposes this approach to arts therapies research generally. Essentially this research is broadly based on grounded theory as developed by Glaser and Strauss (1967) and Charmaz (1995) whereby themes and differences were looked at across participants, transcriptions read through several times to identify meanings and interpreted in the context of each other.

Themes deduced from the data were noted in sequence over time to examine the cumulative experience. Meaning was attributed to participants' comments by analysing for repetitive, dominant or opposing themes (Potter and Wetherall 1987; Bungay and Keddy 1996) and any glaring omissions, for example, there had been no mention of the group being all female (Parker 1992). DMT and group therapy literature informed the analysis, as did the experience of the researcher in DMT group work.

The research used qualitative tools for data collection including questionnaire, semi-structured interviews (based on the findings from the questionnaire and the following interviews) and two reflective journals for individual case profiles. Six interviews with each student were undertaken. One final set of interviews was undertaken during the year following their graduation as practitioners.

Following informed consent and a previously piloted preliminary questionnaire to all research participants to elicit expectations of the DMT group prior to its commencement, 34 semi-structured, one-hour interviews (one each per term over two years and one in the third year) took place. Seven students participated initially, one withdrew from the programme and the research, all were white women between the ages of 25 and 45 years and all British except two.

The students were all fully informed about the research at interview for the programme and knew that they could withdraw at any time without consequences for their training. Communication was directed to their home address and venues for debriefings and interviews were other than the HE institution. In the later stages participants organised these and offered their own homes, which may indicate more ownership of the project on their part. For ethical reasons an interviewer was engaged for all but the final interview. It was ethically possible for this one to be conducted by the researcher (author) since she had left the role of programme leader a year earlier, and had never been directly involved with student-participants' assessments.

All sets of interviews had two sections: an overview of their experiences in the group and questions on themes arising from analysis of data arising from the previous interview and/or journal of one of the two case profile participants. There was an emphasis on relating experience to professional practice at the time. Not being a quantitative study, the number of times an idea repeated was not significant in itself although the first analysis did structure ideas in order of priority according to the number of times mentioned by participants. Sometimes a theme which had its origins in previous research seemed significant. Where there was more than one theme mentioned the same number of times, these were grouped together in the same section. The pattern to appear over the three years was traced from the interviews; where there were conflicting patterns these were also noted.

From the analysis of the fifth interview, clusters were arrived at by a process of discovering an issue arising more than twice in the set of only four transcriptions, due to the absence of three co-researchers. Unfortunately, of these four only two were complete due to a fault on the tape recorder. Three themes from the first two years are now offered for consideration.

Loss

During the third term, as the first year was ending, feelings of anger linked to sadness and disappointment were apparent in relation to the issue of loss:

I finally had a crying release in the DMT group. I felt exhausted and couldn't grieve any more. I sat in a corner and the facilitator suggested I try doing small movements and see what happened to it. Rocking movement and violent movement, directed inwards. I wrote a poem and felt happier. I worked in movement on dying and being reborn, alone.

I feel less close to people now . . . disappointed . . .

I shared my feelings of lack of support and pain in the group. I expressed unhappiness with the group and dealt with it through the movement exercise.

(Third interview)

This can be seen as a precursor to the final ending of the DMT group at the end of the following year. The distance between people is disappointing for some and there was evidence of anger at this loss.

The fourth term produced further indications of profound feelings concerned with the theme of loss. Of particular interest are those connected to anger, that is, the resignation of the programme leader, the absence of group members, the loss of personal relationships, absent fathers, the imminent closure of the group, and a group member having left at the end of the previous term. The following quotations enlighten us to each of these particular losses:

Lots of anger when the programme leader left, a big issue for the group . . .

I was disappointed about the absence of members.

I was disappointed towards the end of term, things stopped.

Pain, bereavement, loss – to do with my Father's death.

A relationship ended. The pain of the past, sorrow, missing others, the absence of other members.

Indeed, the feelings of impending loss of the programme leader preoccupied members and caused anxiety for the most part of this fourth term, in sharp contrast to the minimal expression of anger over this particular loss which was to take place at the end of term four. By the time the fifth term arrived the DMT group experience was characterised by participants' further perceptions of their loss, although this was offset by the new programme tutor arriving and the continued contact with the programme leader through the research process.

Loss was a pervading issue in all the interview transcriptions during term five. Endings concerned the loss of the programme leader, the DMT group together with participants finishing training at the end of the year, only one term away. Noticeable also was a sense of anxiety about the future, in particular how they could practise DMT without the support of an ongoing DMT group experience.

Participants' feelings around the ending of the DMT group revolved around sorting out personal feelings: 'tending to the garden and counting leaves in the garden and awaiting for the growth of the seeds that I planted' (fifth interview). It was important to extend their own living statement, a need to 'extend the seeds of my own individual life', a preparation for leaving the course. The following comment gives a feeling for this stage:

> Like how a baby sort of moves away from its mother and looks back to see that she is there and moves a bit further and comes back. It is sort of to-ing and fro-ing a bit. We only have eight sessions left feels like it's going to be very hard not to have that space. I worry, feel apprehensive about practising and not actually having DMT. I am currently involved in my psychotherapy but the work covered is quite different. The work in DMT is in the learning, learning about my own process and development and about the clients' process, I'm learning in an experiential way. I feel quite worried about the prospect of possibly becoming a practitioner and not having DMT to myself.

Part of the feeling appears to be concerned with giving up group DMT for themselves and yet continuing to provide it for clients. Much of the loss was in their having to let go of learning from an experiential perspective. It was also about the desire to retain the continuity of the group support. Comments illustrated that this was related to practice in that they were aware clients might feel similarly (although they might continue to see each other day to day) and that, as therapists, they may need to guard against 'wanting to carry on with my DMT group'. However, for the profession, being a new and emerging one, there was an especially important loss referred to, that of vital continued professional contact and a place to share ideas. This was probably linked to the ending of their training, rather than solely to the ending of DMT group. Members' own personal therapy (verbal) may have remained in place but they felt it was just not the same process as that offered by the DMT group experience. Then there was the loss of 'the nearly, almost, accepting mother [facilitator] . . .' yet concern was expressed about whether she would miss them:

> We will be missed. In the last session the goodbyes were all directed to us as clients, but when the facilitator was leaving I was aware I felt I hadn't really said goodbye to her – the therapist copping out of goodbye. She

does have to face it with us, individually us to her, and her to us. There was a general goodbye but there was an empty space there.

Fears of this emptiness and needing to 'fill the space up with something' prevailed. Thoughts about courses for the future and even approaching the facilitator to continue the DMT group, were mentioned. And then, in relation to the loss of the programme leader, there were further expressions of anger and feelings of resentment and abandonment in term five, for example:

> I was very angry when the programme leader left. It was very hard on us as we were a new group and had already lost one, and for her not to see us through which was the expectation. To leave prematurely is as big a loss, particularly in terms of our own education as dance movement therapists. She has an enormous wealth of expertise at her fingertips and I started missing [. . .] I have a delayed reaction to loss only when it comes do I actually feel loss. I find it difficult to get in touch with the feelings of loss.

This was in keeping with the lack of anger expressed at the time of the programme leader's actual resignation. Other comments reflected changes in their DMT practice and other experiences of loss as they acknowledged the ending of the group, for example:

> I feel my work has truly changed this term, maybe due to preparing to leave.

> I will be very sad when it finishes, it's a unique experience and very powerful, even if I do find another DMT group it wouldn't be the same. My separation from my mum related to programme leader leaving, she was holding us together. I can lose mum and still be OK, I didn't say goodbye properly to her because I find endings so difficult. I'm not looking forward to the ending next term.
>
> (Fifth interview)

Term six produced the final concerns over the issue of loss. It was recurrent during the final stage in the process of the DMT group, not least because the group terminated at this time, after two intensive years of weekly sessions. Feelings connected with bereavement were evident such as anger and sadness (expressed with tears). Comments pointed to an acknowledgement of a delayed reaction to the ending.

All this was despite the fact that these people were going to meet again due to the research, indicating the loss was solely about the DMT group and/or the programme as a whole; probably the two were inseparable at this stage. It is interesting to note there was a recognition of loss from their experience in the research process as well concerned with transcriptions losing their meaning, highlighted by participants reading them at this time. Anger was related to the programme leader leaving rather than identified as being concerned specifically with the ending of the DMT group. It may have been that it was easier to project anger at this rather than link it to the loss of the DMT group.

The ending was compared, by one participant, to the sister drama therapy programme in relation to their perceived intensity over their group ending. This was in contrast to the apparent lack of intensity which the DMT group seemed to be feeling over its ending, in her perception. Others mentioned endings in relation to their current practice and how they had learned to be aware of the issues surrounding endings as a result of this one. When a group member left abruptly (just before the end) due to a bereavement in her family, others became aware of this as a precursor to the DMT group's ending. Participants felt sad due to having to re-form the group without her and without the opportunity to say goodbye.

Some deterioration in aspects such as personal journal writing (a programme requirement although not submitted or assessed) was evident at this stage. One of the case profile co-researchers said how she did not feel the importance of writing in her journal since the group was soon to finish. This may indicate a depression resulting in lack of motivation to continue the commitment to the personal investment. She and others commented that they did things differently in the last DMT session, initiated by the facilitator, as an acknowledgement that the group was ending. Some felt that people left before the end in some ways; perhaps the final group being perceived as 'different' and the lack of journal writing symbolised this too. The ambivalence of the group about the ending was further illustrated in the light of the confusion they felt because they were meeting up again anyway for the research. The research clearly had effects on the DMT group and in particular the ending process. Their wish to keep in touch was already gratified through the agreed design of the research (follow-up debriefings and further interviews). This comment captures the feeling of the loss not being fully experienced since a sort of group would be maintained by the research to some extent:

> There will be some life around this group until this time next year, and maybe then the total loss of it will be found I think.
>
> (Sixth interview)

Another issue in the final term relating to this feeling of loss was concerned with a loss of opportunity. For example, one person was very aware that she had worked individually for the most part, and wished there had been more group contact on reflection. She wished she had done something more to bring this about. Another group member felt that the group life had not been looked at much at all, nor how each individual 'held' parts of the group

(Foulkes 1964) and the significance of that. She felt she too had evaded the phenomena of how she responded in groups. In relation to this Foulkes wrote:

> All events in the group are understood as being meaningful in the light of the total group matrix.

And:

> A member may meet a manifest but unrecognised part of himself in others, or a repressed aspect strongly contrasting with himself, and he may also find new aspects of his own self in the way others react to him.
>
> (Foulkes 1964: 75, 77)

During term four the fathers of three members' died. It was the parallel process of the programme leader leaving which facilitated their grief. This bereavement became explicit within the DMT group and may link to the felt absence of any male member in this all-female group.

By term six it was apparent that the fact that the group were all women brought out the issue of the lack of men in the DMT group. The deaths of group members' fathers in term three were probably a precursor to this. The lack of male members had not been mentioned in the group so it was probed in the research interviews. The work with fathers was possibly one way in which the DMT group compensated for the lack of men in the group. 'If there were a man in the group he would represent my father' was one response, seeing the group as representing the family again. Others did concede that one way of bringing men into the group was through the work on fathers. Another disclosure concerned a screen memory about being interfered with by father or grandfather; father's face emerged in the movement work.

Physical contact

Term four, the term beginning the second and final year of the DMT group (fourth interview), sowed the seed for physical contact to become a leading theme during the fifth term. In term four the expressed need for physical touch was a minor theme, but still present. Actions such as rocking, hugging, massage, pushing and pulling (and the resistance of pushing and pulling) were commented on as having taken place. Making contact in a physical way such as this or by simply bumping into someone was seen as positive for the group.

However, touch became a major issue in term five, linked to that of space. It arose several times within the ambivalent message of wishing to work together as well as the desire for individuality. Perhaps safety was needed due to increasing vulnerability. One way given by participants of gaining this was fulfilling a need to make more physical contact with group members. However, it was clearly difficult to initiate this for fear of invasion or rejection:

> Lots of times I felt I wanted to make contact but when I looked around in desperation and others were so involved in their own thing I thought – that is the best thing. I haven't done it, I have not really wanted to interrupt someone else's space.

> I would have liked more contact with others, having a safe mum – to hold hands. I haven't felt secure at times in myself because the process for me is so big. Perhaps I needed people a bit closer. I was afraid I would be rejected if I asked for that.

Physical contact had been an ongoing matter for this co-researcher. She comments on her lack of initiative in the area of physical contact, although the following quotation demonstrates a desire to use her body to obliterate the others. This is a good example of how non-verbalised anger might be manifested in the movement imagination ('squash them'). The desire to destroy the group as the ending becomes imminent is not uncommon as a way of dealing with the lack of control of termination not having been chosen by participants (Rutan and Stone 1993):

> I don't initiate much contact in the DMT group although in the final session I wanted to roll over everyone and squash them! It is difficult to have physical contact in the group. I go elsewhere to get that need met, do a lot of contact improvisation, feed elsewhere in a different group. I don't want to get it started.

In contrast to these examples one member said how much easier physical contact had been in the group in term five. Another co-researcher's story speaks of the contact experienced from another participant (client as therapist) as positively supportive, in contrast to the intervention from the facilitator:

> The facilitator prompted me to do something. I was absolutely furious with her [laugh] you know, I just felt 'How dare you?', you know, the fact that I am here is enough and I don't need this, leave me alone. I felt very angry. Then another 'client' actually initiated contact – it felt not like a demand, just two entities, very supportive. At that moment I felt quite unsupported by the facilitator but supported by the group and the space. I expected the support from the facilitator but didn't get it at the time.
>
> (Fifth interview)

Finally, the major theme of safety (Payne 2001) was connected to physical contact as is seen in this example:

> I found the physical contact helped me feel safe and the message in it was 'I am here and I care about you'. There were no demands, I didn't feel the group were focusing on me. One came up to me, which was a message 'I empathize with you' and then she went on her way.

In term six, the final period of the DMT group experience, the theme of sexuality in relation to physical contact emerged for the first time. Sexuality was explored in terms of their own and their clients' sexuality (for example, child sexual abuse and sexual orientation). The hypothetical man was referred to as being able to supply a gender difference. The fact that two members made it clear about their lesbian sexual orientation at the beginning of the group later brought up issues around physical contact and sexuality for the other members. For example:

> That was an issue for me linked with the intimacy issues. Asking about my own sexuality and being unsure about it and if there was a man bringing sexuality and my response to that too. The fact that people had different sexual orientations . . . affected, I think, the intimacy in the group, well, I don't know . . . I remember there was one group I was running and one of the things that came up in supervision was the supervisor suggesting maybe my boundaries, that I was unsure of them and my own sexual orientation yeh . . . [silence]. Maybe I'm fearful about that, and realizing for all of us we have a homosexual part. It's about accepting, not being fearful of it. I have new under-standings. I have not had strong feelings about homosexuals. This was the first time I'd been with people who had actually said 'I am a lesbian.'
>
> (Sixth interview)

Bodily movements were experienced as connected to participants' own sexuality and the difficulties in expressing this in the DMT group such as:

> When I was wiggling my hips one time I was thinking, 'No – this is sexual and I shouldn't be doing that in here at all.' That is the constraint I have, you know. So it helped me when somebody else began talking about being self-conscious, and to be aware of this.
>
> (Sixth interview)

Perhaps there was more fear around the expression of physical contact as well as sexuality because of the sexual orientation of some participants. However, the issue was experienced as having raised an awareness of members' feelings about sexuality in a profound way.

When a participant referred to her experiences of childhood sexual abuse it became clearer how feelings were initially confused then worked through in the DMT group as a result of addressing the issue of sexuality. Intimacy was mentioned (assuming this referred to physical contact as well) in connection with sexuality, for example:

> I would always link it to intimacy if it went far enough and it became sexual.

And:

> I was needing closeness not sexual intimacy so I see how I got these two caught up.

By term six this notion had begun to be linked to their DMT practice; for example, in the comment: 'It has given me more confidence in my work . . . umm . . . concerning clients' sexuality.'

Experiencing the DMT method

By term two, midway through year one, we see the first references to the nature, facilitation method and structure of the DMT group developing. There appears to have been an emphasis on the importance of ritual in relation to the security or safety needs within the group.

> The group has a repetitive format. We move as a group, there is interaction at the start, or we go in partners. Then we're put in a patch alone, then there's discussion of common issues. We all talk individually, for example, about anger. But we can't explore it together because of the structure, because of the reflection time at the end, if it was in the middle there would be time to move again.
>
> (Second interview)

Dissatisfactions in the way the group was set up and run by the facilitator were frequently described, such as the reflection time at the end or the lack of work in a whole group as indicated, for example, in this comment:

> We are doing less as a whole group. I don't feel I always have to be with the group, moving together does happen but is less important.

By term four we can see other messages about the facilitator, such as her initiating connection within the group through a circle formation in contrast to encouraging a focus on one member resulting in other's noticing their neediness. She was experienced as talking only to individuals and not to the whole group in term four, engendering some envy. It was clear to the group members that the facilitator did not always notice when someone needed to be left alone rather than encouraged. The nature of confidentiality and the importance of the facilitator not sharing group information with assessing staff was noted:

> I can share more of myself because it feels safer to share when I know the facilitator won't say it to tutors who are in an educating role, and assessing me, in terms of a trainee dance movement therapist.
>
> (Second interview)

By term three, the end of year one, we can see more of the participants' concentration on the specific aims they perceive the DMT group to have. For example, links are made with issues like the role of personal therapy in relation to the DMT group and the fact that it was an 'as if' group not individual therapy. There was reference to issues surrounding a therapy group as personal development in an educational setting. The notion of whether it was legitimate to have a quasi-therapy group in higher education was something addressed at programme validation. In connection with this idea one participant said:

> I think it can't be totally a therapy group because it is something that is within a college. It's about people's commitment to the programme not the DMT group. More like a course module but for myself too. I don't think I've explored my commitment or views about the DMT group. I am trying to get a view on what sort of group this is. Where does it fit into DMT and bodywork? – I don't know. I use it for myself, for example today I worked with a cushion in terms of a relationship, difficult feelings emerged and I thought, 'Should I be showing this in the group?'
>
> (Third interview)

She indicates here it was different from any other therapy group because of the context; that is, if you are on this course you have to attend the DMT group 'module'. This could be seen to mirror several settings in which a DMT group might be held such as prisons, secure units, day centres and schools. In these settings clients may attend therapy as mandatory if designated as part of their 'care plan' or 'activity'. There are many models of therapy taking place in settings other than health, which do not aim at 'treatment' or the medical model per se where clients 'opt' for DMT. The comment above also draws our attention to the fact that the DMT group is for individual personal development, much as in any psychotherapy training where the PD/training group or experiential group is for the individual trainee therapist as part of their programme.

To return to the issue of commitment (whether reluctance or resistance) referred to in the above quotation, this might relate to the idea of whether attendance at the DMT group should be voluntary or compulsory. The participants did not volunteer for the DMT group as would have been possible outside the context of the programme. However, they were aware of the component (albeit not fully knowledgeable of the implications) prior to registering for the programme, unlike some clients in other settings. They could volunteer for personal therapy, although now trainees are required by ADMTUK to enter personal therapy as a mandatory requirement of their training, in contrast to the British Association for Counselling and Psychotherapy's new guidelines. In therapeutic communities or hospitals, for example, the patients/clients are expected to attend group or individual therapy as part of their treatment/rehabilitation plan, not all therapy needs to be voluntary (Barber 1988).

In term four participants refer to the theme of the nature of the DMT group. A comment about the need for safety to work as a group was less interesting than that about a reticence to initiate working as a whole group for fear their individual experience in DMT would be forfeited: 'If we address group issues we won't get our DMT, it's so precious.' They appear to take responsibility for the lack of whole group experiences by this stage. It was felt they would sacrifice their own DMT experience if they focused on the group. So, in experiencing the method for this particular DMT group they felt a pressure to forfeit the group for individual needs. In contrast they appeared to desire something from the group although a lack of safety may have resulted in a dissatisfaction with group members' resistance to sharing, revealed by comments such as: 'Lots of potential but it doesn't happen that we use one another ... not safe enough so I don't make it happen' or 'Asking for something from the group is very difficult' (Fourth interview).

This quotation above links to the major theme evident in term five – the taking of time and space in the group. It was not so much of an issue in term four, but by term five participants do begin to ask for time but with a sense that there may have been a rejection if they were to ask for too much.

The fear of spillage of inside (group) issues, to the outside world was present in term four. Perhaps this was why there was a reluctance to work on group issues. The following quotation puts it succinctly:

> If stuff between members came out in the group it might affect the work we do with colleagues during the rest of the day ... I hold back in the group because the real stuff between members could be traumatic.

The subtheme of conformity was also evident here (it arose again in term five): 'The thought of breaking ranks from the group is frightening.' Daring not to conform, be different, was seen to be very scary at this stage in the life of the group. This links with the fear of expressing anger in term four. If they were to express this emotion they would be seen as breaking rank perhaps, and so risked the possibility of the fear fantasy of the group breaking apart coming true.

Physical contact was mentioned in relation to helping members to feel connected to the group. The resignation of the programme leader was seen to be 'a big issue' for the group, provoking a fragility and need for further dependency upon each other.

This was indicated in the comment to follow, which may be a reflection of the need for more physical contact, the term 'leaning' not used purely as a metaphor: 'It means we have to lean on each other more.' This participant continues to mention absence from the group in connection with safety: 'The group is a less safe place to take issues because it is not always present in its entirety, people don't look after the group.' And in another comment: 'It should be compulsory to attend. It is important to have all present' (Fourth interview).

The group again became symbolic of a family to some members in term four: 'The group relationships mirror the family and the role I have taken on in it.' In relation to this the idea of becoming more aware of helping others in the group, and the group itself, emerged. For some the group became both the supporter and the helper (group as therapist) as illustrated in the following comments:

> I realize it can be the whole group by itself which can help, rather than the facilitator.

> Links are made within the group themes. I am looking more at others, I'm interested more in what others are doing and saying.

> There's my reaching out to the group and them to me. The group is supportive, sympathetic, friendships are deepening.
>
> (Fourth interview)

Other comments give the impression of an irritation with members' contribution, that they may have seemed over-demanding to others, perhaps a projected fear they may provoke anger or rejection from the group. In addition, for one respondent, when she takes time in the group, this appears to result in a sort of artificiality feeling in which members do not appear to be authentic, repressing what lies behind their 'fidgets'. Whereas when others speak of not being able to be as involved it may indicate a withdrawal into isolation as was prevalent earlier in the group life. It may be that the fear of anger led to such positions becoming adopted. These two quotations crystallise the notion of participants feeling passive and separate from the group in term four:

> I'm feeling guilty about not being able to be an active group member.

And:

> I feel less responsible for the group. I didn't feel part of the group, was
> just there.

(Fourth interview)

Discussion

In presenting this analysis of these themes, over time connections were made
between them in order to make further sense of the way in which participants
experienced the DMT group. This chapter discussed three of the themes
deriving from an analysis of the data from years one and two of the research
(interviews one to six). In terms of connections between them, first there is
the paradox of whether the DMT group promotes the group or the individual.
The tension between these is clearly illustrated by the comments about feelings
of anger and loss. In turn these feelings lead to a fragile state linked somewhat
to the perceived need for more physical contact with each other in the group.
There is some indication that this contact would not be forthcoming, and
there was a hesitancy to initiate it, for a variety of reasons.

Second, leavings, loss and endings were significant. These focused on
fathers, the end of the work-practice group, the programme leader's resignation, one group member leaving early and the imminent ending of the
DMT group itself in term six. By this time, in particular, there was a feeling
that they had not worked enough as a group nor emphasised the group life
and how each individual held parts of it. The focus had been on the individual in the main, it was felt. Some responsibility for this was accepted by
one of the participants whereas others laid it at the door of the facilitator. It
was clearly important to continue to come together after the ending to receive
professional, personal and practical support. The fear that this might not
happen was evident, as was a recognition that they were denying the pain of
separation by focusing on these fantasies.

Safety was a recurring common theme, the lack of it particularly concerning
the expression of anger. The facilitator's attitude, use of physical contact,
permission to take up more physical space and the freedom to be themselves
were the main reasons for feeling there was an increase in safety over time.
The data suggest they were eventually able to trust the facilitator and each
other enough to express themselves uninhibitedly. This notion was supported
by one co-researcher who, after the last interview, requested all transcriptions
to analyse and interpret, and wrote of her later feelings of trust and safety in
the group and the facilitator.

There were some relevant themes during the two years concerning the
DMT group and practice. Some definitely felt their practice had changed by
term six due to, for example, increased confidence in themselves and in their
risk taking. Criticism of the facilitation process was evident at times, as well

as the normal positive comments such as how the facilitator provided security for the group and how they might model this for practice groups. Towards the end some participants identified with the facilitator whereby more speculation of how she might be feeling about the loss of the group emerged.

Participants had an understanding that the DMT group was not 'the' model for their own practice and that the training as a whole aimed to give a wide base of approach. This idea that the DMT group was tailored to the trainee rather than as a method or approach to transfer to client practice is founded on the premise that the student participates 'as if client' in the group. It became clear towards the end that participants understood they were not going 'to get it handed to them on a plate', but that they needed to develop their own models of practice dependent on their client's level of functioning (just as the model of the DMT group was based on their own level of functioning), the setting and their own skills, aptitudes, beliefs and personality. An appreciation of the long-term nature of the DMT process was apparent.

By the final term participants realised the importance of the holding environment (Winnicott 1965) and that consciousness concerning their development/learning in clinical practice paralleled the ending of the DMT group. Examples of the types of countertransferences arising in practice were identified, that is, personal material which could be worked through in the group increasing personal awareness. Being 'as if' in the role of client was seen as necessary for a dance movement therapist in training. From a subsequent analysis there appear to be a number of areas in (a) knowledge, (b) understanding, (c) clinical skills and (d) aptitudes for the developing dance movement therapist to consider when embarking on professional practice in groupwork.

Knowledge is required of:

- the impact of the approach adopted for DMT group work on group process
- the importance of physical contact linked to the role of sexuality and how these might be manifested in connection to group themes emerging, such as fear–safety
- the implications of single and mixed gender groups and the responses they elicit.

Understanding is required of:

- the importance of safety, including ritual and boundaries (such as confidentiality) and how these differ from one to one therapy and in different clinical contexts

- how groups come to represent family for individuals and the expression of this through movement
- the ways in which context, conflict, absence, loss, endings and presence impact on group process
- the importance of movement and stillness, engagement and non-engagement
- the limitations of facilitation at times, the impact of specific group material on the facilitator and the typical projections a facilitator can expect from a DMT group
- the probable feelings to emerge in the group, such as anger/loss, need to conform or break away from the norm, or rejection/fragility/envy and fear
- the nature of empathic attunement (verbal and movement) and how it can be communicated by the facilitator.

Clinical skills could be developed from this type of experiential learning group and might include:

- the capacity to empathise somatically with others, at a body-felt level
- the ability to decide whether/when and how to intervene with a client with movement/stillness or in silence/with words/sounds
- the facility to make contact physically, through movement and words to facilitate a non-verbal dialogue with clients
- the competence to utilise metaphor and symbolic movement processes together with language and the imagination for joining with/building a relationship with others
- the capacity to track feelings and movement in herself and the client, to provide a foundation for an awareness of unconscious somatic countertransference responses
- competence in the verbal reflection of movement processes, active listening, abstinence of questioning, the use of linking skills and verbal interpretation where appropriate (Hyvonen 2005).

Aptitudes might include:

- using the self as a container in the facilitation process
- self-reflection and an awareness of primitive mental/altered states.

Conclusion

This chapter described some of the narratives of trainee dance movement therapists towards their experiences of a DMT personal development group, analysed into three themes. These themes were amongst a number to emerge which were documented over time to provide a process account of the students' lived experience of the group and their perceptions of how it connected to their DMT practice.

References

Aveline, M. (1986) Personal themes from training groups for health care professionals, *British Journal for Medical Psychology* 59, 325–335.

Bachelor, A. (1991) Comparison and relationship to outcome of diverse dimensions of the helping alliance as seen by client and therapist, *Psychotherapy* 25, 227–240.

Barber, P. (1988) Learning to grow: the necessity for educational processing in therapeutic community practice, *International Journal of Therapeutic Communities* 9, 2.

Berrol, C. (2000) The spectrum of research option in dance movement therapy, *American Journal of Dance Therapy* 22, 1, 29–46.

Bischoff, R.J. and McBride, A. (1996) Clients' perceptions of couple and family therapy, *American Journal of Family Therapy* 24, 117–128.

Bungay, V. and Keddy, B.C. (1996) Experiential analysis as a feminist methodology for health professionals, *Qualitative Health Research* 6, 442–452.

Caskey, N.H., Barker, C. and Elliott, R. (1984) Dual perspectives: clients' and therapists' perceptions of therapist responses, *British Journal of Clinical Psychology* 23, 281–290.

Charmaz, K. (1995) Grounded theory, in J.A. Smith, R. Harre and L. van Lagenhave (eds) *Rethinking Methods in Psychology*. London: Sage.

Dinnage, R. (1989) *One to One: Experiences of Individual Psychotherapy*. Harmondsworth: Penguin.

Dosamantes, E. (1990) Movement and psychodynamic pattern changes in long term movement groups. *American Journal of Dance Therapy*, *12*, 1.

Edwards, J.M. (1999) Considering the pragmatic frame: social science research approaches relevant to research in music therapy, *The Arts in Psychotherapy* 26, 281–290.

Elliott, R. and James, E. (1989) Varieties of client experience in psychotherapy: an analysis of the literature, *Clinical Psychology Review*, 9, 443–467.

Erikson, K. and Stull, D. (1998) *Doing Team Ethnography: Warnings and Advice*. Thousand Oaks: CA: Sage.

Etherington, K. (2000) *Narrative Approaches to Working with Adult Male Survivors of Child Sexual Abuse: The Client's, the Counsellor's and the Researcher's Story*. London: Jessica Kingsley.

Forinash, M. (1995) Phenomenological research, in B.L. Wheeler (ed) *Music Therapy Research: Quantitative and Qualitative Perspectives*. Phoenixville, PA: Barcelona Books.

Foulkes, S. H. (1964) *Therapeutic group analysis*. New York: International Universities Press.

Geertz, C. (1973) *The Interpretation of Cultures*. New York: Basic Books.

Gershefski, J.J., Arnkoff, D.B., Glass, C.R. and Elkin, I. (1996) Client perceptions of treatment for depression: helpful aspects, *Psychotherapy Research* 6, 233–247.

Glaser, B.G. and Strauss, A.L. (1967) *Discovery of Grounded Theory*. Chicago: Aldine.

Grafanaki, S. and McLeod, J. (1995) Client and counsellor narrative accounts of congruence during the most helpful and most hindering events of an initial counselling session, *Counselling Psychology Quarterly* 8, 311–325.

Heppner, P. P., Rosenberg, J.I. and Hedgespeth, J. (1992) Three methods in measuring the therapeutic process: clients', counselors' constructions of the therapeutic process versus actual therapeutic events, *Journal of Counselling Psychology* 39, 20–31.

Heron, J. (1971) *Experience and Method: An Inquiry into the Concept of Experiential Research*. University of Surrey: Human Potential Research Project.

—— (1981) Experiential research methods, in P. Reason and J. Rowan (eds) *Human Inquiry: A Sourcebook for New Paradigm research*. Chichester: Wiley.

Hill, C. (1989) *Therapist Techniques and Client Outcomes*. London: Sage.

Hill, C., Thompson, B., Cogar, M. and Denman, D. (1993) Beneath the surface of long-term therapy: therapist and client reports of their own and each other's covert processes, *Journal of Counseling Psychology* 40, 278–287.

Howe, D. (1996) Client experiences of counselling and treatment interventions: a qualitative study of family views of a family therapy, *British Journal of Guidance and Counselling* 24, 367–375.

Hyvonen, K. (2005) Competency and professional development in the dance movement therapy profession, unpublished MSc dissertation, University of Hertfordshire.

Izzard, S. and Wheeler, S. (1995) The development of self awareness: an essential aspect of counsellor training. Abstract of a study at the University of Birmingham at the first BAC Research Conference, February 1995, *Counselling* 6, 3, 227.

Junge, M.B. and Linesch, D. (1993a) An exploration into qualitative research in music therapy, *The Arts in Psychotherapy* 20, 61–68.

—— (1993b) Our own voices: new paradigm for art therapy research, *The Arts in Psychotherapy* 21, 61–67.

Lietaer, G. and Neirinck, M. (1986) Client and therapist perceptions of helping processes in client-centred/experiential psychotherapy, *Person-Centred Review* 4, 436–455.

Lincoln, Y.S. and Guba, E.G. (1985) *Naturalistic Inquiry*. London: Sage.

Lott, D.A. (1999) *In Session: The Bond Between Women and Their Therapists*. New York: Freeman.

Lucchi, B. (1998) *Authentic movement as a training modality for private practice clinicians*. Unpublished dissertation in fulfillment of Doctor of Clinical Psychology, California Graduate Institute.

McLeod, J. (1990) The client's experience of counselling: a review of the research literature, in D. Mearns and W. Dryden (eds) *Experiences of Counselling in Action*. London: Sage.

—— (1994) *Doing Counselling Research*. London: Sage.

McNiff, S. (1998) *Art Based Research*. London: Jessica Kingsley.

Macran, S., Stiles, W.B. and Smith, J.A. (1999) How does personal therapy affect therapists' practice?, *Journal of Counseling Psychology* 46, 419–431.

Martin, J. and Stelmaczonek, K. (1988) Participants' identification and recall of important events in counselling, *Journal of Counseling Psychology* 35, 385–390.

Moustakas, C. (1994) *Phenomenological Research Methods*. Thousand Oaks, CA: Sage.

Newman, G. and Collie, K. (1984) Dramatherapy training and practice: an overview, *Journal of Mental Imagery* 18, 1, 119–125.

Olesen, V., Droes, N., Hatton, D., Chico, N. and Schatzman, L. (1994) Analysing together, in A. Boyman and R.G. Burgess (eds) *Analysing Qualitative Data*. London: Routledge.

Orlinsky, D.E. and Howard, K.L. (1986) Process and outcomes in psychotherapy, in S.L. Garfield and A.E. Bergin (eds) *Handbook of Psychotherapy and Behaviour Change*. New York: Wiley.

Parker, I. (1992) *Discourse Dynamics: Critical Analysis for Social and Individual Psychology*. London: Routledge.

Paulson, B., Truscott, D. and Stuart, J. (1999) Clients' perception of helpful experiences in counselling, *Journal of Counselling Psychology* 46, 317–324.

Paulson, B., Everall, R. and Stuart, J. (2001) Client perceptions of hindering experiences in counselling, *Counselling and Psychotherapy Research* 1, 53–61.

Payne, H.L. (1992) Shut in, shut out: adolescent perceptions of a DMT group, in H.L. Payne (ed.) *Dance Movement Therapy: Theory and Practice*. London: Routledge.

—— (1996a) The experience of a dance movement therapy group in higher education, unpublished PhD thesis, University of London. Copy in LRC, University of Hertfordshire, UK.

—— (1996b) From practitioner to researcher, in H.L. Payne (ed.) *Handbook of Inquiry in the Arts Therapies: One River, Many Currents*. London: Jessica Kingsley.

—— (1999) Personal development groups in the training of counsellors and therapists: a review of the research, *European Journal of Psychotherapy, Counselling and Health* 2, 1, 55–68.

—— (2001) Student experiences in a personal development group: the question of safety, *European Journal of Psychotherapy, Counselling and Health* 4, 2, 267–292.

—— (2002a) *Die wilden Eisbaren – Die kleine Schaferin – Erfahrungen mit der Methode – Hautdichter Kontakt: Studentische Erfahrungen einer TanzBewegungstherapiegruppe* [Ferocious polar bears; Little Bo Peep she lost her sheep; experiencing the method and skin to skin contact: student perceptions of a dance movement therapy group] *Forum Tanztherapie* 1, 22, 60–77.

—— (2002b) A comparison between personal development groups in arts therapies and group psychotherapy training: an international survey. International *Arts Therapies Journal* 1, 1. Online. Available HTTP: http://www.derby.ac.uk/v-art/journal/archives/2002/articles/intsurvey/index.html (accessed 6 June 2005).

—— (2004) Becoming a client, becoming a practitioner: student narratives of a dance movement therapy group, *British Journal of Guidance and Counselling* 32, 4, 511–532.

Potter, J. and Wetherall, M. (1987) *Discourse and Social Psychology: Beyond Attitudes and Behaviour*. London: Sage.

Reason, P. (ed.) (1988) *Human Inquiry in Action*. London: Sage.

—— (ed.) (1994) *Participation in Inquiry*. London: Sage.

Reason, P. and Rowan, J. (eds) (1981) *Human Inquiry: A Sourcebook for New Paradigm Research*. Chichester: Wiley.

Rennie, D. (1990) Towards a representation of the clients' experience of the psychotherapy hour, in G. Lietaer, J. Rombauts and R. van Balen (eds) *Client-Centered and Experiential Psychotherapy in the Nineties*. Leuven: Leuven University Press.

Ryden, J. and Lowenthal, D. (2001) Psychotherapy for lesbians: the influence of therapist sexuality, *Counselling and Psychotherapy Research* 1, 42–53.

Rutan, J.S. and Stone, W.N. (1993) *Psychodynamic Group Psychotherapy*. New York: Guilford Press.

Sands, A. (2000) *Falling for Therapy: Psychotherapy from a Client's Point of View*. London: Macmillan.

Schmais, C. (1981) Group development and group formation in dance therapy, *Arts in Psychotherapy*, *8*, 103–107.

Schmais, C. (1985) Healing processes in group dance therapy, *American Journal of Dance Therapy*, *8*, 17–36.

Schmais, C. (1998) Understanding the dance movement therapy group, *American Journal of Dance Therapy* 8, 17–36.

Schmais, C. (1999) Marion Chace Memorial Lecture Group. A door to awareness, *American Journal of Dance Therapy*, *21*, 1.

Schon, D.A. (1983) *The Reflective Practitioner. How Professionals Think in Action*. London: Basic Books.

—— (1988) *Educating the Reflective Practitioner*. San Francisco: Jossey-Bass.

Seligman, M. (1995) The effectiveness of psychotherapy: the consumer reports study, *American Psychologist* 50, 965–974.

Siegal, E.V. (1995) Dance Therapy: the bridge between the psyche and soma, *American Journal of Dance Therapy*, *17*, 2.

Spaniol, S. (1998) Towards an ethnographic approach to art therapy research: people with psychotic disability as collaborators, *Art Therapy* 15, 29–37.

Small, J.J. and Manthei, R.J. (1988) Groupwork in counsellor training: research and development in one programme, *British Journal of Guidance and Counselling* 16, 1, 33–49.

Steier, F. (ed.) (1991) *Research and Reflexivity*. London: Sage.

Stiles, W.B. (1993) Qualitative control in qualitative research, *Clinical Psychology Review* 13, 593–618.

Torbert, W. (1981) Empirical, behavioural, theoretical and attentional skills needed for collaborative inquiry, in P. Reason and J. Rowan (eds) *Human Inquiry: A Sourcebook for New Paradigm Research*. Chichester: Wiley.

Truax, C.B. and Carkuff, R. (1967) *Towards Effective Counselling and Psychotherapy Training and Practice*. Chicago: Aldine.

Watson, J. and Rennie, D. (1994) Qualitative analysis of clients' subjective experience of significant moments during the exploration of problematic reactions, *Journal of Consulting Psychology* 41, 500–509.

Wilkins, P. (1999) Collaborative inquiry as a teaching and learning strategy in a university setting: processes within an experiential group – the group's story, *Psychology Teaching Review* 8, 4–18.

—— (2000) A group's experience of process in person-centred psychodrama: a qualitative inquiry, *British Journal of Psychodrama and Sociodrama* 15, 1, 231–411.

Winnicott, D.W. (1965) The theory of the parent–infant relationship, in D.W. Winnicott, *The Maturational Processes and the Facilitating Environment*. London: Hogarth Press, pp. 37–55.

Wyatt, J. (2002) Confronting the almighty god? A study of how psychodynamic counsellors respond to clients' expression of religious faith, *Counselling and Psychotherapy Research* 2, 177–184.

Chapter 13

Dance movement therapy with undergraduate dance students

'Special ingredients' in the development of playfulness, self-confidence and relationship

Jill Hayes

Introduction

In this chapter I would like to share the process findings from my recent doctoral study into the perceived effects on self and choreography/performance offered to me by the undergraduate dance students who took part in a dance movement therapy (DMT) experiential group. There are three groups in the study, which are referred to as Cohort One (C1), Cohort Two (C2) and Cohort Three (C3). The majority of the students were in their early twenties, white, British and female, attending a small university in the south of England. The dance experience of these students is varied, yet there is a strong presence of ballet, tap, stage school training and certainly a predominant emphasis upon external forms. The experiential group ran over a period of between eight to ten weeks in the students' final term at university. Students elected to participate. It was not obviously connected to choreography or performance through literature or assessment.

Methodology

The methodology for the study was qualitative and is framed as a multiple case study, offering analysis and reflection on context (Stake 2000). The research questions were:

1   Are there any perceived links between DMT, choreography and performance?
2   If so, what are they?
3   How do they develop?

This chapter responds to the research question concerned with how these links develop. Data for this chapter are taken primarily from the semi-structured individual and group interviews, with particular reference to questions exploring participants' experience of the DMT group and inquiring if it affected them personally and, if so, how?

Thematic analysis (Huberman and Miles 2000) of transcripts involved interpretation of participants' reflections and creation of categories, which the researcher judged to represent the concepts being reflected upon. Similarities and differences were noted (Bungay and Keddy 1996) and predominant themes were highlighted (Potter and Wetherall 1987). Contradictions were sought (Rowan 1981) and categories were continuously cross-checked with the data. Categories changed as a result of these processes.

Findings

The interpreted categories of perceived effect on self (perceived by participants to exist both in the context of the DMT group and as a permanent development) were playfulness, self-confidence and relationship. These were formed from the following dichotomies:

- spontaneous movement versus interrupted movement
- self-awareness and self-acceptance versus alienation from self
- awareness of others versus alienation from others.

Commonly perceived causal factors for these phenomena were play, movement metaphors, acceptance and safety.

Playfulness is defined as free, open, spontaneous engagement with process, often accompanied by enjoyment. *Self-confidence* is perceived as overlapping with playfulness in terms of openness to process, but containing other concepts such as self-value and self-assertion. *Relationship* is defined as connection to others and involvement with others. *Play* is defined as free, childlike movement, frequently involving imaginative experience. *Movement metaphor* is defined as symbolic movement. *Acceptance* is defined as affirmation of self, including experience and feelings. It refers to acceptance by others and also to self-acceptance. *Safety* refers to a feeling of security and containment.

The role of play, movement metaphors, acceptance and safety in the development of playfulness, self-confidence and relationship

Play and the development of playfulness

Play was identified as central to the model of DMT here experienced. Participants spoke of an enhanced ability to play. Play was associated with fluidity and openness, freedom and exploration. Generally, participants valued having time to explore movement free from product making. They felt they had been given permission to be themselves, encouraged to make internal connections and internal decisions. They spoke of 'learning how to play again', 'feeling free', 'being a child again', 'forgetting their troubles', 'having fun', 'letting go' and 'not bothering about what others might think'. These comments on play led to the emergence of the concept of playfulness. It seemed that there were two essential aspects to playfulness being developed in DMT, namely:

• fluidity and openness to process
• a feeling of enjoyment.

Fluidity and openness to process was noticed by participants in comments such as:

> There are times when I get lost in the movement and the movements flow one to another; it comes so naturally.

Openness to process was sometimes connected to childhood play in DMT:

> A regressive childhood thing, age three, finding an inner something, rather than the intellectual; if you go into inner emotions and feelings, the inner creative part, there's a space for that intuitive, childlike, creative thing inside us, that you can tap, the Unconscious, and go with that, let the Unconscious come out a bit, let it flow, and if you can tap into that a bit really, rather than trapping it and getting caught in a web.

Freedom, going back in time, being a child again, intuitive awareness, emotion and creativity are all present in this reflection. Perhaps the emphasis on finding the child within and connecting with feelings through play is particular to the model of DMT here researched. Perhaps the encouragement of play in this model nurtured spontaneous movement infused with childlike, emotional vitality, which contributed to the development of playfulness, as indicated in the following comment: 'In almost every session we were wild and childish; there was a playfulness about us.'

This childlike, emotional vitality was perceived as developing through suspension of intellectual and external concern, and through permission to explore 'inner' realities. The concepts of 'letting go', 'suspending the rational mind', 'playing with metaphors and symbols' have been discussed in relation to therapy (Winnicott 1985; Cox and Theilgaard 1987), in relation to DMT (Payne 1992; Stanton-Jones 1992; Meekums 2002) and in relation to creativity (Arieti 1976; Meekums 1993). Winnicott writes:

> Psychotherapy takes place in the overlap of two areas of playing, that of the patient and that of the therapist. Psychotherapy has to do with two people playing together. The corollary of this, is that where playing is not possible then the work done by the therapist is directed towards bringing

the patient from a state of not being able to play into a state of being able to play.

(Winnicott 1985: 44)

Winnicott refers to therapy as 'playing' in a 'transitional space'. He sees therapy as a mingling of lived and imaginary experience, a meeting of two real/imaginary worlds. Playing, by Winnicott's definition, requires an ability to inhabit an imaginary world and this ability is cultivated by a relationship in which the person feels affirmed and respected as a valuable human being. Where affirmation and respect are present, the person's inner being or 'true self' can emerge in play and be creative.

Students emphasised 'having fun' and 'enjoying' play in DMT. Relishing personal movement in play is a common feature of childhood play (Millar 1976; Garvey 1977). In this instance, having fun seems to have contributed to free-flow movement and reconnection with self in dance as illustrated in the following comment:

> Dance is there to be enjoyed, a way of expressing yourself, and when somebody stops enjoying it, that's very harming. I found that by doing this group [DMT], I thought 'No, I don't care. I might not be able to do that perfectly, but I'll try it and to hell with it'; whereas before it was restrictive.

Enjoyment of movement in play seems to have motivated student involvement with DMT. It lessened anxiety in relation to the unknown quantity of DMT and weakened the restrictive influence of aesthetics and assessment. This finding corresponds to Mills and Daniluk's (2002) recent research into DMT with women survivors of child sexual abuse. In their study, 'permission to play' was identified as significant in providing balance in DMT. The women involved were able to recapture a feeling of playfulness and freedom through play, which constituted a vital counterpoint to the 'heavier' work of reconnecting with painful memories.

Play and the development of self-confidence

Self-confidence may be considered as dependent upon self-trust or the ability to respond to and express internal experience. Winnicott (1985) suggests a sequence of three processes in the development of a 'true' sense of self. The concept of the 'true self' seems akin to the Rogerian (1957) concept of congruence in that the inner life of the person is perceived as motivating external action. Winnicott's sequence is as follows:

(a) Relaxation in conditions of trust
(b) Creative, physical and mental activity manifested in play

(c) The summation of these experiences forming the basis for sense of self.

(Winnicott 1985: 66)

Dissipation of anxiety seems to have occurred through play in this study. The enjoyment and relaxation found in play were identified as facilitating involvement in process. In all cohorts, assertion of self was one of the first themes to emerge, as participants began to connect with inner impulses and feelings, and became more aware of needs, themes and patterns of behaviour. Winnicott writes:

In these highly specialized conditions, the individual can come together and exist as a unit, not as a defence against anxiety but as an expression of I AM, I am alive, I am myself.

(Winnicott 1985: 66)

The freedom afforded by play was acknowledged in comments such as:

It is not structured or set; it is free, you can do what you feel. You are not restricted in any way to do what someone is telling you to do or what you think you should do.

Sometimes participants discussed a process of emotional evolution and self-awareness through play. This process and its relationship to self-confidence are discussed in the next section.

Movement metaphors and the development of playfulness

Movement metaphors were vehicles of play in the DMT group. Thus, playfulness developed through engagement with movement metaphors. Students spoke of 'feeling more free in their bodies', 'feeling looser', 'moving like a child', 'moving spontaneously'. It seems that involvement with movement metaphors contributed to the loss of 'dance-like' movement and to the development of 'free-flow, unself-conscious movement'. One student described the spontaneous evolution of a 'nest' metaphor:

I remember how we made a bird's nest: everyone made a long line and I wanted to be part of it and not long after that everyone started changing and I just stayed where I was and when I sat up there was the bird's nest with the opening towards me, so I just climbed in and curled up.

This recollection captures the playful quality of movement, created in the moment, without conscious desire to craft or organise. This memory of creation of movement metaphor is fairly typical of other recollections of movement creation. The movements are described as 'coming out of nowhere', as 'playful' and 'spontaneous', as well as 'surprising', for example, 'That was weird!', 'It was amazing!'

The phenomenon of surprise in metaphor has been discussed in relation to therapy (Cox and Theilgaard 1987), DMT (Meekums 2002) and creativity (Arieti 1976; Meekums 1993). Cox and Theilgaard have noted the startling quality of metaphor free from rational control; Meekums has warned of the power of movement in DMT to waken sleeping trauma in the body, whilst Arieti has noted the sudden creative synthesis which can occur through metaphor.

Chodorow (1991) refers to DMT as 'moving imagination'. As such, it has affinity with all therapies, which use imagination as a central tool. In DMT participants may feel they can inhabit their imagination and share it with others. Participants in this study engaged playfully with metaphor, often fluidly and openly and sometimes with a sense of enjoyment and humour. There were many metaphors, for example, the nest, the baby in the womb, the cyclone/storm, the embrace, the barrier, the playground and hiding.

It is suggested that in all these examples, participants became involved in symbolic movement, usually without thought of potential meaning. It seemed as though they were immersed in the activity. They were in the nest, in the womb, in the cyclone/storm; they experienced the embrace, the barrier, the playground, and felt what it was like to hide under the stretch cloth, referred to as 'the green protection'. Through make-believe, it seemed that they were able to explore the various dimensions which the metaphor presented to them. They seem to have explored what it was like both inside and outside the nest, womb, storm/cyclone; and seem to have experienced both the joy and sadness of the fleeting embrace and the protection and vulnerability of the barrier. They seem to have experienced the longing to join in as well as the fear of rejection in the playground, to have enjoyed secrecy and freedom which they perceived 'the green protection' to offer them. Sometimes the experience of metaphor led to verbal connection with feelings, thoughts and personal themes, which were either discussed in the group or in individual interviews.

Sometimes, though, the experience of moving, feeling and imagining seemed enough in itself and no verbal sense-making took place:

Interviewer: Did you make any sense of the image? Did you make any connection with going inside the nest?
Participant: I just experienced it.

Cattanach writes:

Play is a symbolic process through which the children can experiment with imaginative choices aesthetically distanced by the creation of this other playing reality from the consequences of those choices in 'real' life.

(Cattanach 1995: 224)

Thus, climbing inside the nest, getting married, tying and being tied, being in the storm and outside it, spinning and stopping, squashing and being squashed were not reflected on (in either group or individual interview), in relation to anything happening in the group or outside the group. They seem to have been experienced playfully in the moment without any compulsion to interpret. It was hard to gauge if 'integration of release and augmented insight' (Cox and Theilgaard 1987) took place through metaphor in these instances, or whether it was simply a process of catharsis. Both processes are possible. What can be argued is that in playing with metaphor, participants were able to experience themselves in a 'fluid, playful' way as in these examples:

> I used to have a problem with balance in Technique and Choreography, but now I feel free and I noticed how different I was. It wasn't just dance; it was me as well.

> It opened me up to something new.

> I'm not so serious in DMT. I can escape from that character and I can move in a different way, freely and with laughter.

Movement metaphors and the development of self-confidence

As discussed above movement metaphors seem to have been vehicles for the development of playfulness. Playfulness in movement was perceived as leading to emotional balance and self-confidence, for example:

> I expressed how I felt through movement and I can concentrate more now. DMT has helped me focus on things, just giving time for myself to sit down and notice how I am. I feel so brilliant. It's just nice to come out of DMT, and we go for a cup of tea and we talk, and X is really relaxed and revitalised and I feel really calm with the whole week in perspective.

Self-confidence was discovered in movement metaphor, perhaps illustrating the concept of re-creation of self in metaphor (Cattanach 1995), as illustrated in this example:

> I really had this strong feeling of what I could do. I felt I could do some really brilliant things. I was feeling really great and getting more positive, and I had this strong feeling of what I could do . . . I don't know whether

I visualised it in my head or whether it was just purely a feeling I felt just through moving. I felt my body could have done some really great things.

Sometimes involvement with movement metaphor led participants to make connections with feelings, for example:

I felt really tired and lethargic and for the first time I stayed with this and moved in that way, I turned and rolled and felt my weight. I felt really annoyed and angry and I didn't realise I felt like that until I said it and it shocked me. As I crawled along I changed my weight emphasis and crawled on my hands really pushing into the ground. In the end I felt relieved, it was a really good release and I felt really calm afterwards.

Participants spoke about 'facing themselves', and sometimes worked with life themes through movement, with growing awareness, as described here:

In the session I was dragging Y around. I felt I was being really manipu-lative. I was dragging her and taking her where I wanted to, and she was doing what I wanted her to do, and I had a sense of being in control, because in my own life I'm really quite weak in the sense that I'll always do things for other people to please them.

Having a tantrum. Yes! Like really, really fast. I remember at one point I was on the floor doing something. It was really exhilarating. It was like being on a roller-coaster ride. I was spinning on the floor and tumbling, quite violent. I've noticed it sometimes when I'm improvising. I do have these violent kind of bashings on the floor. I suppose its some kind of anger coming through, but I can't really figure out where it comes from, although I do in a way.

Metaphors sometimes facilitated a process of association. For example, circular movement seemed to be a dominant movement pattern in C1. One participant recalled the spinning, turning and spiralling and she associated it with the sea and the wind 'a free spirit always returning.' Another spoke about sea and mermaid imagery, associating freedom and beauty with the mermaids. The circle is an ancient symbol of spiritual being, representing the timeless cycle of birth and death, creation and destruction (Cooper 1998) present in spiritual dance forms (Langer 1953). Its spontaneous emergence in this group was associated with infinity, for example: 'I felt as if I could have carried on running round and round for ever', and altered states of con-sciousness 'I was lying on the floor and Y was walking about the space, a circular movement as if she couldn't stop. That was comforting but hypnotic'.

In these two examples, it was as if the participant was caught up in a spin, mesmerised, made giddy and comforted by the whirling movement. One participant described how running round and round caused pain in her legs and how she felt disconnected from physical sensation as the giddiness and fun took over. In this instance circular movement became a vehicle for loss of physical awareness. Paradoxically, circular movement was also associated with heightened emotional awareness. For example, someone felt the pain of her isolation as she moved around the edge of the group, yet choosing to circle round and round became an important landmark in her personal process, symbolising her independence.

It seemed that in some cases, self-awareness led to increased self-confidence in personal life as well as in choreography, as indicated in the following example:

> DMT has made me aware that I want to do and say what I feel from now on, and not lie.
> Before, I had no confidence in choreography, because that thing was there that I couldn't let out, because if I put that in my dance then everyone would see it and it was too personal. I hadn't faced it in myself.

Whilst Gilroy (1989, 1992) argues that self-awareness can inhibit visual art making, she also suggests a correlation between self-awareness and self-confidence. This chapter documents how self-awareness through movement metaphor may contribute to increased self-confidence. It seems that in some instances self-awareness led to self-acceptance, self-nurturing and self-compassion. These self-receptive and self-affirming processes seem to have boosted self-confidence in terms of daily living as well as in terms of artistic agency. Inhibitory effects of self-awareness on art making are discussed elsewhere (Hayes 2004). It seems that sometimes a process of self-awareness was set in motion through engagement with movement metaphor, which subsequently led participants to pay more attention to their feelings. They seem to have attended to their needs more fully and to have experienced a feeling of self-worth as a result, as shown in the following example:

> I expressed how I felt through movement and I can concentrate more now. DMT has helped me focus on things, just giving time for myself to sit down and notice how I am. I feel so brilliant.

Play, movement metaphors and the development of relationship

In playing together the ebb and flow of movement brought people into and out of contact with each other. Relationships were experienced and explored through movement. In the individual interviews, many of the participants remembered 'whole-group' metaphors, indicating a sense of feeling connected to the group. The majority of students spoke about their cohort seeming 'closer' as a result of engaging in the DMT group. In fact, on the basis of frequency and emphasis in the transcripts, perception of increased emotional and physical connection between participants, both in the group and outside of it, is one of the most significant findings of this study. This heightened connection might be compared to Templeton's (1998) definition of 'communitas' as a sensitive connection between group members, including a heightened awareness of each other's physical, emotional, imaginative and spiritual being. A group may be seen as a dynamic constellation of individuals in relationship. The ebb and flow of energy, emotion and imagination in a group depends upon the quality of relationships between participants. In DMT it is believed that movement, emotion and imagination create metaphors that shed light on relationship (Meekums 2002; Stanton-Jones 1992).

The metaphors in Cohort One that received most attention in interview were circles (commented on by four people) and lines (four people). One circle, the nest (four people) had particular significance for participants. Within these metaphors I see the themes of connection and separation (Benson 1987). These interpretations of movement metaphors are influenced by existentialist epistemology. However, inferences were informed by and cross-checked (regularly between 1997–2003) with participants' reflections on their experience of metaphor. Thus, transcript reference to connection and separation informs the existentialist interpretation, inviting consideration of how participants felt during the process of connecting and separating with others; how relationship developed. Nevertheless, it is likely that another therapist or researcher working within a different DMT model would identify other unifying themes and make other interpretations.

Cohort One (C1)

The flux of energy in lines and circles reminded many people of the playground. As in a playground, participants seem to have experienced brief encounters of closeness and intimacy, before breaking apart again in independent movement. Trust and friendship, rivalry, competition, conformity and domination (Yalom 1985; Houston 1993) seemed to be live issues. They seemed to be acted out in playground games such as throwing objects at each other, trying to grab things from each other, exchanging clothes, performing dances about self-assertion and personal pride (for example, Flamenco dancing).

'Lines' as a metaphor were associated with connection and separation. One participant remembered how everyone had been connected in a long line on the floor. She felt ambivalent about this connection, wanting to be separate she stood up, yet wanting to be part of the line she stepped into any gaps that were left. Connection, love and friendship were associated with a line by three people who recalled a moment when everyone was connected in a line on the floor. As they looked up they saw two participants whirling together in a brief embrace and then whirling apart again. The two involved associated different things with this metaphor, one remembering it as 'saying sorry', the other experiencing it as 'parting'. Those who witnessed this moment felt both joy and sadness. It seemed to hold the group together for a moment. Everyone was focused on the duet. Later, it seemed to facilitate discussion of what it felt like to be alone and what it felt like to be in relationship.

In a different session one participant saw and felt the images and music from the film *Brief Encounter* in her mind as lines of people criss-crossed past each other. The image from the film of people coming and going on a railway platform seems to encapsulate much of the movement material of this group. De Maré *et al.* (1991) have theorised that fear of intimacy governs human relationships. The tentative reaching out to and withdrawal from each other present in this group might be seen as an illustration of this.

The metaphor of the nest formed itself out of lines and circles, woven together and apart spontaneously. Perceptions of the nest varied considerably. One person remembered it as a chaotic weaving together, and a desperate trying to escape:

> It was very strange because we were all in a line, very rigid, and then it became chaos. It seemed like something was sorted out and it was fine, and then confusion. Everyone was weaving in and out constructing a nest and yet we were birds trying to get out of the nest. It seemed like everyone was trying to get out but nobody could.

Another person remembered there being a 'calm connection' between group members, and yet another recalled the physical closeness and playfulness present in the weaving of the nest:

> The nest image was in everyone's mind. That was a real moment . . . all that interweaving of arms and legs. I thought it was really playful . . . like threads weaving in and out.

The variety of perceptions of the nest seems to be connected to the variety of feelings amongst individuals about being in this group. One person acknowledged her feelings of 'disconnection' from the group, whilst another felt ambivalence towards joining the group and then enjoyed the feeling of being in the centre:

> When everyone made a long line I wanted to be part of it, but I didn't want to join the line so I made a branch off it. Not long after that it all started changing and I just stayed where I was and when I sat up there was a bird's nest with the opening towards me, so I just climbed in and curled up.

Whilst the metaphor of the nest created fear, confusion and a need to escape in one person, for another it represented the opposite, a containing space or a 'home' where she could 'climb in and curl up'. Anzieu (1984) refers to the potential of the group to become mother to itself, and Houston (1993) uses the image of the nest or womb to encapsulate this concept. It seems that in C1 the group was perceived in this way by some participants, a perception which seemed to arise from individual process (for example, being able to trust and needing to trust) and from the group environment (for example, developing an open and trusting culture, letting go of past mistrust).

In this instance the nest may have symbolised the group as a place where participants would be accepted and nurtured till they were ready to leave. Feelings of wanting to escape from the nest and a recurring theme of longing to be outside the DMT space (gazing out of windows, opening windows) were strongly present in this group, but balanced with a strong sense of feeling safe and supported in the group. Perhaps the sense of safety and belonging as well as the sense of fear of constraint and over-containment facilitated the process of separation and emotional independence in C1. The easeful image of a butterfly emerging from a cocoon in one session seems to suggest a hopeful, willing response to growth and change.

The theme of separation and union present in the nest was a universal theme present in all groups. It surfaced over and over again in metaphor and dynamics. Separation and belonging may be perceived as fundamental to human existence. The tension between a hunger to belong to something larger than the self and the need to assert the self as separate may be considered as the nub of human experience (O'Donohue 1998). The interpreted metaphors of separation and union which reappear throughout the DMT processes in the three cohorts may therefore be seen as manifestations of the essence of human experience.

The response to separation from the group was different in each of the three cohorts: C1 was ready to leave, wanting separation; C2 held on to an illusion of continued union, denying separation; C3 broke apart in anger, hurt and regret, taking refuge in separation. These responses could be attributed to a need to assert a separate identity after intimate group process (C1), a need to continue the process of trust building (C2), and a longing for intimacy strangled by mistrust and fear (C3).

Cohort Two (C2)

Separation and connection seemed to be a theme for this cohort contained in the movement metaphor of 'the mirror'. Mirroring and being mirrored was perhaps particularly important (the only group which had not worked together before, although some group members knew each other) to create a sense of empathy and acceptance as well as strengthening the sense of separate identity and facilitating self-awareness (Stern 1985; Winnicott 1985).

The skipping-rope was a central feature in this group, created by winding up the green stretch cloth. It occupied most of the space, a core group congregating round it and people coming and going from it. For several participants, this activity awakened memories of school, the need to join in a group and the fear of doing so. They re-experienced the anxiety of venturing into a group and felt accepted in their DMT group. In some cases, skipping brought back memories of connection, which were contrasted with current feelings of separation, as in this example:

> While I was skipping, I remembered all about my playground, and how I used to participate in things. Sometimes I feel very distant from people.

There were strong movement contrasts in this playground. One participant recalled quietness and wildness occurring at the same time. Another's dominant memory was of frantic movement in the central space, encircled by pockets of internally oriented activity, extraversion in the centre and introversion on the edges. Others noted the scarcity of whole-group movement.

Group size and stage of development might account for the absence of cohesion. Generally, participants were content with diversity in terms of varied activity and varied levels of connection with feelings and images, perhaps because they were not yet certain that they wanted to enter into a group process. The unity felt in the final session in the circle showed a change towards group interconnection, the metaphor making dynamics visible. This could also be seen as a defiance of ending and separateness (Yalom 1991; O'Donohue 1998).

Cohort Three (C3)

Many people remembered 'playground games' as a metaphor in this cohort, usually games involving rules. Often there were ball games. Other playground themes included watching, showing and 'hanging out'. The playground games were often games of structure, involving the whole group or the majority of the group. They encouraged action rather than feelings. Lindquist (2001) has shown how imaginative play facilitates emotional involvement in dance. In contrast to this, the kind of play often chosen in this group was based on concrete reality, rather than imagination. Some members acknowledged that through such play they wanted to forget their feelings of the moment.

In session two, a participant began a game of British Bulldogs with the intention of bringing the group together into the action. In the penultimate session the majority of participants formed a circle and began to roll a medicine ball with increasing vigour across the circle aiming to touch or knock over the person in the middle, who had to jump out of the way. In both games rules had to be followed in order to play. Group membership was achieved by joining in the game of catching and being caught (strongly and roughly at times). A lot of laughter accompanied these games, in particular in the latter game, which was very loud and boisterous. Other ball games played were baseball and 'catch' in a circle, involving forfeits. These games involved between four to ten people at different times. They too seemed to be all about playing according to the group rules. Such games might be interpreted as manifestation of inclusion, exclusion and conformity, prominent issues in most group process (Yalom 1985).

These games were remembered variously as being fun, providing a focus and an opportunity to release energy and to change mood. Only three people analysed the content of the games in terms of intrapersonal and inter-personal dynamics. One participant saw the passing of the medicine ball in the circle as confirming group membership and, in her case, confirming estrangement from the group. Another participant talked about the difficulty of refusing participation when the ball was thrown to her. Another saw the games as a manifestation of male patriarchal and institutional structures, involving organisation and competition. She considered this to be a threat to creativity and tried to sabotage the games by wrapping the ball in a scarf. It might be argued from participants' reflections that these games were indeed often about avoidance of feelings, whereby rules and rigidity contrasted with creativity and flexibility. Alternatively, competitive games might be seen as structuring feelings with action where participants were 'against' or 'with' each other.

The need for rules and action, rather than free-flow movement and feelings, might be considered as a response to the absence of safety in the group. This group was perceived by a few members to be unsafe for DMT process because of lack of trust (see Rogers 1957). Hostile feelings can be very frightening because of their potential to destroy (De Maré et al. 1991). Flight from such feelings is common through physical activity disconnected with feelings. In the final session, when feelings of hurt and anger at perceived insensitivity spilled out, members felt vulnerable and appalled.

Hiding appeared in many group metaphors. For example, three people huddled under the green stretch cloth, shuffling around the edge of the room until they found a space to settle and draw pictures, still under the cloth. Participants felt that the cloth offered them protection from the majority of the group, which was playing vigorously and aggressively with the medicine ball. Underneath the cloth they made raucous, flamboyant sounds. Paradox was contained in this movement metaphor: simultaneous hiding and showing; blocking connection with the majority group and nurturing connection in the small group.

Watching, massaging and grooming took place frequently in this group, mostly in pairs or small groups of three people. Two individuals experienced watching as separation from those being watched. Most people reflected on the physical and emotional intimacy experienced in pairs and small groups as they massaged and groomed each other. There was one occasion when the whole group formed a massage circle. Group members experienced powerful energy passing round the circle and shared their pent-up feelings and thoughts about the degree programme. One student analysed the tactile, physical culture of this group as a fundamental human need for connection:

> We are relating to each other, grooming each other, rolling over each other, which is not typical, but probably normal human behaviour; but it's not behaviour we are given images of.

Massage occurred frequently in pairs, but only on one occasion in the large group, whilst rough physical contact in whole or large group movement occurred more frequently. Perhaps this was indicative of conjoined affection and hostility, love and hate. Attraction and repulsion was spoken about, for example:

> There are playful elements in the group. As a group we move flirtatiously in the space. We were doing something like the bunny hop, but it was a very aggressive bunny hop; a lot of strength there.

The group metaphors of watching and grooming may demonstrate the polarity of distance and intimacy or merging which characterised this group. Emotions towards others bubbled beneath the surface but were not shared in the large group. One participant spoke of 'something very thin' keeping the group apart, and another described the movement relationships as 'careful'. These two statements conjure up the image of skating carefully over the ice, wary of plunging into the dark water of feeling. The 'something very thin' could also indicate a very delicate protective membrane, which when broken exposes the person's vulnerability. Carefully keeping the membrane intact keeps the person safe. Fear of being hurt was always present in C3 and the resulting wariness of sharing feelings left some participants feeling isolated, sad and confused, for example:

> In almost every session we were wild and childish, but there was a sense of people being isolated. So there is a playfulness and at the same time not quite being a group. I don't think there is enough honesty or openness towards each other and that is why we are separate, which is a shame.

Whilst metaphors of separation and connection seem to be present in all the cohorts, the metaphor of hiding is particular to C3. Whilst fear of vulnerability seems present throughout, it appears to have been offset by development of trust in C1 and C2 and exacerbated by a lack of trust in C3. The themes of belonging and separation were commonly experienced through a variety of metaphors. These metaphors appeared to act both as containers of emotional and psychic realities and as starting points for reflection on personal and group processes.

Acceptance and the development of playfulness, self-confidence and relationship

Rogers (1957) emphasised the importance of unconditional positive regard (UPR) in the promotion of personal growth. In one of his last articles, he wrote:

> When the therapist is experiencing a positive, non-judgmental, accepting attitude toward whatever the client is at that moment, therapeutic movement or change is more likely. Acceptance involves the therapist's willingness for the client to be whatever immediate feeling is going on – confusion, resentment, fear, anger, courage, love, or pride. It is a non-possessive caring. When the therapist prizes the client in a total rather than a conditional way, forward movement is likely.
>
> (Rogers 1986: 199)

In this research participants frequently identified acceptance (by both the therapist and the group) as important in the encouragement of spontaneous participation in group process. Participants stated that they had felt 'under no pressure to perform'. They felt that they could 'be as they were'; 'no need to change themselves to meet an expectation'. They felt that there were 'no rights and wrongs in DMT'. Their experience was accepted as complete in itself and there was 'no pressure to make sense of it'. The therapist's acceptance of participants in the moment was considered as contributing significantly to a playful experience of DMT, as illustrated in the following examples:

> You didn't ask us 'Why did you do that?' It was more like 'What did you feel like? – a different angle.

> I think we felt comfortable knowing that you didn't have to explain yourself. It was just the way it was.

> We only brought up things we wanted to say.

> It was a learning experience. When people were speaking about how they felt when they were moving, I don't think they were thinking 'I hope I'm doing this right so I can get a good mark.'

The latter remark was in fact true: the DMT group was a non-assessed component of the DMT module. Yet the multiple role of the therapist had the potential to undermine the separation of experience from assessment, the module leader's role operating against the intactness of therapeutic experience. However, remarks such as the latter seem to suggest that despite this potential for the blurring of role boundaries, participants did not feel judged or evaluated in what they did. In a culture of acceptance of the 'now', they seem to have found some escape from aesthetic concerns 'It doesn't matter what you look like' – and a welcome opportunity to be playful – 'You can move any way you want'.

Meekums (1998) suggests that 'non-possessive warmth' is essential in working with women survivors of child sexual abuse, helping to undo the experience of judgement and blame familiar to this population. Meekums uses the term witnessing to describe 'being benevolently seen, heard and understood' (Meekums 2000: 77). Being witnessed by other group members was considered by participants in Meekums's study to be a powerful factor in their recovery process. It seems to have forged a strong bond between group members, helping them to feel both compassion and respect for themselves. Prouty (2001) dissects the Rogerian concept of unconditional positive regard (UPR) into the following components: love, care, compassion, non-judgement, acceptance, nurturance, valuing, prizing and respect. Participants in this inquiry often referred to the permissive environment of the DMT group, pinpointing acceptance of and respect for people as pivotal in developing playfulness and self-confidence, for example:

> I'm not really fluent and confident normally, but in this class I don't feel like I was pushed or watched, and I've enjoyed it and said what I wanted to say, and I feel really pleased about that.

In a group situation the responsibility for creating an accepting environment is extended to all group members, as well as the facilitator. Everyone present has the ability to facilitate or destroy therapeutic growth by his or her attitude to other group members. In all cohorts people tried to listen, understand and show compassion, despite the opposing force of criticism and hostility tangled up between some group members. Thus, acceptance by the group was identified as significant in facilitating a process of personal growth: 'Without the acceptance of the group, we couldn't have been so open.' Acceptance and support in the group were perceived as facilitating personal and artistic evolution: 'DMT has helped me get to grips with my dissertation on a personal and an artistic level because I felt supported and accepted by the group.' It seems that a group culture of acceptance of and respect for difference was developed to some extent in DMT: 'There was always a big, big distance, because they did find us strange. They never showed us they wanted to find out. But it's completely different now.' Acceptance by others was perceived as contributing to self-acceptance, which was linked to self-confidence, as suggested by the following example:

> It all relates to confidence. If you're confident when you dance you're OK. You're happy to share it with everyone else; you really give it your all. Dance Therapy helps you to feel OK because it says you're fine as you are.

Self-acceptance seems to have led to greater self-confidence in all areas of life. Acceptance of physical need led students to make more time for physical nurturing, for example, eating good food at regular times, relaxing after strenuous classes.

Acceptance of personal movement seems to have led to an increased motivation to be self-expressive through movement: 'I can't be anything other than me [in my dancing] really.'

Acceptance of emotions seems to have led to greater freedom of emotional expression. Generally, the development of a self-accepting attitude seems to have helped students to relinquish a self-punishing, critical attitude, such as 'When I watch myself on video, I feel completely disgusted'. This seems to have promoted self-confidence, for example:

> In dance therapy I would never get nervous ever. I wouldn't have any anxieties ever. It helped me to deal with the way I felt, which helped me to have a bit more self-esteem.

Self-acceptance seems to have developed alongside acceptance of others, for example:

> I felt fluid and I didn't feel under pressure. I was able to enjoy [technique and choreography]. I've been able to appreciate how other people move. I did observe them before, but now I can fully appreciate how they move.

Acceptance of others seems to have led to empathic awareness of others, for example:

> We have changed; we're more sensitive to each other and more willing to sense how people are feeling. There's not a barrier any more.

Thus, a culture of acceptance seems to have brought participants into contact with each other. The swiftness of this process of acceptance and empathy surprised many, for example:

> A lot of us aren't from the same background, and not all of us are third years. We're a mixed group; a lot of us haven't worked with each other. But now you wouldn't realise that we'd never worked together, eight weeks!

Guidance in the building of an accepting culture can facilitate relationship in groups (Lewin 1936), even when the group has a history of poor communication, as indicated in this example:

> When we first started there seemed to be a really rigid atmosphere in the class, but now it's so open, nobody seems to mind saying what they think.

It is suggested here that a group culture that encourages acceptance of others through the practice of receptivity with self-awareness, modelled by the therapist, facilitates accepting relationships, for example:

> It was a breakthrough session for me because up till now I felt separate from the group. I was trying to be inside the group, but I couldn't feel anybody. I was so much in myself that I wasn't able to. Today was the first time I was feeling the whole group, and letting the group be around me. I don't think I have been able to see people recently. I just wasn't seeing anybody. I needed this. I've had a chance to see you all today.

The concept of receptivity with awareness seems akin to the authentic movement term 'witnessing' (Adler 1972; Musicant 1994, 2001). An overlap between the discipline of authentic movement and the model of DMT in this inquiry might be suggested in this instance.

Safety and the development of playfulness, self-confidence and relationship

Safety seems to have been the axis upon which the playful process of engagement with movement metaphor rested. In this inquiry safety seems to have been created through a process of trust building in an enclosed space protected from intrusion by things outside the group, as suggested in this example:

> You shut the door and that was you, you were there, for that set time, and nobody was going to come and disturb you, stop it or anything. Trusting the rest of the group was really important.

The pivotal significance of safety identified in this study supports and confirms the findings on safety reported in previous studies. For example, Payne (1996, 2001) suggests that safety is the foundation of the therapeutic work, initially dependent on physical, and subsequently on emotional, boundaries. Payne suggests that emotional containment may be present in the rule of confidentiality. Keeping confidentiality may be perceived as a commitment to keeping group members safe, by protecting others' emotional life from intrusion by outside forces.

Meekums, with reference to research with women survivors of child sexual abuse, states: 'The need for safety was the single most often referred to element in recovery by all fourteen research participants in my study' (Meekums 2000: 69). In Meekums's inquiry the associations with safety relevant for this study were confidentiality, respect for difference, sharing, witnessing, appropriateness of activity in terms of timing, need for more time, use of humour, the right to say no and finding a balance between freedom and structure.

Supporting both Payne's (1996) and Meekums's (1998) research findings, this study also suggests that group process is dependent upon members' sense of physical and emotional safety. In this study, as in both Payne's (1996) and Meekums's (1998), confidentiality was named as a significant factor in the creation of safety for therapeutic work, alongside acceptance, empathy and support, as suggested in the following examples:

> When you get this group situation and you are bound and committed, it's total, it's OK to do this [DMT]. No one's going to do you down, so you feel quite relaxed, no fear or phobia. You can vent all your feelings.

> I was able to find myself, having the support of everyone else. It was hard to deal with my feelings throughout, but empathy and support made it possible.

In antithesis to these statements, the perceived absence of confidentiality led to feelings of insecurity and an inability to explore feelings as shown here:

> You were talking about confidentiality and I remember feeling so angry because I saw all those people agreeing who wouldn't respect it. That is why I'm not really comfortable with letting myself go.

The perception of empathy and support in C2 may be compared with the perception of indifference experienced by one participant in C3, which contributed to her unwillingness to share feelings: 'Some people I'm close to and others I'm not. So when asked how I felt, I thought "Who cares anyway?" '

Payne (1996) and Meekums (1998) also found that the creation of a safe exploratory environment was initially dependent on trust in the therapist. This seems to be confirmed by the findings of this study, for example, in comments such as: 'You were a safe person', 'We trusted you'. Perception of therapist acceptance facilitated trust in personal process. The concept of the therapist as 'guide' compared to 'teacher' seems to have been associated with respect for the individual's own judgement, as suggested in the comment: 'It was as if you guided us to become more aware of how we were. You gave us information and ideas and we dealt with them on our own.'

The concept of activating client agency has been the focus of recent research (Bohart and Tallman 1999; Rodgers 2002). The therapist as tool for the client to use in the service of personal growth seems to apply here, in the descriptions of therapeutic relational process offered by participants. In Payne's (1996) study safety was associated with the non-intrusive but active presence of the therapist. In this study many participants seem to have responded to the therapist's guidance. They spoke of her 'opening things up', and 'raising awareness' by her 'observation of the here and now'.

The component of therapist involvement also seems to have been significant in building trust in the process, for example: 'You weren't a watcher; you were a participant'; 'To see you moving around the way we were gave us confidence to do whatever we wanted'. Rogers refers to therapist congruence as being 'freely and deeply' oneself, with accurate self-awareness (Rogers 1957: 97). Lietaer suggests that UPR and congruence are: 'the foundation, the deeper-lying fertile soil, necessary to enable the therapist to respond sensitively to the experiential world of the client' (2001: 90).

In this research the concepts of 'participation' and 'joining in' interpreted from the data seem not to be as 'layered' as the concept of congruence, with its emphasis upon deep sensing and feeling. They would seem to have more affinity with the definition of 'joining in' as active engagement with the group event, as described by Payne (1987, 1992). In interview, participants talked about the therapist being part of the group, not separate from it, not judging or instructing. Participation and involvement seem, in this instance, to be connected to acceptance, rather than congruence.

However, during the process students did seem to need evidence of the therapist's connection with it. They wanted to know if she wanted to be there and how she felt. Participation, on these occasions, seems to have had a greater connection with the concept of congruence. Perhaps participants sensed a lack of congruence, and indicated that they needed to feel the therapist was fully present with awareness in order to dive into sensation and emotion themselves. These requests came at times of insecurity with the process, suggesting that therapist congruence and safety are interrelated in therapeutic work.

As above, the concept of witnessing (Adler 1972; Musicant 1994, 2001) from authentic movement may be considered relevant here. Witnessing in authentic movement seems to combine elements of UPR, congruence as well as empathy, in its emphasis upon receptivity to another's movement, self-awareness and the ability to put aside or own value judgements. In the requests for evidence of my engagement with process, it may be that participants wanted to know that the therapist's involvement was active, as in the concept of witnessing: open both to self and others.

Payne (1996, 2001) and Meekums (1998, 2000) suggest that commitment to experiencing and sharing promotes group trust. This seems to represent experience in this research, as shown in the following example:

DMT has made me aware that I want to do and say what I feel from now on, and not lie, because it's not fair to myself and the rest of the group.

In one session the group was compared to a baby requiring safety (the image seeming to suggest extreme vulnerability), and that safety would be developed by 'being true to ourselves and to others'. A sense of increasing group commitment seems to have influenced individual commitment to the process in C1 and C2. As people began to open up to one another, they relaxed and enjoyed the feeling of being seen and heard. In some cases they were able to give each other critical feedback without feeling threatened, for example: 'You used to have an attitude. I was scared of you!'

Self-confidence seems to have been connected to involvement in a contained group process. Whilst some participants spoke of anxiety due to lack of structured exercises, others seem to have been reassured by the simple structure of the DMT group (Payne 1992, 1996), and to have looked forward to the verbal sharing of different perspectives, which was the final phase of group process. Paradoxically, this sharing of difference seems to have resulted in a feeling of connection and belonging, which seems to have developed self-confidence, for example:

> In the discussion afterwards you sometimes find that everyone feels similar emotions at times. So we are learning to help each other out, to feel better about ourselves. We're all in the same boat.

Finding emotional strength and self-confidence through experience in a safe group has been identified before in relation to arts therapies groups (Meekums 1998). Here too, the sense of 'I am not alone' seems to have both boosted self-confidence and increased commitment to process.

Thus, perception of group safety seems to have brought people into relationship, for example: 'We needed time to build up trust and become a group.' From a starting point of individuality, for example: 'Initially I thought I was an individual in there, amongst a lot of other individuals', those people who experienced a sense of group safety were able to connect with others expressing their feelings as shown here:

> I was glad to be honest with people. We've all got things going on, and to be able to notice and recognise each other's things for me was just, well, we're all human, we're not just dancers.

Recommendations for practice

The findings of this study suggest several recommendations for the practice of DMT. First, safety is at the heart of the therapeutic experience. Without the presence of safety there will be no depth experience of therapy. Second, acceptance is a key to the creation of safety. Acceptance dispels fear of attack, thus opening up the individual to the process of personal as well as transpersonal exploration. Third, play creates a framework in which movement metaphor can emerge and evolve. Fourth, movement metaphor can be a symbolic vehicle for exploration of human experience. Finally, this study recommends that DMT is highly relevant in creative contexts such as dance training and education, with the potential to enhance creativity through personal and social integration of feelings.

Conclusion

In this chapter I have discussed four 'special ingredients' in the development of playfulness, self-confidence and relationship, based on the process and interview reflections. These four factors – play, movement metaphors, acceptance and safety have been presented as interconnected aspects of facilitating experience. It is likely that other researchers might have focused on other 'special ingredients', such as 'the therapist' or 'the student', reframing the interpretation of the data. In my choice of categories I have been mindful of the data, continually cross-checking categories with verbatim comments in order to challenge and alter them. It was intended that the final categories would provide a useful focus for the analysis of DMT process and personal effects.

References

Adler, J. (1972) Integrity of body and psyche: some notes on work in progress, in *Proceedings of the Seventh Annual Conference of the American Dance Therapy Association*, 42–53.

Anzieu, D. (1984) *The Group and the Unconscious*. London: Routledge.

Arieti, S. (1976) *Creativity: The Magic Synthesis*. New York: Basic Books.

Benson, J. (1987) *Working More Creatively With Groups*. London: Routledge.

Bohart, A. C. and Tallman, K. (1999) *How Clients Make Therapy Work: The Process of Active Self-Healing*. Washington, DC: American Psychological Association.

Bungay, V. and Keddy, V. C. (1996) Experiential analysis as a feminist methodology for health professionals, *Qualitative Health Research* 6, 442–452.

Cattanach, A. (1995) Drama and play therapy with young children, *The Arts in Psychotherapy* 22, 3, 223–228.

Chodorow, J. (1991) *Dance Therapy and Depth Psychology. The Moving Imagination*. London: Routledge.

Cooper, J. C. (1998) *An Illustrated Encyclopaedia of Traditional Symbols*. London: Thames and Hudson.

Cox, M. and Theilgaard, A. (1987) *Mutative Metaphors in Psychotherapy: The Aeolian Mode*. London: Tavistock.

De Maré, P., Piper, R. and Thompson, S. (1991) *Koinonia From Hate, Through Dialogue, To Culture in the Large Group*. London: Karnac.

Garvey, C. (1977) *Play*. London: Fontana.

Gilroy, A. (1989) On occasionally being able to paint, *Inscape*, spring.

—— (1992) Art therapists and their art. A study of occupational choice and career development, from the origins of an interest in art to occasionally being able to paint, unpublished PhD thesis, University of Sussex.

Hayes, J. (2004) The experience of student dancers in higher education in a dance movement therapy group, with reference to choreography and performance, unpublished PhD thesis, University of Hertfordshire.

Houston, G. (1993) *Being and Belonging – Group, Intergroup and Gestalt*. Chichester: Wiley.

Huberman, A. M. and Miles, M. B. (2000) Data management and analysis methods, in N.K. Denzin and Y.S. Lincoln (eds) *Handbook of Qualitative Research*. London: Sage.

Langer, S. K. (1953) *Feeling and Form*. London: Routledge.

Lewin, K. (1936) *Principles of Topological Psychology*. New York: McGraw-Hill.

Lietaer, G. (2001) Being genuine as a therapist: congruence and transparency, in G. Wyatt (ed.) *Congruence*. Ross-on-Wye: PCCS Books.

Lindquist, G. (2001) The relationship between play and dance, *Research in Dance Education* 2, 1, 41–52.

Meekums, B. (1993) Research as an act of creation, in H. Payne (ed.) *Handbook of Inquiry in the Arts Therapies: One River Many Currents*. London: Jessica Kingsley.

—— (1998) Recovery from child sexual abuse trauma within an arts therapies programme for women, unpublished PhD thesis, University of Manchester, Faculty of Education.

—— (2000) *Creative Group Therapy for Women Survivors of Child Sexual Abuse*. London: Jessica Kingsley.

—— (2002) *Dance Movement Therapy: A creative psychotherapeutic approach*. London: Sage.

Millar, S. (1976) *The Psychology of Play*. Harmondsworth: Penguin.

Mills, L. and Daniluk, J. (2002) Her body speaks: the experience of dance therapy for women survivors of child sexual abuse, *Journal of Counselling and Development* 80, 1, 77–85.

Musicant, S. (1994) Authentic movement and dance therapy, *American Journal of Dance Therapy* 16, 2, 91–106.

—— (2001) Authentic movement: clinical considerations, *American Journal of Dance Therapy* 23, 1, 17–26.

O'Donohue, J. (1998) *Eternal Echoes: Exploring our Hunger to Belong*. London: Bantam Press.

Payne, H. L. (1987) The perceptions of male adolescents labelled delinquent towards a programme of dance movement therapy, unpublished MPhil thesis, University of Manchester.

—— (1992) Shut in, shut out: dance movement therapy with children and adolescents, in H.L. Payne (ed.) *Dance Movement Therapy: Theory and Practice*. London: Routledge.

—— (1996) The experience of a dance movement therapy group in training, unpublished PhD thesis, University of London.

—— (2001) Student experiences in a personal development group: the question of safety, *European Journal of Psychotherapy, Counselling and Health* 4, 2, 267–292.

Potter, J. and Wetherall, M. (1987) *Discourse and Social Psychology: Beyond Attitudes and Behaviour*. London: Sage.

Prouty, G. (2001) Unconditional positive regard and pre-therapy, in J.D. Bozarth and P. Wilkins (eds) *Unconditional Positive Regard*. Ross-on-Wye: PCCS Books.

Rodgers, B. (2002) An investigation into the client at the heart of therapy, *Counselling and Psychotherapy Research* 2, 3, 185–193.

Rogers, C. R. (1957) The necessary and sufficient conditions of therapeutic personality change, *Journal of Consulting Psychology* 21, 2, 95–103.

—— (1986) A client-centered/person-centered approach to therapy, in I. Kutash and A. Wolfe (eds) *Psychotherapists' Casebook*. San Francisco: Jossey-Bass, pp. 197–208.

Rowan, J. (1981) A dialectical paradigm for research, in P. Reason and J. Rowan (eds) *Human Inquiry: A Sourcebook of New Paradigm Research*. Chichester: Wiley.

Stake, R. E. (2000) Case studies, in N. K. Denzin and Y. S. Lincoln (eds) *Handbook of Qualitative Research*. London: Sage.

Stanton-Jones, K. (1992) *An Introduction to Dance Movement Therapy in Psychiatry*. London: Routledge.

Stern, D. (1985) *The Interpersonal World of the Infant. A View From Psychoanalysis and Developmental Psychology*. New York: Basic Books.

Templeton, E. (1998) Speaking as a dance therapist: dance therapists speaking, paper presented at 31st Annual Conference Congress on Research in Dance, Ohio State University, Columbus, 14 November.

Winnicott, D. W. (1985) *Playing and Reality*. London: Pelican.

Yalom, I. D. (1985) *The Theory and Practice of Group Psychotherapy*. New York: Basic Books.

Yalom, I. D. (1991) *Love's Executioner and Other Tales of Psychotherapy*. Harmondsworth: Penguin.

Chapter 14

Full circle

From choreography to dance movement therapy and back

Rosa Shreeves

Introduction

This chapter comprises reflections on the nature of postmodern dance choreography and creativity in the context of choreography and dance movement
therapy (DMT). Both are clearly different in intention and outcome but the
bedrock of both is dance:

> Dance is a truly unique and direct form of communication.
> Dance is a unifying activity involving the whole self.
> To dance is in the deepest sense of the word to *be* more vividly.
>
> (Shreeves 1990: 12)

For many years, alongside my choreographic work, I was evolving ways
of working therapeutically in dance with a wide range of people. This was
subsequently enriched by my training in humanistic and integrative psychotherapy, which is characterised by an underlying belief in the essential
goodness of human behaviour and, given the right conditions, a capacity for
self-determination and self-healing.

My route into dance movement therapy has been to bring together skills
from performance, choreography and humanistic psychotherapy. My work as
a dance artist informs my therapy work and vice versa. Further influences
include healing, meditation, massage, visual arts, yoga, Alexander technique,
a wide range of dance forms, such as contact dance, release, Latin American
dance, together with experience of other cultures' dance rituals and spiritual
beliefs. My work out of doors, in nature, exploring inner and outer
landscapes has always been central to my process:

> Lying down under the tree I listen to the sound of the leaves.
> The leaves know about falling and dying.
> It seems I can learn something from this place about listening, waiting
> and accepting.
>
> (Bloom and Shreeves 1998: 112)

Over the years, I have been guided and inspired by a whole range of people and ideas from both performance arts and therapy: for example, from the performing world of Steve Paxton (1977), Augusto Boal (1992) and Monika Pagneux; from the voice and movement work of Enrique Pardo and Ria Higler; and from the theory and practice of humanistic psychotherapy including Abraham Maslow (1954), Carl Rogers (1967), Virginia Satir (1978), Albert Pesso (Pesso and Crandell 1991), and particularly Terry Cooper and the formative psychology work of Stanley Keleman (1994). All these different strands have enabled me to deepen and confront my work and to have a conscious language for my process.

Although this chapter separates out the strands of the different disciplines, because of their underlying roots in movement there is endless interplay between them. The experience of dance is many layered. Like looking into a kaleidescope our perceptions grow and change from moment to moment. Writing about movement creates another dimension. It is not the same as the experience of it which is often beyond words; indefinable and more akin to poetry and dreams. This chapter draws together some of the reflections and discoveries arising from my long experience in dance, therapy and related arts. My writing and quotations are prompted by curiosity, insights and memories rather than conceptual approaches and definitive explanations, and my conclusions are open-ended. There are no absolutes, only an infinite variety of response and understanding.

The basis of all my work is the body and my belief that deeper awareness of our bodies inevitably leads to deeper awareness of ourselves. We are our bodies. We often lose that awareness. We have a concept of it but lose touch with the experience. This focus is like an underground stream informing all my work, irrespective of the particular approach I might be employing. I encourage deeper contact with the body, the inner world of imagination, the surroundings and with other people. Separate in words these aspects are simultaneously present in the experience of dance.

And your body is the harp of your soul.

(Gibran 1926: 85)

The essence of movement is the body. We are alive and we move. Our very cells dance to their own pulsations. Breath, heartbeat, thoughts and emotions are all expressed through the body and have their movement patterns and shapes. Dance can be a metaphor for the ways in which we live our lives. The need to move is part of being human and curtailing that need limits our possibilities of development. Over the last half century knowledge of the complex interrelationship of our physical and psychological selves has grown and informed both dance making and DMT:

Living, the whole body carries its meaning and tells its own story, standing, sitting, walking, awake or asleep. For every thought supported by feeling there is a muscle change.

(Todd 1959: 1)

Content and process

This section will compare and contrast aspects of DMT and choreographic process and reflect the interplay between them as I see it. Choreography will usually be concerned with capturing, refining and communicating movement. In choreography the intention is to make a dance. This can be considered as an intimate form of research: a quest, inexpressible in words, to create through movement a meaningful expression of an idea, hardly tangible, that must be drawn from some inner space of the imagination into communicable rhythms and forms. The performing space is the interactive arena for the expression. Other dimensions, for example, video images, script, music or installations, may become part of the communication. The following extract, about choreographic process, is an illustration of a perceptual approach to movement, a fascination with the underlying process of dance making and how it is perceived:

> **By the sea, West Sussex**
> I stop walking and stand very still, becoming more aware of my body and what I am seeing. Through stillness I move onto a different plane of experience.
>
> Eventually, almost without volition I begin to move, following tiny impulses in my body. Gradually I allow myself to follow my spontaneous movement and stillness. One time I begin by slowly bending my knees. Another time I lift one arm, aware of the sensation of lifting, of upward direction and then the slow sinking movement of that arm, the palm of my hand beginning a gentle outward rotation as my trunk bends forwards and downwards. Then stillness again; the end of one phrase and the beginning of another.
>
> I move into unexpected movements, designs and rhythms.

This perceptual approach leads me to reflect on ways into choreography which seem initially to bypass the mind:

> The dance unfolded with its own momentum, rather as a character in a story appears to have a life of its own.
>
> (Shreeves 2004: 26)

As choreographers we may provoke ourselves to step sideways from habitual movement patterns to find fresh movement material. There will be a detailed process of refinement and shaping, in order that our intention is communicated. This is a many-layered process, one which allows a multiplicity of approaches following the skills, background and experience of the maker. Although a dance is generally intended as a communication to an audience, that may not be the primary concern in the choreographic process:

> Dancer and choreographer immerse themselves in the material while keeping in a suspended state of awareness.
>
> (Winearls 1990: 106)

In DMT the basic tenet is that everyone can move and dance and their movement will be meaningful on a personal level. The therapist provides a safe space for disclosure of the feelings and thoughts which arise from the symbolic nature of the dance experience. Symbols have an effect upon us, as signs of an internal resolve:

> A symbol generates itself from the unconscious as a spontaneous expression of some deep inner power of which we are aware but cannot encapsulate in words.
>
> (Fontana 1993: 8)

Personal symbols emerge within the process of both dance movement therapy and choreography. The outcome of dance movement therapy is not goal oriented, although it might well lead to the making of a dance. Sometimes to make a memorable form is very important to clients. In her London seminar, Marti Fromm, of the Miami Dade institute, reiterated that we are not aiming at a goal in therapy but at awareness, stressing how we have a different internal feeling of calm when we are not trying to change clients (Fromm 1990).

People come to DMT for all sorts of reasons, some pragmatic, others profound or painful. Each person will have different needs and expectations. In dance movement therapy we gradually work with the client's upswellings of personal movement and rhythms. We encourage immersion into a flow of movement. The content of the session will arise from the client: the client is the content. Just simply to focus on one's own movement begins a process of change and understanding.

There will be a multiplicity of approaches used, for example, breathing and slowing down, body awareness, choosing and repeating a movement, following an image, an emotional feeling, or a personal story. Writing, drawing or other art forms might support the process. Sometimes we might use movements or ideas derived from other disciplines like yoga or meditation (Bloom and Shreeves 1998; Shreeves 1998).

By their inner awareness of themselves and an attunement to their clients, dance movement therapists resonate with their clients' experience and gain clues as to how to proceed. In so doing the client's subtle, hardly visible movements expressive of thoughts or attitudes may be observed by the therapist and become part of their intimate and creative interaction.

A reflective space is opened up. The reflecting back by the therapist to the client is the main characteristic of DMT. To be understood and integrated, feelings need a human response. This may be through movement or words, but most importantly through the therapist's attentive presence. Reflecting back or mirroring the client's movement is like an active listening. It is a way of honouring and reinforcing what the client is 'saying' in movement. The client may begin to have a different experience of himself, for example, more powerful, less anxious, more confident, more visible to themselves.

This is an extract from two participants' views from a DMT group entitled 'Dreams and Movement'. Here the group members reflect back to each other: After a period of individual exploration and deepening of their dance, participants continued in groups of three. One person danced, the other two witnessed this dance and then mirrored phrases from it back in movement. One participant commented: 'I just loved the way I saw my dream and myself. It was amazing, really satisfying to be seen.' Another said: 'I had felt very sad. I saw how sad I felt, like you really knew me.'

The reflective relationship is the catalyst for the client's growth. The latter may begin to make conscious choices, literally trying out a different dance. Here there is a parallel to the 'step sideways' in the choreographic process. The ability to listen, to be curious, to wait, reflect, play, speak or be silent are some of the therapeutic skills involved. Suggestions for movement might be made. Filling out a movement phrase goes hand in hand with feelings of emotional completion and satisfaction.

To form attachments, to have meaningful relationships in life, is an imperative of being human. In DMT the nurturing of contact in relationship to others is paramount. It is the *feeling* of contact; that of a living, breathing closeness and warmth that we all hunger for. In sharing our movements and thoughts with others we may feel closer to them. I have observed how moved and excited people can feel in self-motivated dance, and how quickly in a non-judgemental space they may feel warmer towards others. I have noticed in my work with psychiatric patients how important is this sense of being together, of sharing an experience, quite apart from whether we are literally moving together as a group or in actual physical contact:

> Intimacy is based upon sharing internal excitement. . . . This pulse of excitement is the foundation for forming a subjective and personal love. It is a pattern that has to do with being able to give and to receive.
>
> (Keleman 1994: 2)

In choreographic contexts moving freely with awareness in and out of contact with others may be used to generate performance material. This may be through literal physical contact as in contact dance or in stressing the relationship between dancers. For example, Enrique Pardo, who acknowledges the influence of James Hillman (1999) on his work, uses a mixture of directed and spontaneous voice and movement frameworks to create visual and audible images. These are then moulded into the wider context of the performing space. This is from his workshop at Warwick University, October 1999:

> Go, keep going, four people are leaders, mirror them from wherever you are, keep changing, you must have a response to that person passing you, where are you in the space, keep going – Go, Rosa go, all the way to Africa!

Authenticity is important in DMT where we aim to support people to find their own personal dance, which is in response to themselves rather than to a particular style of movement, although the latter may arise in the course of the work. On one occasion rock and roll with a client, and on another a group Merengue session, led to reflections on contact with the self and others. Moving towards authenticity in DMT and also in choreography is a process of becoming surer about yourself, finding your own voice, guided by an internal sense of rightness rather than a focus on others' expectations. This sense of rightness can be recognised on a bodily level, perhaps as an experience of inner spaciousness, calm or balance.

Albert Pesso, originally a dancer and then co-founder of psychomotor therapy, created the idea of the 'possibility sphere'. He writes that this creates an atmosphere for a client where something important can happen for them where they have opportunity to be completely themselves:

> The possibility sphere invites out the parts of the clients that are in trouble – that are hurting, that are tense and aching for resolution – and parts that are not yet found, like power.
>
> (Pesso and Crandell 1991: 51)

I have used the notion of the 'possibility sphere' as a starting point for movement exploration in DMT. Each person walks at a slow pace around a chosen small circle on the floor and stands within it; then outlines their own possibility sphere, by reaching out with fingertips and toes into the space and on the floor around them. Within their designated circles, clients move in the space however they choose, with eyes closed, not intruded upon by others, allowing movements, symbolic processes and feelings to emerge.

The cycle of creativity

Creativity is part of being alive. We make and produce things all our lives. We use our imagination to shape and form our very selves. We change literally through moving; the movement of heartbeat and breath, the little shifts of muscles and bones, the subtle movement of our inner organs, all are part of our own individual dance. Like nature of which we are a part, we are in a continuous process of growing and changing. Throughout time in many cultures and in many ancient beliefs we learn how dance and ritual have always been in people's lives and marked their journey through the seasons of the year.

Creativity is on the whole an illogical process. Imagination connects disparate aspects; mistakes become wonderful discoveries; blind alleys open into vistas; unexpected obstacles arise; things are not what they at first appeared to be. In DMT and in choreography if we can stay open to curiosity rather than criticism, all manner of opportunities may arise.

In humanistic psychotherapy, the use of 'reframing,' a concept from neuro-linguistic programming, has affinities with the above (Bandler and Grinder 1990). It encourages the client and the therapist to turn a problem round and to try out different possibilities of responding. Action leads to internal change. The reframing may be verbal, through movement, through drawing or through use of gestalt (Clarkson 1993).

As a dance movement therapist I use my creativity to support and deepen the client's experience. As a choreographer my creativity is focused on shaping my insights and designing movements in the service of the dance. I do not try to shape my clients.

In the complex cycle of creativity, the notion of *'Experience, Recognise, Deepen and Communicate'* occurred to me very early on in my career when I was beginning to work with groups. It was a helpful marker in recognising stages of the creative process. I noticed how quickly people tried to know, to label, exactly what they were doing, rather than giving themselves time to experience intimately the nature of the movement; a way of knowing through the body: to take each aspect in turn.

Experience

We gradually feel more connected to our bodies, being more aware of the ground beneath us, of our breathing and the creating of space around ourselves; on being in the moment of now. Experiencing is an immersion into the rhythmic stream of movement, an emptying and opening, a focusing on bodily sensation through movement.

Recognise

Here we begin to recognise what we are doing and how we are doing it: for example, tracking our movement internally and saying to ourselves, 'Now I am lifting my head, now I am turning, softening in the centre of my body or sinking slowly towards the earth.'

Deepen

With recognition we deepen the content, taking time to inhabit each movement fully, to try out possibilities and to reflect on the growing expression. We might slow down the movement process, wait or through repetition explore foreground phrases. We use intuition, trial and error. We gradually become more specific, paying attention to detail and nuance. In this stage we may feel confused and uncertain. We are in transition between what we are aware of and what is emerging.

Communicate

Here there is a clarity of movement and form and intention begin to emerge. We reconnect to the idea's core or essence which can be so easily lost in the process. The dance begins to communicate, to make sense to both the creator and to others. In DMT this might be where the client begins to integrate aspects of their experience and share insights with the therapist. In choreography the dance content and the form it takes become an inseparable whole.

In this cyclical process of 'Experience, Recognise, Deepen and Communicate' the words are not intended as a plan or formula for a piece of work. Too much definition can be counterproductive in the creative process. We may move fluidly back and forth between the different aspects. In DMT they may be implicit in the therapist's process. For example, when a client rushes into an interpretation, it may be useful to return to the experience and allow recognition and meaning of the image, the feeling or the story gradually to emerge. These aspects can also be recognised within the examples from practice in this chapter. Similarly, I remember many occasions in choreography when I felt dissatisfied with a particular movement phrase and needed to go right back to rediscovering the original experience which motivated it; finding and deepening the heart of the movement, returning to its essence.

It is important at this point to reiterate the significance of the deepening process, so crucial to creativity. Here, 'extending the ground' is a metaphor for the deepening process. We have an opportunity to 'extend the ground' by allowing more space and time between the initial movement impulse and the forming and embodying of the idea. In our need to have goals, we may forget to listen to our bodily wisdom, thereby cutting short our creative process.

We can 'extend the ground' by a period for reverie and contemplation, like a dreaming space. We can slow down and wait, creating inner space for images and movements to emerge. DMT clearly provides and encourages space for this. Choreography often operates within time restraints; a dance has a completion time deadline from external requirements. But dreaming time has less to do with chronological time than with a yielding attitude to one's own pace. It appears an integral part of creative process. There seems to be a paradox between the dreaming time and the very pragmatism of making dance for performance. In my experience unfettered imagination and pragmatic movement go hand in hand. Dreaming precedes action; action is made fertile by the roots of dreaming. Interestingly, 'Dreamtime' in Australian Aboriginal beliefs was when the shapes and patterns of the earth began to form (Chatwin 1987).

Our dancing can be a journey of adventure. Along the way we may feel anxiety or fear, where nothing is clear. We have left behind the safety of what we know and are stepping over the edge of darkness into the unknown. On this route we need to trust our creative process:

> No matter how large the garden – if you are directly planting, you do so by patting and patting the earth, taking little handfuls of it up. Be gentle, be economical. This is how to treat the land, thoughtfully, with presence of mind: Whatever happens to this field in some way also happens to us.
>
> (Pinkola Estes 1995: 26)

Understanding and integration

This section reflects on transcendent moments, the relationship of client and therapist and of the audience and performer, and how these are intrinsic to understanding and integration. We may all be familiar with that moment in our practice when everything seems to come together: time stands still, the moment expands, we have a sense of wholeness. We feel an altered state of consciousness. There are times in working with dancers on their choreographic process and also in DMT when I am aware of that transcendent moment, which expands and vibrates in the space between us. Here is an example from practice during a course in southern Spain – a moonlit rooftop dance:

> The dance begins with a clear shared movement, leading into individual expression and then coming back together again into a unison ending. The light, the surrounding landscape and everyone's heightened awareness creates a particular, intense ambience. The dance is the container for spirituality, nature and of communion with others. It is repeated on several occasions, a symbol of the group's identity.

The client/therapist relationship is integral to the transcendent moment in DMT. In the therapeutic relationship moments of heightened awareness can inform the session. Some observation or image begins to resonate as relevant to the client's process. Something of importance is emerging. Awareness deepens. As therapists we may see tiny visual clues or sense a change of energy between ourselves and our client. We resonate with the client's experience. The intention of the one moving and the attention of the therapist witnessing intensifies the movement experience. The dance is the container for the experience. It is a shared moment, subtly deepening our experience

and understanding. It moves me when even within just a moment of movement I might receive a clue to someone's history and current concerns, their
essence encapsulated in movement. Here is an extract from DMT practice on
a beach in North Wales:

> P leaned his back against the breakwater and using the support slowly
> moved himself along it changing the shape of his body and creating clear
> movement images. I suddenly saw how this dance was an expression of
> his core need for support in his life, and how with this physical support he
> manifested more of himself. In that space he became more visible to me
> than ever before. Subsequently he shared his experience, his insights and
> his wish for support with the group and, for a short while at his request
> they lifted and carried him high above their heads, literally giving him an
> experience of total support.

In a similar way the performer/audience relationship is integral to
heightened awareness and transcendent moments in choreography:

> Dances will be made for different reasons, in different settings, with dif-
> ferent people. But above all dance is a communication. As we watch we
> can have a sense of rightness, deeper than appreciation where the experi-
> ence of choreographer and audience meet. The dance becomes alive, or is
> brought into being by the participation of all those involved in it.
>
> (Shreeves 2004: 26)

When a dancer performs to an audience, that experience is part of the
continued deepening of the choreography. Dances need an audience to bring
them to fruition. It is not just a matter of showing them per se. In the act of
performing changes occurs within the dancer. There may be a heightened
sense of rhythmic connection to the piece. All aspects become heightened in
performance and the dancer's response to himself is part of the growing
process. The dancer actually completes the forming of himself and the dance
through the alchemy of the performer/audience relationship. Changes are
literally imprinted on the body's memory and are interwoven into the dance.
Through the interaction of the dancer with the performing space a further
powerful dimension is created where the space becomes a landscape redolent
with images. Choreography may give an audience new and often unexpected
perspectives changing their internal experience:

> She seemed hardly to move. It wasn't a group of gestures or a fixed
> pattern of steps . . . It had little to do with dance and yet it was the
> essence of all great dancing. . . . to convey a feeling, to make a suggestion
> and when it was done, we were different.
>
> (Watson 1976: 203)

Healthier dancers

Support for dancers in the UK has had until recently a focus on the physical health of dancers. Now it appears the overall well-being of dancers has been highlighted, researched and documented since the two 'Healthier Dance Conferences' in 1990 and 2000, instigated by the organisation Dance UK. A wide range of topics was presented and discussed, ranging from nutrition for dancers, issues of anorexia, alternative approaches to training and dancers' emotional issues. I have noticed how concern about body image, low self-esteem, dealing with criticism, ageing and performance anxiety often feature in my therapeutic work with professional dancers. I also have on occasion heard from dancers how a focus on body awareness work in DMT has indirectly influenced their approach to their own work. Sometimes the training of dancers and structures within the performing world can show a lack of understanding about factors influencing a dancer's personal growth and achievement. Perhaps more dreaming time is needed?

The conferences have illustrated how, for instance, psychotherapy, massage and visualisation techniques can be very supportive to the dancer. In this whole area dance movement therapy with its flexibility and holistic approach can be very helpful. Dancers have an opportunity to explore their personal concerns rather than their performance, often reframing their view of themselves, with time to reflect, to be curious rather than critical. There are so many possible approaches, all using movement as a primary mode of discovery. An extract from DMT practice illustrates this point:

> T was very anxious about an upcoming audition, worrying that he would dry up, appear foolish, be far less able than other people, etc. With the help of some body awareness work he realised how his anxiety led him to tighten up muscularly, to restrict his breathing and generally feel worse. Recognising that after all he did not know, but only imagined what the audition would be like, he decided to play with the movement, words and images arising from his internal process. Along the way, he discovered an alternative, optimistic scenario. He said that this was a kind of rehearsal for an event, a positive rather than a negative act of the imagination. He felt changed within himself – more open – relaxed and less anxious. For a short while he danced freely, just for the pleasure of moving.

As a dance artist, in the area of choreographic mentoring, I support dancers in their choreographic process, using skills and observations honed over years of experience in the diverse world of choreography and performance including collaborations with musicians and visual artists. My intention here is first of all to provide a safe and non-judgemental space for the exploration and creation of the dance work. Dancers will ask for different kinds of support: for example, to work on particular movement patches which do not feel right; to clarify through moving and talking an initial idea for a piece; to share personal difficulties; to have an opportunity to dance through and have feedback about the movement, the feeling, the rhythm, or the whole communication.

I am very drawn to this area of my work. I observe and empathise, listening and understanding through my own body in an intuitive, inner mirroring process. I notice detail. I see what is just beginning to emerge in the movement, what patterns are left like echoes in the space, what is the timbre of the underlying rhythm. I ask questions, occasionally mirror movements or alternatives and remain still and silent a lot, waiting for the dancer's intentions and clarity to unfold. In this situation I am a mix of helpmate, mentor and audience in one. This dimension adds to the growth of the dancer and the dance. I am very clear that this is his dance, not mine. I resonate with the difficulties and share the excitement of the 'ah-ha' moments. In a postcard to me Jenner Roth (2004), a founder of humanistic and integrative therapy in Europe and the UK, said:

> I was so struck by your description of how you work with someone doing their own choreography: following closely behind them as they create and find their own movements and being there to support and validate what they've made. It seemed to me a perfect description of how I like to think of therapy; with an intimacy and relationship, with an exploration. It stays with me.
>
> (Roth 2004)

Dance performers and choreographers have many transferable skills which could be used in therapeutic situations and many do go on to train as dance movement therapists. Whereas, for example, dancers might bring a familiarity with improvisation structures and movement observation skills, dance therapists will be skilful in 'reading' underlying psychological roots of movement or recognising the personal implications of using a particular dance form.

We need to stay aware of false paradigms. As stated earlier there are differences of intention and practice between therapy and choreography, but at times there is a crossover between them. Any experience we have will become part of who we are and inevitably inform our future actions. If sources from personal history are used in a choreography there is a choice to include or recognise this or not. There are no absolutes in creativity; process may become part of performance. I have noticed in my conversations and interactions with cutting-edge dance artists how some appear to be exploring the subconscious and interweaving movement with other forms. Whereas in dance movement therapy personal outcomes are foreground, in choreography it is what you design in movement that is paramount and the communication of that to an audience.

In addition, in professional dance, the value of talking about the creative process involved, as a way of both enhancing and clarifying the communication, has long been a debating point. It can be very helpful to the artist in the process of forming the dance. For example Chisenhale Dance Space in London has an ongoing programme of artist-led, process-based projects, with an emphasis on process rather than on finished work, enormously enriching to all concerned:

> What matters are not the things that happen, it's the times between. Possibly the thing that matters, that you are looking for, is like the roots of plants, hidden and happening in the gaps of your knowledge.
>
> (Milner 2000: 44)

Summary

This chapter has drawn on personal experience to reflect on roots of dance common to DMT and choreography. Dance as a universal and ever-changing art will continue to grow and diversify in all its forms and on the way uncover new meanings and fresh questions. DMT has an important role in that process.

References

Bandler, R. and Grinder, J. (1990) *Frogs into Princes*. New York: Gavcel.
Bloom, K. and Shreeves, R. (1998) *Moves*. Amsterdam: Harwood.
Boal, A. (1992) *Games for Actors and Non Actors*. London: Routledge.
Chatwin, B. (1987) *The Songlines*. London: Vintage Press.
Clarkson, P. (1993) *Gestalt Counselling in Action*. London: Sage.
Fontana, D. (1993) *The Secret Language of Symbols*. London: Pavilion.
Fromm, M. (1990) Extract from seminar 'Working with Clients', Spectrum Centre for Humanistic Psychotherapy, London.
Gibran, K. (1985) *The Prophet*. London: Heinemann.
Hillman, J. (1999) *The Force of Character*. New York: Ballantine.
Keleman, S. (1994) *Love: A Somatic View*. Berkeley, CA: Center Press.
Maslow, A. (1954) *Motivation & Personality*. London: Longman.
Milner, M. (2000) *A Life of One's Own*. London: Virago.
Paxton, S. (1977) *The Small Dance*. Dartington College Theatre Papers. The first series, no. 4. Totnes: Dartington Hall College of Performing Arts.
Pesso, A. and Crandell, J. (1991) *Movement Psychotherapy: Theory and Application of Pesso System/Psychomotor Therapy*. New York: Brookline.
Pinkola Estes, C. (1995) *The Faithful Gardener*. London: Random House.
Rogers, C. (1967) *On Becoming a Person*. London: Constable.
Roth, J. (2004) Personal communication. London.
Satir, V. (1978) *People Making*. London: Souvenir Press.
Shreeves, R. (1990) *Children Dancing*. London: Ward Lock.

—— (1998) *Imaginary Dances*, London: Ward Lock.
—— (2004) Valley of small things, *London Dance UK News Issue* 53, 26–27.
Todd, M. (1959) *The Thinking Body*. New York: Dance Horizons.
Watson, L. (1976) *Gifts of Unknown Things*. London: Hodder and Stoughton.
Winearls, J. (1990) *Choreography: The Art of the Body*. London: Dance Books.

Appendix

Professional associations

Association for Dance Movement Therapy in the United Kingdom (ADMT.UK)
The Administrator
ADMT.UK
32 Meadfoot Lane
Torquay
Devon TQ1 2BW
UK
Email: queries@admt.org.uk
Internet: http://www.admt.org.uk/

American Dance Therapy Association (ADTA)
ADTA National Office
Suite 230
2000 Century Plaza
Columbia
ML 21044
USA
Tel: 410 997 4040
Fax: 410 997 4048
Internet: http://www.adta.org

Dance Therapy Association of Australia (DTAA)
PO Box 641
Carlton South
VIC 3053
Australia
Tel: 0419 531 218
Fax: (613) 9598 0636
Email: dtaa@alphalink.com.au

International Dance Therapy Institute of Australia
PO Box 274
Elsternwick
Melbourne
VIC 3185
Australia
Tel: (613) 9578 7109
Email: mbraban@bigpond.com

IDTIA studio
Danceworks Studio
29 Macquarie Street
Prahan
VIC 3181
Australia
Tel: (613) 9578 7109
Email: mbraban@bigpond.com

Dance Therapy Association of Finland
Suomen Tanssiterapiayh distys ry
PL 1366
FIN-00101 Helsinki
Finland
http://www.tanssiterapia.net

Art Therapy Italiana
Art Therapy Italiana
Via Barberia 13
40123 Bologna
Italy
http://www.arttherapy.it

Japanese Dance Therapy Association (JDTA)
Tokyo Welfare Special School
2–7–20 Seisinchou Edogawaku
Tokyo 134–0087
Japan
Tel and fax: 81 3 5605 8283

Dance movement therapy professional training programmes UK

Goldsmiths College
University of London
New Cross
London SE14 6NW
Tel: 020 7919 7171

Roehampton University
Erasmus House
Roehampton Lane
London SW15 5PU
Tel: 020 8392 3000

University of Derby
Mickleover
Derby
DE3 5GX
UK
Tel: 01332 514323

European Professional Training Programmes

Italy

Dr Rosa Marie Govoni
Art Therapy Italiana
Via Barberia 13
40123 Bologna
Italy
Email: r.m.govoni@freesurf.ch; rosamariagovoni@tiscalinet.it

Netherlands

Hogeschool voor Muziek en Dans
Kruisplein 26
3012 CC Rotterdam
The Netherlands

Annalies Schrijnen-van Gastel
Postgraduate Programme in Dance Therapy
Codarts University of Professional Arts Education
Kruisplein 26
3012cc Rotterdam
The Netherlands

Portugal

Isabel Figueira
University of Lisbon
Portugal
Email: isabelfigueira@hotmail.com; dance_therapy_portugal@hotmail.com

Slovenia

Dr Breda Kroflic
Associate Professor Convenor of Postgraduate Arts Therapies Education
University of Ljubljana
Faculty of Education
Kardeljeva pl. 16
Si–1000 Ljubljana
Slovenia
Email: breda.kroflic@guest.arnes.si

Spain

Heidrun Panhofer
Autonomous University Barcelona
C/d'en Grassot 26, 3, 1,
08025 Barcelona
Spain
Email: info@en-e-mocion.com

Sweden

Prof. Erna Gronlund
University College of Dance
Sweden
Email: erna.gronlund@telia.com; erna.caresia.gronlund@danshogskolan.se

Journals

International Journal of Body, Movement and Dance in Psychotherapy
University of Hertfordshire
Meridian House
32 The Common
Hatfield
Herts AL10 0NZ
UK
Tel: 01707 285861
Email: BMDP@herts.ac.uk
Internet: http://www.tandf.co.uk/journals/titles/17432979.asp

The Arts in Psychotherapy
Customer Service Department
6277 Sea Harbor Drive
Orlando
FL 32887-4800
USA
Tel: +1 (407) 345-4020
Fax: +1 (407) 363-1354
Email: usjcs@elsevier.com
Internet: http://www.elsevier.com/locate/artspsycho

American Journal of Dance Therapy
Suite 230
2000 Century Plaza
Columbia
ML 21044
USA
Internet: http://www.springerlink.com/link.asp?id=105545

German Journal for Dance Therapy
Forum Tanztherapie
DGT
Konigsberger Str 60
50259 Pulheim
Germany
Tel: 02234 83008
Internet: http://www.dgt-tanztherapie.de

Author index

Acierno, R. 50, 69
Adair, G. 115, 128
Adler, J. 10, 13, 138, 141, 147, 148, 225, 227, 229
ADMTUK 13, 47
Aginsky, Y. 138, 147
Allen, J.G. 54, 69
Alperson,, E.D. 150, 152, 165
Anderson, T. 99, 149, 150, 165
Ansdell, G. 32, 46, 47
Antinori, D. 126, 128
Anzieu, D. 218, 229
Aposhyan, S. 2, 12
Arieti, S. 209, 212, 229
Arjunwadkar, K. 151, 165
Arpin, J. 125, 128
Atkinson, P. 67, 68, 69
Austin, J.H. 123, 128
Aveline, M. 185, 203

Bachelor, A. 185, 203
Baggott, R. 41, 47
Baker, W. 69
Bakka, E. 104, 110
Bandler, R. 113, 128, 238, 244
Bannerman-Haig, S. 6, 88, 99
Barber, P. 198, 203
Barker, C. 203
Barnes, C. 32, 47
Baron, N. 102, 110
Barrett, E. 170, 181
Bartel, L. 2, 12
Bartenieff, I. 59, 69
Bateson, G. 12, 13, 117, 127, 128
Beard, C. 63, 170, 181
Beckett, D. 168, 181
Behar-Horenstein, L. 13
Beiswanger, G. 11, 13

Bender, M. 17, 28, 29, 69
Benson, J. 17, 29, 216, 229
Berrol, C. 9, 10, 13, 187, 203
Besio, K. 125, 129
Best, P.A. 113, 128, 167, 181
Bick, E. 88, 95, 96, 97, 99
Bion, W. 88, 93, 94, 99
Bischoff, R.J. 185, 203
Blakely, T. 69
Bliss, J. 37, 47
Blom, L.A. 11, 13
Bloom, K. 232, 235, 244
Boal, A. 233, 244
Boas, F. 61, 69, 112, 115, 124, 125, 126, 128
Boas, S. 6, 61, 112, 115, 124, 125, 126, 128
Bohart, A.C. 227, 229
Bourdieu, P. 127, 128
Bowlby, J. 55, 69
Britton, R. 93, 99
Brooks, D. 10, 13
Brun, B. 64, 69
Bruschweiler-Stern, N. 166
Buckland, T.J. 102, 111
Buckroyd, J. 10, 13, 169, 175, 181
Bunce, J. 6, 71, 85, 86
Bungay, V. 187, 203, 208, 229
Butz, D. 125, 128
Byrne, P. 35, 47

Callaghan, K. 52, 55, 56, 69, 126, 128
Carkuff, R. 185, 206
Caroll, R. 19, 29
Caskey, N.H. 185, 203
Cattanach, A. 212, 213, 229
Chaiklen 69

Chaiklin, S. 34, 39, 47, 52, 81, 86, 131, 166
Chaplin, L.T. 11, 13
Charcot, J.M. 74, 86
Charmaz, K. 187, 203
Chatwin, B. 240, 244
Chico, N. 205
Chodorow, J. 10, 13, 90, 99, 148, 212, 229
Clark-Rapley, E. 127, 129
Clarkson, P. 48, 238, 244
Coffey, A. 67, 68, 69
Coker, E.M. 125, 129
Collie, K. 185, 204
Conzolino, L.J. 146, 147
Cooper, J.C. 2, 11, 13, 214, 229, 233
Corbin, J. 48
Coseo, A. 126, 129
Costinos, C. 99
Cox, M. 209, 212, 213, 229
Coyne, L. 54, 69
Crandell, J. 233, 237, 244
Crickmay, C. 10, 11, 12, 15
Cruz, R. 9, 10, 13, 52
Cubero, M. 125, 129
Curzon-Hobson, A. 170, 181

Damasio, A.R. 3, 13, 19, 29, 171, 182
Daniluk, J. 210, 230
Dasgupta, G. 10, 14
Davies, L. 151, 165
Davis, A.D. 34, 42, 47, 85, 86, 125, 129
De La Mata, M.L. 125, 129
DeLozier, J. 113, 114, 121, 129
De Mille, A. 64, 69
Department of Health (DOH) 33, 36, 41
Dilley, B. 11, 13
Dilts, R. 113, 114, 121, 129
Dinnage, R. 185, 203
Dokter, D. 126, 129, 131
Dosmantes, E. 203
Droes, N. 205
Dunin, E. 104, 111

Early, E. 63, 64, 69, 107, 148
Edwards, J.M. 187, 203
Eichel, V. 130
Elliott, R. 185, 203
Emanuel, R. 77, 86
Epstein, S. 58, 69
Erikson, K. 187, 203, 204
Escobar, T. 137, 147
Escott, C. 166

Etchegoyen, R.H. 140, 146, 147
Etherington, K. 185, 203

Fadiga, L. 182
Feder, B. 13
Feder, E. 13
Fisk, N. 166
Foa 52, 69, 70
Fogassi, L. 182
Forinash, M. 187, 203
Fortin, S. 12, 13
Foster, S.L. 12, 14
Foucault, M. 168, 182
Foulkes, S.H. 193, 203
Fraleigh, S.H. 11, 12, 14
Frankl, V. 152, 165
Freedland, A. 166
Freud, S. 7, 74, 132, 133, 135, 136, 146–148
Friedman, M.J. 69, 70
Fromm, M. 151, 165, 235, 244
Fromm-Reichman, F. 165

Gallese, V. 182
Ganet-Segal, J. 10, 13
Gard, M. 125, 129
Gardner, H. 113, 129, 170, 182
Garrard Post, S. 129
Garvey, C. 210, 230
Gebru, H. 125, 129
Geertz, C. 186, 203
Gendlin, E.T. 114, 129, 171, 182
Gerhardt, S. 3, 14
Gershefski, J.J. 185, 203
Gibran, K. 233, 244
Giddens, A. 127, 129
Gilligan, S.G. 114, 129
Gilroy, A. 215, 230
Glaser, B. 47, 114, 129, 187, 203
Glasman, J. 38, 47
Glittenberg, J. 125, 129
Glover, V. 166
Goldberg, S. 182
Goleman, D. 151, 165
Gomez, L. 137, 138, 148
Good, B.J. 84, 118, 129
Goodill, S.W. 1, 13
Grafanaki, S. 185, 203
Graff Low, K. 150, 166
Greben, S.E. 170, 182
Green, J. 12, 14, 150, 165
Grinder, J. 113, 128, 238, 244

Guba, E. 187, 204

Habermas, J. 118, 129
Hager, P. 168, 181
Hall, E.T. 29, 111, 127, 130, 165, 244
Halprin, A. 2, 11, 14
Hanna, J.L. 126, 130
Hanniford, C. 19, 29
Hartley, L. 12, 14
Hatton, D. 205
Hayes, J. 14, 230
Hedgespeth, J. 204
Henderson, B. 117, 130, 166
Henwood, K. 50, 70
Heppner, P. 185, 204
Herman, J.L. 171, 182
Heron, J. 186, 187, 204
Hersen, M. 69
Hervey, L.W. 9, 115, 130
Hetcht, T. 12, 14
Hickey, C. 168, 182
Hill, C. 130, 185, 204, 230
Hillan, E. 150, 165
Hillman, J. 237, 244
Hinshelwood, R.D. 97, 99, 140, 147, 148
Hodnott, P. 164, 165
Hofstede, G. 119, 120, 125, 130
Holden, U. 17, 29
Holliday, A. 50, 69
Horowitz, M.J. 58, 69
Houston, G. 216, 218, 230
Howard, K.L. 185, 205
Howe, D. 185, 204
Huberman, A.M. 208, 230
Hurlbut, W.B. 129
Hyvonen, K. 202, 204

Izzard, S. 185, 204

James, E. 185, 203, 237
Jankowitcz, D. 156, 165
Johnson, D.R. 34, 35, 38, 42, 44, 45, 48, 127, 130
Jones, P. 2, 14, 155, 165
Joseph, A. 169, 175, 182
Junge, M.B. 187, 204

Karkou, V. 5, 31, 34, 36, 38, 40, 47
Kashyap, T. 1, 14
Keane, T.M. 69, 70
Keddy, V.C. 187, 203, 208, 229
Keleman, S. 233, 236, 244

Kelly, G.A. 156, 165
Kestenberg, J. 6, 39, 48, 85, 86, 88, 89, 90, 97, 99
Kinchin, D. 51, 69
Kirschenbaum, H. 117, 130
Kitwood, T. 17, 27, 28, 29
Kitzinger, J.V. 150, 165
Klein, M. 7, 93, 99, 100, 140, 147
Koch, N.S. 126, 127, 130, 131
Koltai, J. 10, 11, 14

Laban, R. 2, 6, 14, 34, 38, 43, 48, 86, 88, 90, 95, 99, 136
Lally, V. 170, 181
Lamb, W. 72, 85, 86
Langer, S.K. 214, 230
Latour, B. 125, 130
Lawrence, F.C. 70, 86, 175, 182
Le Goff, J. 130
Leamon, J. 163, 165
Levy, F. 10, 14, 30, 34, 48
Lewin, K. 225, 230
Lewis, D.P. 47, 59, 69, 99, 181
Libet, B. 71, 86
Lietaer, G. 185, 204, 206, 227, 230
Lincoln, Y. 70, 187, 204, 230, 231
Lindon, J. 107, 111
Lindquist, G. 12, 14, 219, 230
Linesch, D. 187, 204
Llewellin, S. 36, 41, 48
Lohn, A. 69, 131, 166
Loman, S. 86, 89, 99
Lord, D.L. 150, 165
Lott, D.A. 185, 204
Loughran, E. 114, 130
Low, K. 33, 48
Lowenthal, D. 185, 206
Lucchi, B. 185, 204
Luckmann, T. 118, 131
Lycouris, S. 11, 14

MacDonald, J. 4, 5, 47, 49, 69, 86, 99
Machel, G. 102, 111
Macran, S. 185, 205
Mahler, M. 182
Mahtani, A. 129
Manthei, R.J. 206
Marranca, B. 10, 14
Marris, P. 86
Martin, J. 185, 205
Maslow, A. 233, 244
May, H. 17, 28, 29, 128, 131, 165

Mayo, E. 115, 130
McBride, A. 185, 203
McKibben, H. 6, 15
McLeod, J. 113, 115, 130, 185, 204
McNiff, S. 9, 14, 115, 130, 187, 205
Mearns, D. 180, 182, 204
Meekums, B. 2, 4, 7, 14, 34, 38, 48, 89, 99,
   167, 171–174, 182, 209, 212, 216, 223,
   226–228, 230
Mehta, M. 151, 152, 165
Melville-Thomas, R. 89, 99
Merry, S.E. 13, 113, 130
Milburn, M. 166
Miles, M.B. 208, 230
Millar, S. 210, 230
Mills, L. 210, 230
Milner, M. 244
Miyaji, N.T. 125, 130
Monaghan, L. 117, 131
Monk, M. 47
Moodley, R. 125, 130
Moore, C., 19, 29,
Moore, P. 126, 128
Moustakas, C. 50, 70, 187, 205
Muran, C.J. 118, 130
Musicant, S. 225, 227, 230

Nadel, M.H. 11, 13, 15
Nagrin, D. 11, 15
Neirinck, M. 185, 204
Nellhaus, T. 127, 130
Newman, G. 2, 15, 185, 204
NHS 32
NICE 33, 154, 165
North, M. 18, 89, 97, 99, 241

Ogborn, J. 47
Orbach, S. 180, 182
Orbe, M.P. 125, 130
Orlinsky, D.E. 185, 205
Ott, B.R. 28, 30

Pallaro, P. 10, 15, 148
Palley, R. 3, 15, 71, 72, 85, 86
Panksepp, J. 3, 15
Papadopoulos, N. 61, 70
Park, J. 69, 70, 130, 170, 182
Parker, I. 187, 205
Parkes, C.M. 77, 86
Parkinson, J. 4, 6, 15, 71, 73, 74, 75, 77,
   79, 81, 83, 85, 86
Paulson, B. 185, 205

Paxton, S. 15, 244
Payne, H.L. 1, 2, 4, 7, 10, 15, 30, 34,
   38, 48, 69, 88, 89, 99, 102, 103, 111,
   113, 130, 133, 134, 148, 167, 169, 173,
   182, 184, 185, 187, 195, 203, 205, 209,
   225–228, 230
Pearson, J. 2, 13, 15, 102, 111
Penfield, K. 4, 7, 132, 135, 148, 167, 182
Perrett, D. 183
Perrin, T. 17, 29
Perry, B. 56, 70
Pesso, A. 233, 237, 244
Peterson, K.C. 52, 70
Pidgeon, N. 50, 70
Piper, R. 229
Pollard, R. 69
Potter, J. 187, 205, 208, 231
Prain, V. 168, 182
Predock, J. 11, 15
Prout, M.F. 70
Prouty, G. 223, 231

Quality Assurance Agency 31

Raphael-Leff, J. 149, 151, 152, 162, 165
Read Johnson, D. 52, 70
Ready, R.E. 28, 30
Reason, P. 130, 186, 187, 205, 231
Reeve, S. 124, 128
Regel, S. 31, 48
Reich, W. 55, 57, 70, 81, 86, 97, 100
Rennie, D.L. 185, 205
Rieber, R.W. 102, 108, 111
Ritter, M. 33, 48, 150, 166
Rizzolatti, G. 173, 182
Roberts, D. 31, 48
Robertson, A. 154, 166
Robson, C. 90, 100
Rodgers, B. 227, 231
Rogers, C.R. 82, 86, 117, 120, 130, 173,
   183, 220, 222, 227, 231, 233, 244
Roll, S. 11, 15
Rosch, E. 131
Rosenberg, J. 204
Roth, G, 2, 15,
Roth, J. 243, 244
Rothschild, B. 19, 30, 52, 55, 57, 70
Rousseau, C. 125, 130
Rowan, J. 186, 204, 206, 208, 231
Royal Colege of Psychiatrists 32
Runberg, M. 69
Rutan, J.S. 194, 206

Ryan, A. 168, 183
Rycroft, C. 141, 148
Ryden, J. 185, 205

Sacks, O. 74, 86
Sager, P. 10, 11, 13
Sakiyama, Y. 126, 131
Sandel, S. 17, 19, 30, 34, 35, 38, 42, 44, 45, 48, 69, 114, 130, 131, 151, 166
Sanderson, P. 34, 36, 38, 40, 47
Sands, A. 185, 206
Satir, V. 233, 244
Scarth, S. 167, 183
Schatzman, L. 205
Schechner, R. 127, 131
Schloss, J. 129
Schmais, D. 10, 15, 34, 38, 47, 136, 148, 184, 206
Schon, D. 187, 206
Schore, A.N. 56, 70
Schutz 118, 131
Schwartz, R.A. 70
Scott Hollander, A. 17, 19, 30
Segal, H. 100
Seligman, M. 185, 206
Senghas, R.J. 117, 131
Sergiovanni, T.J. 118, 131
Sharp, P. 170, 183
Shaw, R. 2, 15, 167, 171, 183
Shayer, M. 115, 131
Sheets-Johnstone, M. 15, 57, 70
Sherborne, V. 39, 48
Shields, C. 55, 70
Shilling, C. 125, 131
Shreeves, R. 8, 9, 232, 234, 235, 241, 244
Siegel, E. 35, 39, 48, 148, 151, 166
Simkin, P. 150, 166
Singer, A.J. 6, 101
Slade, P. 166
Sloan,T.S. 118, 131
Small, J.J. 185, 206, 244
Smith, B. 183
Smith, J. 15, 205
Smith-Autard, J.M. 11, 15
Snyder, S. 50, 70
Sossin, M. 86, 99
Spaniol, S. 187, 206
Sparkes, A. 168, 183
Spiby, H. 150, 154, 161, 166
Spiegel, D. 55, 70
Stake, R.E. 50, 70, 207, 231

Standal, S. 82, 86
Stanton, T. 2, 9, 12, 15, 34, 48, 209, 216, 231
Stanton-Jones, K. 9, 10, 15, 34, 48, 209, 216, 231
Stark, A. 10, 13, 148
Steier, F. 187, 206
Steinman, L. 11, 15
Stelmaczonek, K. 185, 205
Stephens, T. 61, 70
Stern, D. 151, 166, 218, 231
Stevenson-Hinde, J. 86
Stiles, W.B. 187, 205, 206
Stockley, S. 17, 19, 30
Strachey, J. 137, 148
Strauss, A. 11, 14, 37, 47, 48, 114, 129, 187, 204
Stromstead, T. 54, 56, 70
Stuart, J. 205
Stull, D. 187, 203, 204
Subramanyam, A. 126, 131
Suddendorf, T. 183
Sullivan, H.S. 34, 48

Tallman, K. 227, 229
Teixera, J. 150, 166
Templeton, E. 216, 231
Theilgaard, A. 209, 212, 213, 229
Thompson, S. 131, 204, 229
Thorne, B. 180, 182
Todd, M. 234, 245
Todes, C. 73, 74, 86
Torbert, W. 187, 206
Torp 104, 110, 111
Totton, N. 2, 12, 15, 171, 183
Trevarthen, C. 170, 183
Truax, C.B. 185, 206
Truscott, D. 205

Underwood, L.G. 129

van der Hart, O. 55, 70
van der Kolk, B.A. 56, 68, 70
Van Hasselt, V.B. 69
Varela, F. 123, 131
Vigilante, D. 69
Violets, M. 18, 19, 22, 30
von Durckheim, K.G. 171, 183

Waddell, M. 93–95, 100
Wadsworth Hervey, L. 9, 10, 15
Walsh, D. 149, 166

Warnier, J-P. 125, 131
Watson, J. 185, 206, 241, 245
Weber, S. 150, 166
Westbrook, B.K. 6, 15
Wetherall, M. 187, 205, 208, 231
Wheeler, S. 185, 204
White, E. 10, 15, 63, 136, 148
Whitehouse, M. 88, 100, 137,
   148
Whiten, A. 183
Wiener, A.J. 151, 166
Wilkins, P. 185, 206, 231
Williams, J.H.G. 173, 183

Willman, A. 125, 129
Wilson, J.P. 170, 181
Winearls, J. 235, 245
Winnicott, D. 62, 69, 70, 152, 166, 201,
   206, 209–211, 218, 231
Wood, I. 182
Woods, P. 90, 100
Wyatt, J. 187, 206, 230

Yalom, I. 41, 42, 48, 177, 180, 183, 216,
   219, 220, 231
Yamamoto, K. 19, 29
Yip, K. 32, 48

Subject index

ADMTUK 1, 3, 4, 5, 12, 47, 198
alienation 208
anger 42, 43, 51, 58, 59, 63, 77–81, 133,
    170, 178, 188, 189, 191, 192, 194, 196,
    198, 199, 200, 202, 214, 218, 220, 222
antenatal 7, 149, 150, 152, 154, 155–158,
    161, 162, 164–166 *see also* birth
    preparation, holisitc
anthropologists 117, 126–127
anthropology 113, 114, 118, 125, 128,
    130, 131
anxiety 22, 73, 77, 94, 151–157, 161, 166,
    189, 190, 210, 228, 240; Parkinsons 72;
    therapist contains 81; baby's 93;
    reduction in 150; at the start of DMT
    172; disruption of 211; re-experience
    of 219; performance 242
arts therapies 2, 9, 31, 33, 36, 37, 103,
    109, 173, 184, 185, 228, 230
assessment 18–20, 22, 25, 27, 28, 34, 47,
    70, 85, 86, 89, 127, 143, 144, 146, 174,
    175, 185, 207, 210, 223
Association for Dance Movement
    Therapy 12, 48
attitude 5, 26, 31, 42, 43, 77, 80, 84, 85,
    123, 137, 151, 154, 157, 161, 174, 179,
    200, 222–224, 228, 239
authentic 11, 165; movement 7, 10,
    13–15, 132, 134, 135, 137, 141–144,
    147, 148, 185, 225, 227, 237 *see also*
    choreography, dance, improvisation

bereavement 74, 83, 84, 189, 191–193 *see
    also* loss
birth, 7, 45, 54, 75, 84, 124, 127, 149,
    150–158, 161–166, 214; preparation
    152, 154, 156, 158, 163, 165 *see also*
    antenatal, holistic

body 1, 3, 11–13, 19, 21–25, 30, 31,
    53–57, 59–62, 70, 71–73, 77–85, 87–98,
    105, 112, 115, 117, 119, 121–125,
    127–131, 137–139, 143–147, 150, 152,
    157, 161–165, 173–180, 194, 202, 212,
    214, 229, 230, 233, 234, 238, 243;
    action 34, awareness 2, 6–8, 10, 12, 19,
    26, 68, 78, 82, 151, 175, 235, 242–244;
    body-mind 38, 52; memory 241; of
    knowledge 35; reinhabit the 65;
    changes10, 21; image 242; shape 24;
    wisdom of 167–171
boundaries 6, 40, 56, 82, 83, 105, 108,
    112, 118, 119, 124, 125, 181, 195, 201,
    223, 225
breath 7, 151, 153, 156, 164, 238;
    breathing 56, 149, 150, 152, 156, 164,
    235, 238, 242

care home 18, 22, 29; workers 22,
    49–70
case study 5, 50, 85, 90, 174, 207
chaos 35, 44, 156, 217
children 4, 6, 87, 89, 99, 101–104,
    106–110, 119, 212, 229, 230 *see also*
    special schools
choreography 6, 8, 10, 11–15, 207, 215,
    224, 230, 232, 234, 235, 237–239,
    241–244 *see also* creative movement,
    dance, improvisation
circle 9, 19, 23, 25, 43, 44, 60, 105, 124,
    141, 176, 196, 214–216, 219, 221, 232,
    235, 237, 239, 241, 243, 245
co-creation 127, 181
combined methodology 31 *see also*
    research, inquiry
communication 6, 12, 17–19, 22–28, 33,
    78, 83, 84, 87, 90, 96, 119, 122, 123,

125, 126, 130, 158, 235; activities 17,
18, 27; verbal 17, 19, 24, 122
community dance 3, 36–39
competence 7, 112, 116, 123, 126, 128,
202
complex 4, 5, 49, 51, 52, 55, 57, 68, 71,
84, 89, 107, 114, 118, 142, 146, 155,
170, 181, 233, 238 see also post
traumatic
consciousness 12, 72, 73, 83, 114,
123–126, 129, 134, 136, 137, 201, 214,
240
contact 7, 8, 12, 27, 41, 54, 95, 96, 112,
120, 163, 164, 169, 189, 190, 192–195,
199, 200, 202, 203, 205, 215, 224, 232,
233, 236, 237; improvisation 169, 194
see also communication, physical
contact, touch, play
container 38, 39, 56, 63, 64, 77, 80, 83,
93, 202, 240 see also holding, therapist
coping strategies 7, 150, 161, 164, 166,
169
counselling 3, 9, 10, 12, 42, 125, 130, 185,
204, 205 see also psychotherapy
countertransference 7, 130, 132, 135, 140,
141, 143, 145, 146, 174, 176, 202
creative movement 3, 83, 109 see also
improvisation, dance, choreography
creative process 8, 11–12, 13, 72, 108,
238, 239, 240; creativity 6, 10, 11, 14,
101, 104, 106, 110, 167, 209, 212, 220,
229, 232, 237–239, 243
culture 6, 7, 8, 17, 35, 112–131, 218, 221,
223–225 see also transcultural

dance 1; multi cultural trends in 2, 3–5;
mainstream 8; world of 9, 10, 11;
consciousness through 12, 13–18, 22,
23; clients ability to 26; engage
through 27, 30–39, 41, 44–47, 49, 52,
55, 57, 60, 61, 63–65; skills in 68, 69,
71, 80, 84, 87–91, 95, 98, 100, 101–105,
107, 108, 110, 112, 114, 122, 125–127,
129–131, 133, 135, 139, 143, 144,
147–150, 164–171, 174, 175, 182, 186,
191, 197, 201, 203, 205–207, 209–211,
213, 214, 215, 217, 219, 221, 223; to
make 224, 225, 227; training and
education in 229, 230–236, 238–241;
artist 242; performers in 243;
movement therapy see DMT,
ethnography 101–104 see also

choreography, creative movement,
ethno
data analysis 114, 187
data collection 187
death 44, 77, 142, 149, 157, 189, 214
deepen 233, 238, 239
dementia 4, 5, 17, 18, 19, 22, 25, 26–28,
79, 83
Department of Health (DOH) 29, 47 see
also Author index
development 1; personal 2, 6–8; of
understanding 12, 14; of group 23, 28;
of theory 31, 35, 38, 41, 42, 45, 46,
48, 54, 55, 62, 64, 71, 72, 82, 83, 85,
88–91, 96, 101–103, 105, 107–110,
112–115, 117, 118, 120, 125, 127, 133,
147, 148, 161, 169, 171, 173, 184–186,
190, 197, 201, 204–211, 213, 215, 219,
221, 222, 224, 225, 229, 230, 233 see
also personal
differentiate 9, 10, 58, 73
disclosure 193, 235
dissociation 54, 61, 146
DMT 1, 2, 3; other terms 4–8, 9; dance,
research 10; personal development 11;
dance 12, 14, 17, 18, 28, 29, 31, 32–33;
approaches 36; community 38;
assumptions 39; as distinguished from
34–43, 45; interactive 46–50, 52, 53;
individual 57, 58, 65, 68, 71; effects 72;
pre verbal, physical symptoms 73,
74–83; groups 75, 77–86, 87;
psychoanalysis 87–88; infant
observation 89–92, 95, 96, 97; flow 98,
99, 101, 102, 103; dance ethnography
104, 109; training 110, 112; profession
113; researchers 116; transcultural 117,
120, 121; cognitive skills 123, 124, 125;
training 127, 128, 132; the unconscious
133; movement psychotherapy 134;
authentic movement 149;
psychoanalysis 150; kinaesthetic
empathy 151–153, 167–171;
embodiment 171; process 172; warm
up 173–181, 183, 184; personal
development, DMT students,
approach, group therapy 185, 186;
humanistic 187–192, 193; physical
contact 194; ending 195, 196; method
197–200, 201; and practice 203, 205,
207; dance students 208–209; play,
model 210; childplay 211; metaphors

212, 213, 215–223, 225–229; process 231, 232; dance 233, 234; choreography 235, 236; contact 237; authenticity 240; tanscendence 244

DMT group 7, 8, 14, 35, 43, 75, 82, 83, 85, 120, 126, 127, 152, 153, 173, 175, 178, 180, 184–198, 200–202, 205, 207, 208, 211, 216, 219, 222, 223, 228, 236 *see also* group

drama therapy 185, 192 *see also* arts therapies

eating disorder 169, 174, 175, 181

echoing 179

effort 39, 75, 81, 144, 170

ego 62, 63, 121

embodiment 2, 3, 7, 12, 15, 65, 128–130, 148, 167–171, 174, 181

emotional 8, 10, 11, 27, 47, 53–56, 61, 63–65, 71, 72, 78–83, 85, 87–89, 93, 94, 97, 102, 105, 106, 138, 139, 149–151, 163, 170, 171, 209, 211, 213, 215, 216, 218–220, 222, 225, 226, 228, 235, 236, 242

empathy 11, 13, 120, 121, 150, 170, 173, 218, 224, 226, 227

enduring mental health difficulties 33

energy 62, 74, 143, 146, 153, 216, 220, 221, 240

ethics 1, 123

ethno 6, 107, 108, 110

ethnography 6, 110

evaluation 17–19, 22, 23, 26, 41, 42, 47, 98, 103, 104, 114, 155, 156, 180 *see also* research, inquiry

event 6, 22, 50, 55, 58, 104, 109, 134, 140, 142, 143, 146, 227, 242

exercise 122, 128, 168, 189

expression 3, 10, 11, 17, 19, 23, 24, 26, 27, 57, 61, 65, 71, 72, 74, 81, 83, 88, 90, 105, 109, 120, 135–138, 141, 146, 151, 152, 177, 180, 189, 195, 200, 202, 206, 211, 224, 234, 235, 239, 240, 25 *see also* movement

eye contact 92, 94–96, 117, 137, 179

family 32, 33, 35, 73, 75, 78, 80, 83, 102, 108, 118, 119, 121, 142, 145, 158, 161, 164, 174, 175, 179, 192, 193, 199, 202–204

femininity 119

fieldwork 101, 103, 104

fragmented 5, 68, 93, 94, 95, 126

free association 7 *see also* psychoanalysis

games 90, 105, 107, 108, 216, 219, 220

gender 119, 162–164, 181, 195, 201

gesture 43, 72, 85, 138, 143, 144, 177 *see also* movement

goal 44, 55, 57, 115, 119, 175, 176, 235

grounded theory 5, 31, 36, 50, 114, 187

grounding 36, 151, 174

group 3, 7, 8, 11, 19, 22–27, 33–35, 38–40, 42–46, 53, 74–82, 84, 85, 91, 103–106, 115, 119, 120, 122, 124, 127, 128, 130, 149, 152, 153, 163, 164, 169, 171, 173–180, 182, 184–203, 205, 207, 210, 212–214, 216–223, 225, 226–228, 230, 236, 241; dynamics 19, 23, 46 *see also* personal, development, DMT

Hawthorne effect 115, 128

hierarchy 41, 120

holding 22, 23, 25, 44, 55, 62, 65, 91, 93, 97, 119, 133, 151–153, 164, 191, 201 *see also* container

holistic 5, 7, 28, 61, 114, 118, 149, 152, 154, 156, 163, 165, 166, 186, 242 *see also* birth preparation

hormones 153

humanistic 34, 38, 41, 46, 113, 186, 232, 233, 238, 243

identity 50, 58, 110, 117, 123, 124, 126, 129, 147, 182, 183, 218, 240

images 43, 80, 138, 180, 217, 221, 239, 242

improvisation 2, 7, 8, 10, 12, 90, 115, 116, 124, 175–177, 243 *see also* creative movement, choreography

impulses 136, 143, 153, 211, 234

individuation 179

inquiry 1, 2, 4, 6–8, 112, 113, 115, 116, 118, 123, 126, 130, 151, 187, 206, 223, 225, 226 *see also* research

integration 3, 5, 19, 27, 35, 58, 60–62, 68, 71, 73, 85, 88, 93–95, 97, 101, 102, 146, 213, 229, 240

interaction 2, 6, 23, 24, 27, 28, 38, 39, 46, 61, 78, 88, 98, 107, 114, 118, 137, 196, 236, 241 *see also* communication

interpretation 6, 61, 67, 127, 132, 140,

141, 202, 208, 216, 229, 239 *see also* psychoanalysis

interviews 8, 18, 19, 80, 83, 107, 112, 113, 149, 155, 156, 163, 173, 187, 188, 200 *see also* research, inquiry

joining 24, 80, 202, 217, 219, 227

journal 5, 49, 53, 54, 56–59, 62–65, 68, 131, 186–188, 192, 205

Kestenberg Movement Profile (KMP) 85, 99

kinaesthetic 3, 73, 113, 151–153; empathy 169, 170

Laban Movement Analysis(LMA) 6, 88, 95, 136

labour 150, 151, 152, 157, 161, 163, 164 *see also* birth

language 1, 24, 30, 34, 43, 72, 73, 89, 102, 103, 105, 108, 110, 120, 122, 131, 132, 135, 136, 147, 168, 202, 233

leadership 41, 43, 84, 115, 127, 130, 177

learning 2, 6, 7, 11, 13, 22, 27, 49, 55, 56, 58, 69, 80, 87, 92, 105, 111, 136, 164, 167, 169, 170, 171, 173, 180, 181, 182, 185, 186, 190, 201, 202, 206, 208, 222, 228; difficulties 69, 80

life changes 149

Links Movement and Communication (LMC) 17

loss 8, 17, 19, 42, 44, 72, 74, 75, 77, 78–80, 83, 84, 99, 102, 175, 178, 179, 184, 188–192, 200–202, 211, 215 *see also* bereavement

love 57, 63, 70, 93, 116, 123, 133, 142, 216, 221–223, 236

meaning 5, 6, 35, 58, 68, 77, 78, 90, 97, 98, 117, 131–134, 138, 151, 158, 179, 192, 212, 233, 239

meditation 153, 235

mental 2, 4, 5, 8, 29, 31–35, 39, 42, 46, 48, 49, 58, 70, 77, 82, 85, 90, 94, 110, 122, 134, 141, 146, 150, 162, 163, 170, 210; health 2, 4, 5, 29, 31–35, 39, 42, 46, 48, 49, 70, 110, 122, 146, 162

metaphor 5, 11, 65, 73, 125, 141, 168, 202, 208, 211–219, 221, 225, 229, 233; metaphorical 56, 64

methodology 4, 28, 31, 36, 41, 90, 102, 103, 186, 203, 207, 229

mirror 9, 173, 197, 199, 237, 243

mobility 18, 19, 22, 23, 26

modelling 112–114, 170

mother 6, 35, 53, 57, 59, 61, 62, 65, 87, 93, 94, 96, 108, 142, 143, 150, 151, 177–179, 190, 218

movement 1–11, 13, 15, 17–20, 22–49, 51–72, 74, 76–96, 98–101, 103–112, 114–120, 122, 124–140, 142–150, 152–154, 156, 158, 162–170, 172–178, 180, 182, 183, 186, 188–198, 200, 201–226, 228–245 *see also* authentic movement, creative movement, dance, choreography

movement observation 6, 85, 89, 90, 98, 243

movement observer 78, 81

multi-modal inquiry 7, 113 *see also* research, qualitative

music 1, 23, 32, 32, 46, 47, 52, 53, 84, 115, 134, 135, 150, 176, 179, 180, 187, 203, 204, 217, 234

narrative 14, 56, 57, 63, 65, 107, 136, 138, 183, 204

National Health Service (NHS) 49, 156

neurolinguistic programming (NLP) 113, 114, 121, 129

neuroscience 7, 14, 19, 128, 146, 148, 183

non-verbal communication 27, 72, 83, 88, 89, 94

Object Relations 148, *see also* psychotherapy

older people 17, 19, 29 *see also* dementia

pain relief 150, 153, 156

parapraxis 133

pattern 63, 104, 138, 146, 188, 214, 236, 241

perceptions 5, 14, 50, 58, 83, 93, 99, 110, 184–186, 189, 203–205, 217, 230, 233; of students 203, 205

person-centred 17, 82, 133, 185, 206

personal, development group 7, 10, 173, 182, 184–186, 202, 205, 230; expression 17; therapy 136, 139, 185, 190, 197, 198, 205 *see also* DMT group

physical contact 8, 56, 184, 193–196, 199–201, 221, 236 *see also* touch

play 3, 5, 8, 11, 12, 14, 29, 50, 68, 84, 87, 89, 90, 94, 95, 107, 108, 110, 120, 126,

136, 143–145, 163, 208–211, 219, 229, 230, 236, 242

position 4, 25, 43, 63, 92, 114, 118, 121, 149, 157, 163, 164, 167–170, 177, 178

post traumatic 70 *see also* complex

posture 19, 21, 54, 72, 73, 85, 152, 153, 164

power 35, 41, 64, 74, 75, 112, 120, 122– 124, 126, 127, 136, 144, 147, 153, 167, 168, 187, 212, 235, 237

primacy 57, 70

processes 2–4, 7, 9, 34, 35, 88, 90, 91, 98, 102, 103, 110, 133, 138, 146, 151, 152, 165, 167, 169, 170, 171, 172, 181, 202, 204, 206, 208, 210, 213, 215, 218, 222, 237

professional culture 126; development of 113–131

profiles 35, 188

projection 7, 40, 132, 135, 140, 141, 146; projective identification 94, 147

psyche 55, 61, 88, 166, 229

psychiatry 10, 125, 130

psychoanalysis 149, 150

psychobiology 52, 70

psychodynamic 34, 35, 41, 46, 147, 152, 206

psychological 2, 3, 10, 15, 17, 19, 32, 36, 53, 56, 58, 61, 63, 64, 68, 72, 73, 75, 78, 82, 83, 89, 105, 110, 133, 136, 150, 177, 185, 233, 243; psychology 2, 3, 12, 17, 27, 88, 107, 109, 113, 114, 118, 128, 129, 233

psychosis 34; psychotic 69, 206

psychotherapy 2–4, 7, 9, 12, 34, 39, 42, 57, 69–71, 129, 132–136, 142, 144, 146, 148, 167, 169, 171, 177, 180, 184–186, 190, 197, 203–206, 232, 233, 238, 242 *see also* therapy

qualitative research 90 91, 98, 101–104, 109–113, 115, 116, 119–121, 125–130, 147, 149, 150, 154–156 *see also* inquiry, research

quantitative 188

reflective space 236

refugee 101–104, 109, 110

rejection 12, 82, 117, 176, 178, 180, 194, 198, 199, 202, 212

relaxation 7, 57, 68, 149, 150, 151, 153, 154, 161, 164, 166, 211

Repertory Grid 165

research 1–14, 18, 19, 22, 28, 31, 36, 46, 50, 52, 56, 67, 68, 71, 72, 74, 75, 79, 85, 87, 89, 90, 91, 98, 101–104, 109–116, 119–121, 126–130, 147, 149, 150, 154–156, 161–164, 167, 168, 170, 171, 173, 181, 184–189, 191–193, 200, 203–207, 210, 222, 226, 227, 231, 234 *see also* inquiry, qualitative

resistance 27, 60, 166, 193, 198

rhythm 20, 23, 45, 57, 76, 81, 82, 120, 243

ritual 45, 64, 127, 150, 175, 196, 201, 238

safety 8, 14, 43, 59, 62, 79, 83, 135, 151, 172, 173, 175, 182, 193, 195, 196, 198–201, 205, 208, 218, 220, 225–230, 240

schizophrenia 33–35, 42

self 2, 3, 5–8, 10, 11, 19, 23, 24, 40, 41, 54, 58, 68, 69, 72, 73, 77, 79, 80, 82, 83, 87, 97, 105, 114, 118, 121, 124–129, 134, 136, 140, 143, 145, 152, 153, 155, 157, 161, 162, 170, 173, 176, 178, 185, 187, 193, 195, 202, 204, 207, 208, 210, 211, 213, 215, 216, 218, 222–225, 227–229, 232, 236, 237; awareness 204; sense of 5, 95, 124, 210

sensation 56, 215, 227, 234, 238

separation 44, 45, 56, 74, 75, 143, 179, 191, 200, 216, 218–221, 223

sex 43; sexual abuse 53, 171, 173, 182, 195, 196, 210, 223, 230; sexuality 119, 195, 196, 201, 206

somatic countertransference 181

somatic intelligence 7, 12, 167, 170, 171, 173, 175, 181; issues 2, 7, 11, 12, 13

soul 63, 68, 71, 121, 126, 233

special schools 186 *see also* children

speech 1, 72, 183

spirit 44, 54, 65, 121, 153, 171, 214; spiritual 3, 19, 53, 54, 121, 150, 151, 152, 214, 216, 232

supervision 7, 25, 49, 57, 84, 91, 103, 112, 116, 123, 125, 126, 167, 182, 186, 195

symbol 214, 235, 240; symbolic 2, 60, 62, 64, 164, 199, 202, 208, 212, 229, 235, 237

synchrony 23, 45, 99

teach 154, 168

techniques 11, 15, 40, 49, 125, 150, 151, 152, 157, 161, 242

thematic analysis 155
themes 7–9, 11, 15, 44, 64, 98, 110, 114, 137, 138, 155, 174, 179, 180, 184, 187, 188, 199–201, 203, 208, 211, 212, 214, 216, 219, 221
therapeutic alliance 3; environment 17; space 46, 63, 65; support 18
therapist 3, 5, 7, 18, 19, 21–23, 25, 27, 35, 38–42, 44, 46, 55–57, 61, 62, 65, 68, 71–73, 77, 78, 80–84, 88, 89, 91, 93–95, 98, 101, 104, 109, 114, 117–120, 122, 125–128, 132, 134–138, 140, 141, 143, 146, 167, 173, 174, 179, 181, 182, 184–186, 190, 194, 197, 199, 201, 203, 204, 206, 209, 216, 222, 225–227, 229–231, 235, 236, 238–240
therapy 1–3, 5–7, 9–11, 13, 15, 17, 20, 24, 26–28, 30–36, 38, 40, 42, 44, 46, 47–49, 52, 54–56, 58–66, 68–71, 73, 74, 76, 78, 80, 82, 84–90, 92, 94, 96, 98–101, 103–106, 108–112, 114, 116, 118, 120, 122, 124, 126, 127–131, 133, 134, 136, 138–140, 142–150, 152, 154, 156, 158, 162, 164–167, 169–178, 180, 182, 183, 185–201–207, 209, 210, 212, 214, 216, 218, 220, 222, 224, 226, 228–238, 240, 242–245 *see also* arts therapies, DMT, personal, psychotherapy
touch 19, 64, 79, 81, 82, 96, 149, 152, 191–193, 219, 233 *see also* physical contact
training 1, 4, 7, 8, 10–13, 17, 18, 22,
25–27, 29, 49, 55, 101–103, 105, 108, 109, 112, 115, 118, 125, 127, 128, 133, 136, 139, 144, 147, 154, 167, 169–171, 173, 175, 177, 179, 181, 183–186, 188, 190, 197, 198, 201, 203–207, 229, 230, 232, 242
transcultural 4, 125, 126, 128–131; competence 6, 112–131
transference 7, 57, 66, 77, 130, 132, 133, 135, 140–143, 146
transformation 5, 9, 11, 68, 125
transpersonal 229
triangulation 50
trust 8, 24, 80, 117, 137, 153, 173, 176, 181, 200, 210, 218, 220, 221, 225, 226–228, 240

unconscious 2, 11, 34, 53, 55, 58, 61, 65, 71, 72, 78, 86–88, 90, 132–135, 138, 143, 146, 147, 151, 152, 179, 202, 235
unknown 36, 210, 240

variations 43
video 6, 18, 19, 23, 42, 44, 72, 85, 103, 147, 162, 163, 224, 234

well-being 5, 8, 10, 11, 15–18, 28, 29, 42, 47, 78, 148, 150, 165, 242
workshop 104–108, 115, 128, 237

yoga 7, 149–151, 152, 154, 156, 158, 232, 235